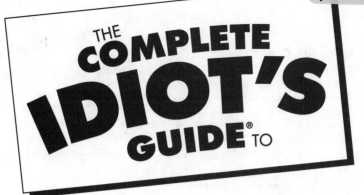

THE COMPLETE IDIOT'S GUIDE® TO

The World of the Bible

by Donald P. Ryan, Ph.D.

ALPHA

To Samuel McKean Maurice Ryan

International Standard Book Number: 0-02-864447-6
Library of Congress Catalog Card Number: 2002117444

05   04   03   8   7   6   5   4   3   2   1

Interpretation of the printing code: The rightmost number of the first series of numbers is the year of the book's printing; the rightmost number of the second series of numbers is the number of the book's printing. For example, a printing code of 03-1 shows that the first printing occurred in 2003.

Printed in the United States of America

Note: This publication contains the opinions and ideas of its author. It is intended to provide helpful and informative material on the subject matter covered. It is sold with the understanding that the author and publisher are not engaged in rendering professional services in the book. If the reader requires personal assistance or advice, a competent professional should be consulted.

The author and publisher specifically disclaim any responsibility for any liability, loss, or risk, personal or otherwise, which is incurred as a consequence, directly or indirectly, of the use and application of any of the contents of this book.

Publisher: *Marie Butler-Knight*
Product Manager: *Phil Kitchel*
Senior Managing Editor: *Jennifer Chisholm*
Senior Acquisitions Editor: *Randy Ladenheim-Gil*
Development Editor: *Lynn Northrup*
Copy Editor: *Michael Dietsch*
Illustrator: *Jody Schaeffer*
Cover/Book Designer: *Trina Wurst*
Indexer: *Brad Herriman*
Layout/Proofreading: *John Etchison, Becky Harmon*

Contents at a Glance

Contents

Foreword

It is a truism that one cannot properly understand the Bible (both Old and New Testaments) without knowing something of the world in which it came to be. Yet this is a somewhat daunting task, not only because the Bible's texts teem with the mention of little-known peoples and places, but because the Bible was not composed all at once, but rather over a period of several centuries in several ancient languages. Thus, it cannot be read easily as a monolith, but rather must be read with some effort and as the product of many changes, historical as well as theological. Moreover, today we are removed from these changes by more than two millennia, a period over which numerous developments and discoveries have changed the way we interpret the Bible. Translations of the Bible abound, as do interpretations of its varied texts, but even when it is read in its original Hebrew, Aramaic, and Greek, many things remain difficult to understand or mysterious at best. Therefore, to appreciate more fully the Bible's many fascinating messages, contemporary readers must sift through layer upon layer of interpretive history and gather the tools, knowledge, and languages necessary for reconstructing the ancient worldview in which the Bible's texts were written.

Indeed, context is everything in biblical scholarship. It both determines and expands the interpretive value of biblical passages. What might be deemed insignificant or mundane upon a casual reading of the Bible often turns out to be of profound importance once the context of a passage is elucidated. Even a cursory knowledge of the plants and animals of the biblical world can reward the reader with a literary and theological sophistication seldom realized, and even a rudimentary understanding of Israel's history and geographic neighbors can offer deep insights. The Bible's ancient writers were deliberate in their choice of words, in their selection of topographical references and tribal affiliations, and in the ways in which they composed their texts. As contemporary readers of the Bible, therefore, we must familiarize ourselves with the biblical world if we truly want to understand the Bible on its own terms.

In *The Complete Idiot's Guide to the World of the Bible*, Donald Ryan helps us explore this world. He introduces us to ancient Israel's physical environment, its cities and diverse peoples, its fauna and flora, its geographic landscape, and even its climate. He sheds light on how the ancients lived; how they reckoned time; how they built their homes; what they ate; and how, where, and whom they worshipped. He discusses the intellectual world of the Bible as well by explaining the numerous languages and scripts employed in the ancient Near East and the contributions Israel's superpower neighbors have given to world history. With an eye toward the Bible's interpretive history, Ryan provides information on a number of Bible translations and carefully explains the terminology that occupies modern scholarship, often accenting his discussions with insights derived from archaeology.

In addition, he provides a number of contemporary tools for understanding this world, including references to useful books, magazines, and websites that will enable readers to investigate the biblical world further after completing this book. Ryan's even-handed approach and accessible style allow readers to appreciate the diversity inherent in a number of religious traditions and to understand the origins and interpretive differences that distinguish one religious tradition and denomination from another. This book, then, opens a door not just to one world, but to two: the historical world of the Bible writers and the world of interpretative history.

Scott B. Noegel, Ph.D.

Dr. Scott B. Noegel is associate professor of biblical and ancient Near Eastern languages and civilizations at the University of Washington–Seattle. He received his Ph.D. in Near Eastern languages and literatures from Cornell University in 1995. Dr. Noegel is the author of nearly 50 articles on diverse topics concerning ancient Near Eastern languages and literature; 5 dozen book reviews; and several books, including most recently *Nocturnal Ciphers: The Allusive Language of Dreams in the Ancient Near East* (American Oriental Series, in press); *Magic and the Bible* (Peabody, MA: Hendrickson Publishers, in press); and *Historical Dictionary of Prophets in Islam and Judaism* (Historical Dictionaries of Religions, Philosophies, and Movements, 43; Prévessin, France: Scarecrow Press, 2002), the latter of which he co-authored with Dr. Brannon Wheeler.

Dr. Noegel is also the editor of *Puns and Pundits: Wordplay in the Hebrew Bible and Ancient Near Eastern Literature* (Bethesda, MD: CDL Press, 2000); and co-editor of *Prayer, Magic, and the Stars in the Ancient and Late Antique World* (Pennsylvania State University Press, projected date, 2003); and *The Linguistic Cycle: Selected Writings of Carleton T. Hodge* (CDL Press, 2003). His research and publications have earned him a place in *Contemporary Authors* (Gale Group, 2002) and in the *International Directory of Distinguished Leadership* (American Biographical Institute, 2002).

Introduction

Welcome to the fascinating world of the Bible. Whether you know very little about the Good Book or you've read through it several times, there is always a lot more to learn. For example, although many people have heard of the Philistines (and may have some pretty negative impressions from reading such stories as David and Goliath), you might not know that they appeared in the Promised Land not very long before the coming of the Israelites. They were seafaring refugees from the Aegean area in the Mediterranean, and despite their reputation as callous thugs, they were actually quite culturally sophisticated!

Or how about those Hittites and Ammonites, or the kings named Herod and the Pharisees during the time of Jesus? What did the folks back then eat and how did they conduct their lives? And where do scholars come up with some of this information that adds additional life to the Bible? We'll look at these topics and much more.

How This Book Is Organized

In this book, we're going to do a little survey of the world of the Bible and take a gander at some of the many fascinating ancient cultures that play a role in its pages.

In **Part 1, "Introducing the Bible and Its World,"** I'll provide some basic information about the Bible and how scholars, including archaeologists, go about trying to illuminate its pages. Then we'll learn a little geography and natural history of the Bible lands. And to top things off, we'll discuss some important Bible stories that aim to explain the world we live in.

In **Part 2, "Residents of the Promised Land,"** you'll meet some of the various people who lived in the ancient region of Palestine, including the Canaanites, the Philistines, and, of course, the Israelites.

In **Part 3, "The Empires Nearby,"** we'll take a look at some of the powerful civilizations that played a major part in many Bible stories: people such as the Egyptians, the Babylonians, the Persians, and the Greeks. And you'll read about one of the most important inventions to come out of the Bible lands: writing.

In **Part 4, "Daily Life in the Holy Land,"** you'll discover how ancient Israelites lived their lives from birth to death and how they organized their society and worshipped God. We'll also take a closer look at the very special city of Jerusalem.

In **Part 5, "The Holy Land in the Time of Jesus,"** we'll grab a glimpse of the complex world of Jesus and some of his followers. We'll also see how the teachings of Jesus began to spread far and wide.

In **Part 6, "The World of the Bible Today,"** I'll provide some information about how you can further explore the world of the Bible.

You'll also find three appendixes—a glossary, bibliography, and resources—that will assist you in your investigation of the Bible world.

Obviously, it's a lot of ground to cover and this book can only etch the surface, so to speak. But we'll be covering enough territory to give you a general idea of the subject and some of its many facets. I hope it will inspire you to want to learn more.

Keep in mind that Bible scholars and archaeologists can be an argumentative bunch. New discoveries and interpretations appear regularly and a lot of what is in this book can be argued in a variety of different ways, and that's part of the scholarly process. In this book, though, you're going to get some very basic information on the subject, and later on, if you want to learn more, you can check into the ins and outs of whichever topics strike your fancy.

Extras Along the Way

Throughout the book you'll find little boxes that offer all kinds of information you won't want to miss: explanations, definitions, quotations, and interesting tidbits to help you in your understanding of the Bible.

Is That So! _____
Here you'll find some interesting facts and occasionally provocative bits of information.

Logos _____
Logos is the Greek word for *word*. We will use Logos boxes to define technical or generally unfamiliar words or concepts used in this book.

Thus Saith _____
These boxes present quotations and insights from the Bible and elsewhere.

This and That
These boxes will present miscellaneous items of interest related to the Bible and its world.

People and Places
In these boxes, you'll find information about some of the interesting people and places of the Bible world.

Acknowledgments

Many thanks are extended to Sherry Ryan and my enthusiastic assistant Samuel; Mr. and Mrs. M. D. Schwartz; Randy Ladenheim-Gil, Lynn Northrup, and the other fine folks at Alpha Books involved in the editing and production of this book; my various scholarly cohorts, including Brian Holmes, Daris Swindler, Thor and Jacqueline Heyerdahl, and Barbara Mertz; my many excellent colleagues in the Humanities Division at Pacific Lutheran University; my loyal supporters, including Denis Whitfill, Darrell Baker, Jeffrey Belvill, Johnny Rockne, Joshua Jeroboam Alper, Drs. Liisa and Richmond Prehn, John and Lynn Cole, Lester and Shirley McKean, Patricia Armstrong, Jane Hayes, and Jane Ho; and special thanks to three fine scholars and teachers whose advice has been outstanding and greatly appreciated: Rev. Hugh Crowder, Dr. Ralph Gehrke, and Rabbi Mark Glickman.

Trademarks

All terms mentioned in this book that are known to be or are suspected of being trademarks or service marks have been appropriately capitalized. Alpha Books and Penguin Putnam Inc. cannot attest to the accuracy of this information. Use of a term in this book should not be regarded as affecting the validity of any trademark or service mark.

Part 1

Introducing the Bible and Its World

In commencing our exploration of the world of the Bible, we need to start at the very beginning and lay a foundation, and that's exactly what we're going to do. First, we'll begin with a bit of information about the Bible itself. Next, we're going to discuss how we can gain insights into biblical times and the meaning of the Book itself. As you'll see, research tools such as archaeology can add a lot to our knowledge.

And to end this first part of the book, we're going to look at some very early stories from the Bible's first book, Genesis. These stories strive to tell us of the very origins of our world, those who live there, and to some extent, why we are the way we are. As such, these stories set the stage on which much of the biblical drama plays out.

Chapter 1

The Enduring Fascination of the Bible

In This Chapter

- One important book!
- The divine library: the Old and New Testaments
- The origins of the Bible
- A book for all people
- Who wrote the Bible?
- The search for meaning

The Bible remains one of the most influential books ever written. Billions of copies have been printed in thousands of languages, and its contents are revered as holy by three of the world's great religions: Judaism, Christianity, and Islam. The Bible is a book of origins and laws, morals, and values. It is a book of inspiration, history, and literature and one of the foundation documents for Western civilization.

As a matter of introduction to tackling the ancient world of the Bible, let's take a brief look at this vitally important book and its contents. We'll examine a few highlights of its history as a book and take a flying glance at what it might all mean.

A Book Like No Other

The *Bible* is held in high regard by a good portion of the world's population. The Hebrew Bible is held sacred by 15 million Jews as well as more than a billion Christians who have added Scriptures to the volume. Although viewing their special book, the Koran, as the ultimate word of God, a billion Muslims respect the Bible as a source of earlier divine revelations.

In addition to being the most printed book in the world, it is also the most studied. For centuries, theologians and other scholars, and average humanoids, have continually studied the Bible in order to ferret out its mysteries and meanings. Every word has been examined over and over again, and there may be more books written about the Bible than probably any other subject.

So what is it about this very special book? What kind of book is it? The Bible is ...

♦ A book of beginnings that explains, in its own way, the origins of our planet and all things on it, including people, and offers insights into why things are the way they are.

♦ A history book that tells the story of some of the events that took place in the Near East up until about 2,000 years ago.

♦ A book of laws, morals, and values that provides guidelines for individual and community behavior.

♦ An inspirational book that has provided guidance, hope, and motivation to many—often for good (although occasionally for evil).

♦ A book of fine literature, from sagas to beautiful poetry.

♦ A book of wonders; miracles and divine interventions abound in the Bible, supporting the faith of believers and bolstering the incredulity of its detractors.

Logos

The word **Bible** is derived from the Greek word *biblia,* which means "books." The Greek word gets its origin from the Phoenician port of Byblos, which was known for its export of paper made from papyrus in ancient times. The word *Tanach* is the Hebrew name for the Hebrew Bible or "Old Testament."

Thus Saith

You can learn more about human nature by reading the Bible than by living in New York.
—William Lyon Phelps, English professor and journalist, in a 1933 radio speech

The Divine Library

The Bible is actually a library of books. The books of the Old Testament, or Hebrew Bible, tell the story of the Jewish people and their relationship with God and fellow people. The Christian addition to the Bible, the New Testament, contains stories about, and the teachings of, Jesus and some of his followers. Muslims consider both the Old and New Testaments as sacred Scripture, and add an additional volume of holy revelations, the Koran. Let's take a brief look at what is to be found within the pages of the Old and New Testaments.

Is That So!

Some people don't like the term "Old Testament" because it might imply that the Old has been superseded by the New Testament. Jewish people, who don't accept the New Testament as Scripture, simply call the Old Testament "the Hebrew Bible." It has been suggested that the expressions First and Second Testament be used, or Hebrew Scriptures and Christian Scriptures. The term "Old Testament," however, has been in use for such a long time that its use as the name for the Hebrew Bible is commonly accepted, at least by non-Jews.

The Hebrew Bible/Old Testament

The Hebrew Bible or Old Testament (written primarily in the Hebrew language) is divided into three sections: the Torah (law), the Prophets, and the Writings. The Torah, sometimes referred to by its Greek name, the Pentateuch, consists of the first five books of the Hebrew Bible and is considered the fundamental source of law for the Jewish people. Its first book, Genesis, tells the story of God's creation of the earth and all living things, especially people, who often disappoint their Creator. At one point in Genesis, God destroys most life on the planet in a great flood and starts over. Eventually, God chooses a mortal, Abraham, with whom an agreement, or covenant, would be struck. In exchange for exclusive worship and obedience to but one God, God would in turn bless Abraham and his descendents and through them bring divine blessing into the world. They would become known as the Hebrews, the Israelites, or the Jews.

The covenant with God is affirmed numerous times in the Bible, and in the book of Exodus, the Hebrews are delivered out of slavery in Egypt. God then presents a series of commandments and laws for living and worship; a blueprint for life under his leadership. The Torah lays the foundation for the rest of the Old Testament, and the spiritual development of the descendants of Abraham.

Along with the Torah, the other books of the Old Testament contain historical and prophetic stories that show the successes and foibles of God's people, and God's reactions thereto. God delivers the Hebrew people from slavery and assists them in conquering and settling "the Promised Land," where they eventually establish their kingdom. Both marvelous blessings and tragic setbacks occur, and along the way come some prophets, who as messengers of God provide warnings should God's laws not be obeyed. Other Old Testament books contain wise adages, poetry, and praises to God.

This and That
For a good overview of the contents of the Bible, read *The Complete Idiot's Guide to the Bible,* now in its second edition, by Jim Bell and Stan Campbell (see Appendix B).

Throughout the Hebrew Bible, the power of God is demonstrated through miracles and divine interventions while humans struggle to behave properly and deal with the notion of one Supreme Being. The religion that developed within the context of the Hebrew Bible is Judaism, and the Jewish people continue to thrive in a modern world radically different from that of their origins during biblical times.

Is That So!

Apart from the hundreds of millions of Bibles printed in such major languages as English, Spanish, and French, the Book has been translated into such obscure languages as Mta Manobo in the Philippines, the Hanga language found in Ghana, Africa, and the Peruvian Amuesha language. Wycliffe Bible Translators works with the goal of providing the Bible in all languages of the world. Since its founding in 1942, it has been involved in translating the New Testament into more than 500 languages.

The New Testament

The New Testament contains the story of the life of Jesus of Nazareth and some of his followers who believed that Jesus was the Son of God sent to Earth as prophesized in the Old Testament. It was originally composed in the Greek language. The first four books, referred to as "the Gospels," tell of significant activities in the life of Jesus, especially teaching and healing. The execution of Jesus was followed by his resurrection from the dead.

After the Gospels comes the Book of Acts, which tells the story of the followers of Jesus in the immediate aftermath of his death and resurrection. Jesus ascends to Heaven with a promise to return and his followers begin to spread "the Word." Much of the rest of the New Testament consists of letters, especially by a believer and missionary named Paul, that elaborate on and further develop the teachings of Jesus. The final book, Revelation, is a symbolic work which is often used to predict dire times preceding the return of Jesus, or "The Second Coming."

By the way, not all Bibles are the same. Christian Bibles contain both the Old and New Testaments, and although they include all of the books of the Hebrew Bible, several of the books appear in a different order. Some Christian Bibles, including those of the Catholics, contain several additional books, known as "the Apocrypha," which although considered worth reading, aren't included in modern Hebrew and Protestant Bibles.

Hebrew Bible/ Old Testament		New Testament		
Genesis	Song of Solomon	Matthew	1 Peter	
Exodus	Isaiah	Mark	2 Peter	
Leviticus	Jeremiah	Luke	1 John	
Numbers	Lamentations	John	2 John	
Deuteronomy	Ezekiel	The Acts	3 John	
Joshua	Daniel	Romans	Jude	
Judges	Hosea	1 Corinthians	Revelation	
Ruth	Joel	2 Corinthians		
1 Samuel	Amos	Galatians		
2 Samuel	Obadiah	Ephesians		
1 Kings	Jonah	Philippians		
2 Kings	Micah	Colossians		
1 Chronicles	Nahum	1 Thessalonians		
2 Chronicles	Habakkuk	2 Thessalonians		
Ezra	Zephaniah	1 Timothy		
Nehemiah	Haggai	2 Timothy		
Esther	Zechariah	Titus		
Job	Malachi	Philemon		
Psalms		Hebrews		
Proverbs		James		
Ecclesiastes				

The Books of the Bible (Protestant arrangement of books).

How Did We Get the Bible?

Like much with regard to the Bible, its origins are a subject of controversy. The earliest material containing the Creation and stories of the first people, along with their genealogies, were probably passed down by oral tradition for many generations. Writing is only about 5,000 years old, which is much too late even for those who believe that the earth is only about 6,000 years young.

Writing It Down

It's not known when all the various books of the Bible were first written down and collected, although there is a tradition that holds that it was the Jewish scribe Ezra who gathered the Old Testament books into their standardized form around the mid-fifth century B.C. We don't have the original manuscript of any of the books of the Bible, but instead have copies that might date from a few thousand to a couple hundred years after the events that are described in them.

A rabbi scrutinizes a portion of the text of the Torah handwritten on a scroll.

(Photo by Josh Miller)

The Hebrew Bible, a.k.a. the Old Testament, was written mainly in Hebrew although some was in Aramaic. Around 250 B.C., a group of 72 scholars assembled in Alexandria, Egypt, to translate it into Greek. The result was called "the Septuagint," which presents a surviving rendition of the Old Testament of that time. The process of *canonization*—that is, decisions as to which books to include in the Holy Book—was completed by A.D. 70 for the Hebrew Bible, if not well before. The books comprising the New Testament were canonized by the mid-fourth century A.D. and both the Old and New Testaments were translated into Latin by a Christian scholar named Jerome by the year A.D. 405.

Logos

Canonization was the process by which potential parts of a book, or a group of books, were accepted or rejected for inclusion in the Bible.

Start the Presses

Until the invention of the printing press, all Bibles were copied by hand. In later Jewish tradition, very strict rules govern the copying of religious texts to ensure accuracy (see Chapter 18). Even today, handwritten Torah scrolls are used in synagogues.

Christian monks labored for years to produce copies of the Bible, and it must have been a relief to all when the movable-type printing press was invented by Johannes Gutenberg in 1456. The first book printed on that press was the Bible in Latin, and this became known as the Gutenberg Bible.

A page from the Gutenberg Bible.

(Photo by Josh Miller)

Spreading the Word to All People

In Christian Europe, the fact that the Bible was printed in Latin gave a certain power to the relatively few who were literate and could read it. Keeping the Bible out of the hands of the masses was one way of controlling the interpretation of the Great Book. The Bible was eventually translated into such languages as English and German, although this initially happened against the wishes of the authorities.

William Tyndale (1494–1536), who translated, printed, and distributed copies of the New Testament in English, was pronounced a heretic by English church officials and burned at the stake.

German theologian and reformer Martin Luther (1483–1546) not only translated the Bible into German, but insisted that it be written in the kind of language that the average individual could understand and appreciate. Eventually, most people came to accept that the Bible could indeed be a book for all people. From then on, the mysteries of the Bible would be made public for all to examine and contemplate.

A great milestone was achieved when an official English language translation of the Bible, commissioned by the English monarch King James, was published in 1611. The King James Version became a standard that's still widely in use today. There are many who claim that this translation was inspired by God and is the authoritative Bible to be consulted. Another important translation, the Revised Standard Version, appeared in English in 1952 after years of work by scholars. Other translations followed, and a visit to a local religious bookstore will usually reveal an amazing variety of translations, including the New International Version, the Jerusalem Bible, the Good News Bible, the New American Standard Bible, and the New King James Version. And along with those, there are plenty of specialty editions addressed to specific audiences, including the Life Recovery Bible, the Daily Walk Living Bible, and the New Adventure Bible for young people. The text of the Bible can be found on audio cassettes read by the likes of Charlton Heston, and it's also available on CD-ROM for computer study and on the Internet as well.

> **This and That**
>
> There are a number of Bibles that are paraphrases; that is, they tell the stories without an exact translation. The Living Bible is one such presentation. There are even translations that incorporate slang or regional dialects in order to make the Bible accessible to more people. A recent translation of the New Testament into Hawaiian pidgin, for example, is called Da Jesus Book.

Who Wrote the Good Book?

Given its popularity and influence, one might expect an easy answer to one of the most important questions: Who wrote the Bible? Well, like everything else you might find in the Bible, it's not necessarily that simple. Some of the books have their authors identified by name, for example, the book of Isaiah is presumed to have been written by Isaiah, the book of Luke by Luke, and so forth. Others maintain a tradition of authorship, such as the Torah having been written by Moses. For several books, the authors are decidedly unknown.

Let's look at some general issues regarding the author or authors of the Bible and its divine authority. There are a number of possibilities across a broad spectrum, including the following:

◆ The Bible was written by God and dictated to the likes of Moses, who recorded it verbatim.

- The Bible is the inspired Word of God transmitted through human scribes who, being human, aren't necessarily infallible and are capable of creating and perpetuating errors.

- The Bible was written by wise and pious people as a profound expression of their understanding of their origins and God's will.

- The Bible was written by humans, but nonetheless contains timeless wisdom and items of historical and literary interest.

- The Bible was written by humans belonging to particular cultures at a particular time and is not necessarily a universally relevant document.

The first couple possibilities view the Bible as infallible; that is, the Word of God is accurate as written. This being the case, there is little to argue about with critics regarding its authority. At the other end of the spectrum, someone who holds the last viewpoint might regard the Bible as an interesting collection of antique Near Eastern myths, legends, and superstitions.

What Does It All Mean?

Pick up a telephone directory from any large U.S. city and turn to the Yellow Pages. Now look at the listings under churches. What do you see? An amazing and lengthy array of names and places. In Tacoma, Washington, for example, one can find listings for Anglicans, Assemblies of God, Bible Missionary churches, Brethrens, Disciples of Christ, Churches of God in Christ, Covenant churches, Episcopalians, Foursquare Gospel churches, Full Gospel churches, Lutherans, Methodists, Nazarenes, Presbyterians, Roman Catholics, Seventh-Day Adventists, and the United Church of Christ—and that's just a sample.

Among the group of Christian believers known as Baptists, you have the choice of attending a variety of congregations including the American Baptists, Baptist Bible Fellowships, Conservative Baptists, General Conference Baptists, Independents, Missionaries, Baptist National Convention of America churches, Reformed Baptists, Regular Baptists, and Southern Baptists. In certain major cities, you'll also find quite a diverse selection of Jewish congregations listed under "synagogues"

> **People and Places**
>
> The Gideons International is an organization founded in 1899 with the goal of making the Bible as widely available as possible. They distribute Bibles and New Testaments all over the world, including in hospitals, prisons, and, yes, motel rooms.

including Reform, Conservative, and Orthodox. Although the Bible is used as a spiritual handbook by them all, their interpretations can be so different that one wishes that God had left more detailed instructions and unambiguous directions.

Why all the variation? A summary explanation would take at least a book the size of this one, if not several. Much of it has to do with theological interpretation, while some of it is cultural, historical, and political. What we can see here is that the Bible is a very powerful, influential, and even somewhat mysterious book even thousands of years after the events it presents took place.

If everyone thinks they've got the spin on God, Jesus, religion, or whatever, who's correct? A black-and-white perspective would say it would have to be one, and that the others are amiss or wrong one way or another. On the other hand, could it have been God's intention that religion be practiced and explored in different ways by different people? This a question to ponder, debate, and likely leave unanswered until the time comes when you meet your Maker and get the straight scoop.

Given all the viewpoints and choices, I should make the general stance of this particular book clear. Although a variety of perspectives will be presented here, my own outlook is basically more conservative than otherwise. In short, I see the Bible as a rich and relevant spiritual document that contains great historical value.

Thus Saith

There are many theological questions which can be asked—even interesting ones, for which the truest answer this side of the grave is, "I don't know."

—James A. Pike, *Beyond Anxiety* (1953)

Some believers subscribe to the belief that the Bible contains the answers to all of life's most profound questions, past, present, and future. Ask some rabbis a difficult question, for example, and if they don't have an answer already, a careful study of the Scriptures will probably result in one, perhaps after a bit of arguing back and forth. "What do I do?" and "Why?" questions are especially appropriate.

Finding Your Way Around the Bible

Before moving on to the various fascinating subjects in the chapters ahead, there are a couple things to get used to in case you aren't already in the know: how to find things in the Bible and the translations of choice used in this book.

Chapter and Verse

As you now know, the Bible is composed of many books, each with a given name. These books have been divided into numbered chapters and verses that enable us to precisely locate a given word, phrase, or story of interest. For example, John 3:16 refers to the sixteenth verse of the third chapter of the Book of John, which happens to be found in the New Testament. Keep in mind that a Jewish Bible does not contain the New Testament and that the New Testament is sometimes published by itself without the Old Testament.

Name Your Source!

As I've noted, there are many different translations of the Bible from which to choose. When quoting a Bible verse, it's a good idea to let people know which version you're using, so here are some abbreviations you might find used in this book and elsewhere which will tell you the source of the quotation:

- KJV is the King James Version.

- RSV is the Revised Standard Version.

- NIV is the New International Version.

In this book, the biblical quotes are from the Revised Standard Version unless otherwise indicated.

The Least You Need to Know

- The Bible is the most influential book ever assembled. Billions of copies have been printed in an incredible number of languages.

- The Bible is actually a library comprising a great variety of spiritual insight, history, and literature.

- The Old Testament/Hebrew Bible is the foundation of Judaism. The New Testament/Christian Scriptures build on the Old Testament to present the message of Jesus.

- There is an immense variety of opinions regarding the true nature of the Bible, its authorship, and how it should be understood.

- Although composed many centuries ago, the Bible continues to touch the hearts and minds of billions of people today.

Searching for Insights

In This Chapter

- ◆ Scrutinizing the word: looking for meaning
- ◆ Digging up facts
- ◆ Determining the age of archaeological remains
- ◆ A review of time terminology
- ◆ The dynamic and controversial field of biblical archaeology

Even though it is profoundly popular and important, the Bible is not necessarily the easiest book to understand. It was written over a period of hundreds of years by many authors at times and in cultures far removed from our own. So how do we make sense of these profound and provocative texts?

Such a challenge has been addressed continuously for numerous centuries by theologians and other scholars as well as the average reader or believer in God. There are a number of ways of shedding light on the subject, and in this chapter, we're going to see how many students of the Bible carry out their search for meaning and understanding.

Looking at "The Word"

Despite these centuries of study, and hundreds of thousands of books and articles on the subject, there is no one consensus on what the Bible or any of its numerous books or parts of books might really mean. Two scholars analyzing the same biblical verse might come to completely opposite conclusions, while others will say that the message can't be studied directly, but only by reading between the lines. At the very root of study, of course, are the words themselves.

Old Languages

As I mentioned in Chapter 1, the Bible as we know it was written primarily in Hebrew and Greek. If you want to be a real Bible scholar, you're going to have to be able to read and understand those languages and scripts competently if you hope to evaluate the source material on your own; otherwise you'll have to rely upon a translation as most people do. There are also some Old Testament texts written in Aramaic, a language related to Hebrew, and some early Christian writings can be found in languages other than Greek such as Syriac and Coptic. If you have a broad interest in the ancient world of the Bible, other languages of the old Near East might also be of interest, including Akkadian (the language of the Babylonians and Assyrians) and Egyptian. You'll learn a lot more about ancient languages and texts in Chapter 14.

> **People and Places**
>
> American professor and archae-ologist William Foxwell Albright (1891–1971) was a true master of Biblical scholarship. He was an amazing expert on many languages of the ancient Near East and a major force in the world of biblical archaeology.

Under the Microscope

With biblical texts, there are a variety of things to sort out, especially with the older documents. Who wrote them, when, and where? Some actual surviving ancient manuscripts are fragmentary or otherwise damaged and difficult to read. But apart from these sorts of questions and problems, the ultimate goal is to determine what it all means. What are the words trying to tell us? The process of analyzing and deriving meaning from the text of the Bible is called *exegesis*. Competent members of the clergy, for example, will study a text in great detail before developing an interpretation and sharing their views with their congregations, eager for enlightenment. Such studies include a word-by-word and grammatical analysis, hopefully in the original language, along with a consideration of the historical, cultural, and even geographical context of the verses. What comes before and after the verses of interest is important as well, along with an interest in where other related material might be found elsewhere in the Bible. The huge range of interpretations possible, however, clearly demonstrates that exegesis is not an exact science, but a scholarly process.

Logos

Exegesis is the process of analyzing and deriving meaning from the biblical text.

Tools of the Trade

Fortunately, many good reference works make this seemingly intimidating effort less difficult. *Concordances*, for example, list words in the Bible and all the places where they occur. Other volumes allow side-by-side comparisons of different translations of the same phrases. A wealth of Bible encyclopedias and handbooks also assist the process. Some of these valuable reference works are now available on CD-ROM for ease of use, including searching for items of interest.

Thus Saith

It is one of the glories of the Bible that it can enshrine many meanings in a single passage. ... Each man marvels to find in the divine Scriptures truths which he himself has sought out.

—St. Thomas Aquinas De Potentia (1263)

Outside Sources

Apart from the Bible itself, other written sources can shed some interesting light on the Bible, its people, and its times. Inscriptions and documents from places such as Mesopotamia occasionally help explain if not actually confirm certain things in the Bible. Apocryphal and other books not in the biblical canon can sometimes prove useful, as do local traditions that survive today in some of the biblical lands. Ancient historians occasionally provide additional commentary, as do collections of Jewish religious commentary and tradition, and the Koran.

Studying the Past

Cultural *anthropology* has much to say of interest to those examining the Bible. Anthropologists observe and attempt to explain culture, typically in an objective, nonjudgmental way. Such scholars might ask what roles religion and history serve in a culture. What social, intellectual, and psychological needs do they meet? To understand Jesus, for example, and what he was saying and doing, you really need to understand the historical and cultural context of the times. Jesus was a Jew living in Palestine under Roman occupation.

The field of *archaeology* has contributed mightily to the study of the Bible. Archaeology is the study of the remains of the human past, and the examination of leftovers such as ancient artifacts, bones, and texts can provide some real insights.

The notion of *biblical archaeology* at face value doesn't appear to be a difficult one. Biblical archaeologists are interested in what archaeology can tell us about the Bible. But there are others who prefer other terms. Because the majority of the story involves the life and history of the Jews in the area of modern-day Israel, there are some who prefer to call it the archaeology of the land of Israel.

Others find that term politically charged, and these people might prefer the term Syro-Palestinian archaeology, or Palestinian archaeology. Still others see those terms as likewise problematic and too restrictive, given that the Bible includes tales of Egypt, Mesopotamia, and other places in the region, and refer to themselves as archaeologists of the lands of the Bible or the Near East. Plus, these areas certainly contain important archaeological material that dates well before and after most biblical events.

Logos

Anthropology is the study of human cultures. **Archaeology** is the interdisciplinary study of the human past. **Biblical archaeology** attempts to use archaeological techniques to illuminate the world of the Bible.

Modern-day Israel seems to be one big archaeological site. Interest in archaeology is a matter of national pride, and numerous excavations take place there every year. Biblical archaeology is popular in much of the world. Several magazines cater to a public thirst for more information, and many scholarly journals address the subject, under various names (see Chapter 23). To keep things simple, let's just use the term Biblical archaeology to refer to any archaeology that relates to the Bible and its peoples in both the Old and New Testaments.

Coming of Age

Some of the earliest attempts to explore the ancient world were inspired by the Bible. Nineteenth-century excavations in places such as Palestine and Mesopotamia were often inspired by the desire to demonstrate the accuracy of the Bible and learn more about the people described therein. Many of these early excavations were certainly crude by modern standards and were mostly dirt-removal exercises in search of interesting objects. A lot has changed since, and archaeology has evolved into a sophisticated science. Great care is used today in an effort to extract as much information from the remains of the past as possible. Specialists abound and some are experts in such subjects as dating pottery, reading inscriptions, and studying bones, soil, and plant remains.

It's certainly not the purpose of this book to describe the hows and whys of the many facets of archaeology. Such details can be readily found elsewhere. But there are a couple things that will be important in understanding some of the issues in the chapters ahead. One is a quick understanding of the archaeological record. The other is a brief knowledge of how archaeologists tell how old things are.

> **People and Places**
>
> Sir William Matthew Flinders Petrie (1853–1942), an Englishman, is considered by many to be the father of both modern archaeology and the archaeology of the Palestine region. He advocated that archaeologists practice precise scientific methods in their work, and he demonstrated such procedures during decades of excavations in both Egypt and the Holy Land.

Tell Me About Pots!

Two of the most important things that biblical archaeologists study are *tells* and pottery. Tells are mounds which are the accumulated debris of years and years of people living in one spot. Tells tend to look like big hills, and the archaeologist who dares to excavate these places is bound to find an amazingly complex series of layers, features, artifacts, and structures dating back thousands of years! Trying to relate one part of a site to another can be complicated, and digging a tell can be like sorting out a massive three-dimensional puzzle.

Pottery was a mainstay of many human cultures, and in places like the Bible lands it serves as a vital tool to the archaeologist. Even though they are baked hard, pots are constantly breaking and being replaced. Their pieces tend to survive, however, for a good long time so they provide a good tool for archaeological analysis, especially in terms of identifying who made them and when.

> **Logos**
>
> A **tell** (also spelled tel) is a mound made up of the accumulated debris of human occupation. Tells are commonly found all over the Near East.

Ceramic pots can shatter into dozens of pieces but not all shards are equally useful to archaeologists. Handles, rims, and decorated fragments can be very diagnostic in providing information about their age and manufacture.

Tells are the accumulated remains of the human past. From a distance, they often look like hills on the landscape. This tell is the site of Gezer in Israel.

(David Moyer collection)

The Archaeological Record

First of all, what archaeologists are really digging up are some of the material remains of the human past. Note that I used the word *some*. It's very important to understand that not everything people do leaves a mark or record that we can find later. A lofty conversation, for example, leaves no trace in the ground. Furthermore, many things don't survive very well through time. Depending upon environmental conditions, all, some, or none of what has resulted from human behavior might survive the ages. Even so, it becomes a good bit of detective work for the archaeologist to make sense of that which survives.

Archaeological excavation is typically destructive in the sense that it disrupts the original order in which things are found. That's why it's crucial that archaeologists accurately record everything that is found, because they have only one chance to do it correctly. And they should publish their results, too, so that others may examine their work.

Some archaeologists choose not to completely excavate large archaeological sites. By leaving a portion of the area alone, they argue, it saves something for the archaeologists of the future who might have better techniques than we have now.

How Old Is It?

Determining age, or dating, is a crucial element within archaeology, and there are a number of ways to go about it. Let's take a quick look at three of the most important that are used in biblical archaeology.

Layers of Time

Analyzing layers, or strata, in an archaeological site is known as *stratigraphy*. By looking at how layers of dirt and debris are positioned in an archaeological site, it's usually possible to tell which layer with its accompanying objects is older than another. The older ones tend to be below the younger ones, but it's sometimes not that easy because things can get mixed up through a variety of processes. Excavating a tell in the Holy Land is like cutting through a complicated layer cake!

Sorting out the many layers in a tell can sometimes be a very difficult task! Here, the late great archaeologist Douglas Esse explains the complex strata at the site of Ashkelon, Israel.

A Matter of Style

Another very important way to date old objects is by their style. You can tell that a Model T automobile is older than a Camaro by the way it looks. So, too, with many other kinds of objects because styles tend to change through time. This is where the broken pot shards of the Bible lands become useful. A knowledge of changing pottery styles allows an expert to pick up a piece of pottery and tell whether it is a tenth-century Philistine pot or a much later Roman amphorae. With old texts, the writing style and the choice of words can often determine when a document was written.

Famous and Radioactive

Radiocarbon dating, or carbon-14 dating, is famous and receives a lot of attention. Without going into tremendous detail, this dating method is based on the notion that all living creatures absorb a kind of radiation from the atmosphere. When they die, this radioactive material begins to decay at a known rate. The amount of radioactive material remaining in an archaeological sample can be measured, and, thus, it can be determined how many years it has been since the sample was in a living state.

Although this technique works very well, it's not perfect. It only works accurately with uncontaminated organic materials, and the older the sample, the wider the spread of possible dates. The technique is good only for objects dating between about 400 and 50,000 years, which isn't much of a problem for most of what is found of biblical interest.

The analysis of pots and pot shards can provide archaeologists with much useful information.

Linking It Up

Sometimes we can get dates for biblical times and events from what we know about other cultures. The Bible might mention a foreign individual whose existence is known from outside sources, or an outside source might mention a biblical individual, thus providing a link in time. We know specific calendar years for the invasion of

Palestine by the Assyrians and Babylonians, and we know when the Persian King Cyrus reigned, so this sort of information helps us tie things down. Foreign objects of known age are tremendously helpful, too. An Egyptian object found in a certain layer of a tell and dating to the reign of a known pharaoh will tell you at least that that particular layer probably doesn't predate that pharaoh.

> **Is That So!**
>
> Although archaeological excavations continue to take place in the Holy Land, there are quite a few whose results remain unpublished and thus unavailable for study by other scholars. This is considered to be a major scandal. This includes important work that took place even decades ago!

Time Terminology

Because we are discussing time and dating, let's take a moment to review a few terms that are useful in placing things in their historical context. The calendar in common use today was created by Christians and begins its numbering system with the birth of Jesus.

The Traditional Terms

The term B.C., or "Before Christ," refers to the number of years before the birth of Jesus. The term A.D. has confused a few. Some people think that because B.C. means "Before Christ," then A.D. must mean "After Death." Not so. First of all, if that were the case, you'd have to add about 33 years to your actual date to account for the tenure of Jesus' life on earth and then come up with a special term for dealing with those years. And according to Christian Scriptures, Jesus was only dead for a couple days before being resurrected anyway.

Fortunately, we don't have to worry about all that: A.D. is actually an abbreviation for the Latin phrase *anno Domini*, which means "Year of Our Lord." From the perspective of a Christian calendar-constructor, every year since the birth of Jesus would be a Year of Our Lord.

> **This and That**
>
> When our present calendar was created, a mistake was made in calculating the date of the birth of Jesus by a few years. Although this doesn't much affect our ability to organize and discuss time, it had some interesting implications regarding the celebration of the new millennium and the accompanying predictions for the end of the world.

The Same but Different

Now some folks out there don't care for the theological bias of these terms. Perhaps they don't share Christian beliefs or simply feel that religion should not be imposed on such a universal apparatus as a calendar. To address those concerns, there is an alternative pair of terms that essentially mean the same things. The terms recognize that our current Christian calendar is entrenched and in common use and is not going away, but the theological implications are neutralized. *B.C.E.*, or "Before the Common Era," means the same as B.C., and *C.E.*, or "Common Era," is the equivalent of A.D.

The term *Common* refers to the calendar dates that we all use in common, regardless of their origin and irrespective of our personal beliefs. The B.C./B.C.E. and A.D./C.E. distinction is mostly known in academic circles, where it is unevenly applied. It's often a matter of personal choice and occasionally it is an editorial policy in some journals, but B.C.E. and C.E. are being used more frequently, so it's best to recognize and understand them for what they are.

The important thing is to have a system that everyone can understand. In this book, we will use the traditional B.C./A.D. terms that are familiar to more people.

Counting Backward

Another occasionally useful way of noting a point in time is with a B.P., or "Before Present," date. Essentially, B.P. means "years ago." So if this is the year A.D. 2000, and I'm talking about 10 years B.P., I'm referring to the calendar year A.D. 1990. Or to make matters slightly more complicated, if this is the year A.D. 2000, and I'm talking about 2500 B.P., I'm referring to the year 500 B.C.

Why would anyone want to do this? In some scientific methods, such as radiocarbon dating, the age of an object is assessed from the time of the laboratory procedure. A date produced in the laboratory 10 years from now would be different (by 10 years) from a date provided today.

This and That

For a good introduction to the subject of archaeology, check out my book *The Complete Idiot's Guide to Lost Civilizations* (see Appendix B).

Round About Then

One last term of time is *circa*, usually abbreviated with a simple "c." or sometimes "ca." Circa means "about that time." It is useful for rounding off dates for a general discussion or for referring to dates we can't pin down exactly.

A Framework of Time

Useful frameworks constructed to organize time and history have developed for the cultures of the ancient Near East. They allow us to place things in their proper chronological order and relate events across time and space. The archaeological history of the Palestine region, where most of the Bible stories take place, is organized into groupings based on time and technology:

- **Paleolithic (c. 1,000,000 years ago–8000 B.C.).** A time period when humans were primarily hunters and gatherers making use of stone tools.

- **Neolithic (8000–4500 B.C.).** The time period when humans began to develop agriculture and settle in permanent villages.

- **Chalcolithic (4500–3300 B.C.).** The Neolithic with the addition of the use of the metal copper.

- **Bronze Age (3300–1200 B.C.).** The time period in which bronze metal technology was available. It tends to appear with the building of urban cities.

- **Iron Age (1200–586 B.C.).** The time period in which iron technology becomes available, a metal superior in some ways to bronze.

This time-classification scheme was developed in Europe in the early nineteenth century and then applied to various places as archaeology developed. It's very culturally specific, though, as in some places, such as Africa, you might have hunters and gatherers living in a region in which iron-users also flourish. In biblical archaeology, many of these "ages" are subdivided into specific time periods; for example, Late Middle Bronze Age II refers to the years 1800 through 1650 B.C. and Iron Age Ia is 1200 through 1125 B.C. The dating is occasionally subject to dispute and revision, so don't be surprised if you see different dates for different time periods in different books. The time periods following the Iron Age can also be arranged by the dominant power in the region; for example, the Neo-Babylonian Period (586–539 B.C.), the Persian Period (539–332 B.C.), the Hellenistic or Greek Period (332–63 B.C.), and the Roman Period (63 B.C.–A.D. 360).

Archaeologists hard at work excavating a big tell in Israel.

Great Expectations

Is it appropriate to use archaeology to prove the details of a book such as the Bible? Biblical archaeology is almost always controversial. Should archaeology be used to explain the Bible or should the Bible be used to explain the archaeological record? And what happens when the text of the Bible and what's dug up seem to disagree? Should one take precedent over the other? It's a matter of intense debate. Ultimately, though, archaeology is merely a tool that can shed light on the past. It can't on its own impart religious lessons or define miracles or the nature of God.

> **Thus Saith**
>
> The gospel story is full of miracle and miracles; yet not one bit of that "evidence" would have been visible to a newsreel camera or the observation of a scientifically trained reporter. A miracle is visible only to the heart it touches.
>
> —M. Holmes Hartshorne, *The Promise of Science and the Power of Faith* (1958)

The Bible contains many stories of God's direct intervention in human affairs including what we might call miracles. Miracles are divine interventions or even the suspension of the usual physical laws of the universe. Such amazing phenomena are, however, really impossible to "prove" in the archaeological record. In the story of the Israelite conquest of Jericho, we are told that God intervened to cause the walls of that city to collapse. Although it's possible to find fallen walls in the archaeological record, the "handprint" of God would not be detectable in the archaeological record. And if God utilized natural forces to carry out desired results (earthquakes, storms, etc.), the role of divine intervention would likewise be difficult to discern.

A Matter of Debate

Given the controversial nature of the Bible, it's not surprising that attempts to apply archaeology to "test its truth" have led to great arguments.

Among those who study the Bible and archaeology, there are two widely opposite viewpoints, and lots of other folks in the middle who believe something in between. The biblical *maximalists* believe that the Bible is an accurate account of history and that archaeology can, does, and will confirm this truth. Many of these scholars, but not all, subscribe to the fundamentalist belief that the Bible is the inspired word of God and every word should be taken literally.

On the opposite extreme are the biblical *minimalists* who see the Old Testament in particular as historically unreliable, and as such, much of it is best viewed as cultural mythology, fable, and literature. Minimalists argue that there is little archaeological evidence for much of what is said in the Bible. Where are the ruined cities of Joshua's conquest, they'll argue, and where is the evidence for the likes of King David, not to speak of hundreds of other biblical characters? Deluxe skeptics they are, with a "show me the archaeological evidence" approach. They certainly seem to enjoy a vigorous debate.

This might be an appropriate time to bring up a special term that's useful in describing the debates about the various controversial parts of the Bible, including such issues as the Creation, Noah's Ark and various miracles. The word is *apologetics*, and those who engage in apologetics are called *apologists*. Now in modern English, that word *apology* tends to mean that one is sorry for something or remorseful. Not so when it comes to such things as Bible study. The earlier meaning of the word has to do with defense, and biblical apologists are those who ardently defend the integrity of the Book. Are they sorry? No way! They'll gladly serve up some answers to your most challenging questions and then it's up to you what to make of it. Some of the masters of apologetics are outstanding debaters, so if you want to pick a fight, you better be prepared with some intellectual and spiritual ammo! And you'd better know your Bible!

As you can see, the study of the Bible is a vibrant process with a variety of disciplines contributing to the search for understanding. The more we learn about the dynamics of the past, the more insights we might gain from the texts; a good reason for studying archaeology and history no matter what your spiritual viewpoint.

Logos

Apologetics is the defense of one's beliefs. **Apologists** are the practitioners of apologetics.

The Least You Need to Know

♦ Scholars have studied the text of the Bible for centuries in order to better understand its history and meaning.

♦ The archaeology of the world of the Bible is a wonderful and controversial subject.

♦ Archaeologists employ a wide range of methods to tell how old things are and to interpret artifacts.

♦ Archaeology can assist in the understanding of biblical times and places, but can't be expected to solve all questions or prove miracles.

♦ You can expect lots of interesting discoveries and insights from the dynamic field of biblical archaeology.

Meet the Holy Land

In This Chapter

- ◆ The Middle East defined
- ◆ The region of Palestine
- ◆ Geographical features
- ◆ Biblical peaks
- ◆ Earthquakes and storms

A little knowledge of geography goes a long way in understanding the world of the Bible. Knowing what's where and how things relate physically really helps one to put the picture together. In many ways, the lay of the land and its climate have had a tremendous effect on the course of history and the ways people lived.

In this chapter, we're going to take a general look at the geography of the Bible from a couple different levels. First we'll look at the broader region known as the Middle or Near East. After that, we'll turn our attention more specifically to the land of Palestine and some other interesting biblical natural features.

What Makes Up the Middle East

Apart from the latter events of the New Testament during which Christianity is spread into the fringes of Europe, the events in the Bible take place in a region that goes by several names. The term "Middle East" is commonly used today although "Near East," which means essentially the same thing, is more popular in the academic world. The "Middle East" is basically the predominantly Islamic and Arabic-speaking countries found bordering the Eastern Mediterranean and parts farther east. This includes Egypt, Jordan, Syria, Lebanon, Saudi Arabia and the Gulf States, and Iraq. I'll generally be using the term "Near East" for this wider region in this book.

The small Jewish nation of Israel is geographically mixed in with the Arab world as is Iran, which although Islamic, is not Arab. The Arab countries in North Africa (Morocco, Algeria, Tunisia, and Libya) are usually included because of their cultural relationship to the others, as are Sudan and Turkey because of their non-European culture and their proximity to the others.

Map of the Ancient Near East.

(Adapted from: Alfred Hoerth et al., 1994, Peoples of the Old Testament World, *p. 16)*

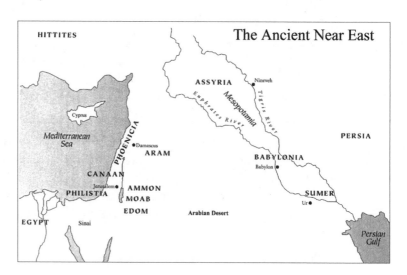

The terms "Middle East" and "Near East" have no natural meaning. The "East," of course, can be anywhere depending upon where you happen to be on the face of the planet. The terms were contrived by European geographers who found the Eastern Mediterranean east of their homes and places such as China and Japan to be very far to the east. Thus the terms "Middle" or "Near" East and "Far" East.

Another term one finds on occasion is Levant. The Levant refers more specifically to the countries bordering the Eastern Mediterranean, and that would include Egypt, Israel, Lebanon, and Turkey.

Lands of Ancient Greatness

The Near East was home to several of the earliest and greatest ancient civilizations. Egypt, of course, was the land of pharaohs, pyramids, and the Nile River. It was the Nile that allowed Egypt to develop and thrive. And to the east, in the vicinity of modern-day Iraq, lay Mesopotamia. As in Egypt, the civilizations there developed along a river, in this case two, the Tigris and Euphrates. In Mesopotamia, the earliest civilization, that of Sumer, arose along with perhaps the greatest intellectual invention of all time: writing. Even farther east was Persia, in the area of modern-day Iran. In the area of Turkey, there was the Hittite civilization.

> **People and Places**
>
> Not all Arabs are Muslims, and not all Muslims are Arabs. Although both Iran and Turkey are predominantly Islamic and are located in the Middle East, their inhabitants are not Arabs. Arabs are those who speak Arabic as their native language or have Arab culture as their own.

Palestine

The majority of the action of the Bible takes place in an area about the size of New Jersey; a region generally known as Palestine. The term *Palestine* refers to a geographical region which more or less incorporates the area of the modern state of Israel and the territory east to the Jordan River. (Some will include parts of western Jordan east of the river as well.) The word has its roots in the word *Philistine*, which was the name for a group of people who lived along the coast (and whom you'll meet in a later chapter). The name Palestine was in general use to describe the region for many years until the modern state of Israel was formed in 1948. The use of the term *Palestine* in this book is geographical and unrelated to the contemporary political situation in the region.

> **People and Places**
>
> Many Arabs who feel dispossessed by the creation of the modern state of Israel, or who live in territories occupied by Israel after a series of wars, call themselves "Palestinians." The area was, in fact, known worldwide by the name *Palestine* until the state of Israel was declared in 1948.

A Land of Many Names

Palestine is located at a crucially strategic crossroad. This slim band of land is a bridge between the continents of Africa and Asia, with Europe nearby. And it is situated between great ancient civilizations, including Egypt to the southwest and Mesopotamia and other great powers to its north and east. Located on the Mediterranean, parts of it were accessible by sea and the territory was also readily traversed by land. As such, it was often overrun by other powers within the region including the Egyptians, Assyrians, Babylonians, Persians, Greeks, Romans, Islamic conquerors, European crusaders, and the Turkish rulers of the Ottoman Empire.

In the Bible, this territory is not referred to as Palestine, but is given different names as history progresses. During early times, before the Israelite kingdom was established, it was often called the Land of Canaan. As such, its borders generally incorporated the territory of the modern state of Israel and the West Bank of the Jordan River and sometimes included Lebanon (ancient Phoenicia) and part of Syria. With the coming of the Israelites, the land would be divided among their twelve tribes and eventually united under a king of the Land of Israel. After a political split between the tribes, "Israel" would refer specifically to an alliance of ten tribes in the north. The two other tribes in the south, including that of Judah, would survive despite brutal attacks by foreigners and deportations.

Logos

The term *Jew* is derived from the name **Judah,** an Israelite tribal district in Palestine and a name used for the same by Persians, Romans, and others. The original district was that assigned to the descendents of Judah, one of the sons of the biblical patriarch Jacob.

When the Persians incorporated Palestine into their empire, they called the place Judea after the Israelite tribal district of *Judah*. The Romans would follow suit by naming a province of that region Judaea. The region would later be referred to as Syria-Palestine and eventually just Palestine.

After World War I, the region became a British protectorate. Conflicts between the local Arab population and large numbers of immigrating Jews brought about the division of Palestine by the United Nations in 1947. When the modern state of Israel was declared in 1948, conflict immediately broke out.

The region of Palestine is also known as the Holy Land. Sites of utmost sacredness to Jews, Christians, and Muslims can be found there. It was there that the Hebrew patriarchs left and it was there where their descendents returned and settled and built kingdoms after the Exodus. Jesus lived his life in Palestine, and Mohammed later came to visit. The ancient city of Jerusalem was the site of the great Jewish temple, was a place where Jesus was active and spent his final days, and was where Mohammed ascended to heaven on his Night Journey. The Bible has ensured that the history of this area is not to be forgotten and nearly every identifiable site related to its most precious stories is considered special today.

The Lay of the Land

Let's take a closer look at the layout of Palestine. The region can be divided into several areas: the coast, the foothills, the highlands, the Jordan Valley, and the Jordanian highlands.

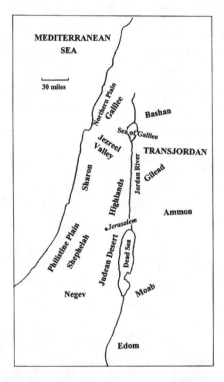

MEDITERRANEAN
SEA

30 miles

Northern Plain
Galilee

Bashan

Sea of Galilee

Jezreel
Valley

TRANSJORDAN

Sharon

Highlands

Jordan River

Gilead

•Jerusalem

Ammon

Philistine Plain

Shephelah

Judean Desert

Dead Sea

Negev

Moab

Edom

A general geographical map of the Palestine region.

The coastal area of Palestine is typically divided into the Northern Plain, the Plain of Sharon, and the Philistine Plain in the south. Because of dunes and swampy conditions, many areas right next to the Mediterranean were unsuitable for agriculture. There are few reasonable harbors, so it's no surprise that the inhabitants of Palestine were not known as great mariners. Just to the north, however, in the land of Lebanon, the Phoenicians were masters of great seagoing enterprises. Heading east from the Philistine Coast, the terrain rises, and woody foothills known as the Shephelah region segue into the southern highlands.

Is That So!

Using Roman technology and engineering, the Jewish King Herod built an impressive artificial harbor on the coast of Palestine in the years 22 through 10 B.C. Being a virtual servant to the Romans, he named the port Caesarea after the emperor, Augustus Caesar.

Palestine is bisected north to south by highlands. From the north, one finds the Galilee region, in the center is the hill country of Ephraim or Samaria, and the Judean mountains in the south. Heading farther east, one finds desert wilderness and a drop down to the Jordan River and the Dead Sea. And to the very south lies the vast expanses of the Negev Desert. The great fertile and strategic Jezreel Valley cuts across the highlands and provides west to east access from the plains to the Jordan Valley.

Towns and cities in ancient Palestine were connected by various paths and roads. There were, though, two great international byways that passed through the vicinity by land. The Via Maris, or "Way of the Sea," traversed in a south/north direction a bit inland from the coast. The so-called King's Highway passed in a similar direction overland in the area of the Jordanian plateau from Damascus in Syria to Aqaba on the Red Sea.

People need fresh water. The fact that it can be so scarce in the Near East makes water supply a great concern for many who live there. Fortunately, Palestine has some good lakes, rivers, streams, and wells. The largest and most famous freshwater lake in the area is the Sea of Galilee in the north. The Sea of Galilee is also known by other names. In Hebrew, it's called Kinneret. The Romans called it the Sea of Tiberius after one of their emperors.

The Jordan River, of course, is very well known. It formed a kind of west/east boundary both in ancient and modern times. The Israelites crossed it to enter the Promised Land, and Jesus was baptized in it. It flows from the far north, into the Sea of Galilee, and then empties into the Dead Sea.

The strategically and religiously important Jordan River.

(David Moyer collection)

Other rivers and streams flow down from the highlands toward the coasts. Springs were important sources of water. Jerusalem, for example, has a beautiful spring whose waters were transported into the ancient city by a tunnel during times of conflict. Wells and oases in the desert allowed for long-distance travel and humans and beasts of burden.

It's Dead!

The Dead Sea is one of the most remarkable natural features in the Near East. It lies in the Great Rift, a massive geological feature that stretches from East Africa into Syria. At about 1,300 feet below sea level, the Dead Sea is the lowest spot on earth. Its waters are so thick with salt and other minerals that no fish can survive. Water from the Jordan and other sources evaporates in the very arid environment.

The Dead Sea today is on the tourist maps and there are health spas and beaches along its shores. The chemical consistency of the lake is such that it is impossible to sink, so a common stunt is to have one's picture taken reading a newspaper while floating near the surface.

> **People and Places**
>
> At En-Gedi, near the scorching and arid western shore of the Dead Sea, a little oasis thrives in the desert. Natural springs provide waterfalls, freshwater pools, lush vegetation, and even a habitat for wild ibex!

The salty Dead Sea is the lowest spot on earth.

(David Moyer collection)

Lands to the East

The lands to the east of the Jordan River and the Dead Sea are geographically known as Transjordan, "across the Jordan." These territories are also quite important in biblical history and geography and were home to some of the opponents of the Israelites. Mountains and plateaus rise dramatically on the east side of the Jordan Valley, and this area can be divided into five areas separated by east-to-west rivers. From north to south these areas are Bashan, Gilead, Ammon, Moab, and Edom.

Closer to Heaven

Mountains are special places in many cultures all around the world. They rise above the land in the direction of heaven and, thus, are seemingly that much closer. They can also invoke fear, provide obstacles to travel, and provide a bird's-eye view of action below. Some of the more famous biblical mountains include the following:

- ◆ Mt. Ararat, where Noah's Ark landed

- ◆ Mt. Sinai, where Moses obtained the Torah, including the Ten Commandments

- ◆ Mt. Nebo in Transjordan, where Moses was allowed to view the Promised Land before he died

- ◆ Mt. Moriah in Jerusalem, where the Jewish temples were built

- ◆ Mt. Carmel, a prominent landmark on the coast of northern Israel, where Elijah challenged the prophets of Baal

- ◆ Mt. Gilboa, where the Israelites fought the Philistines

- ◆ The Mount of Olives, near Jerusalem where Jesus was betrayed

Is That So!

The hills and mountains of Palestine are riddled with caves. In prehistoric days, they provided shelter for early inhabitants and could also serve as burial places and good places to hide from enemies. The famous Dead Sea Scrolls were found hidden away in caves for safekeeping.

You might be surprised to learn that the locations of a couple of the most well-known biblical mountains is a matter of debate. Although there are peaks traditionally identified as Ararat and Sinai, arguments have been posed that the famous biblical events actually occurred on other mountains in the Near East.

How's the Weather?

Although the Middle East has a reputation for being a hot, miserable place, this isn't always so. In Egypt, for example, they can get a lot of rain in the north during the winter and snow does fall and accumulate in mountains of the great desert wilderness of Sinai!

In Palestine, it tends to be warmer during the summer and cooler and wetter during the winter. The farther east and south one goes, the hotter it tends to be, with the opposite situation toward the north and west. The sea breezes along the coast tend to keep things fairly moderate during the summer, whereas the Judean wilderness and the Dead Sea region can be brutally scorching at the same time. It's not uncommon for Jerusalem, at an elevation of around 2,500 feet above sea level, to get a little snow during the winter. There is even a ski area on Mt. Hermon in the far northeast corner of modern Israel that opens when there is enough snow!

Catastrophes!

Weather and other natural phenomena have the potential of causing great human misery and destruction. Too much water or too little is worthy of great fear. The story of Noah has God wreaking mass destruction with a great flood. Famine was certainly serious business in a land such as Palestine that depended much upon natural cycles of rain for its crops to flourish.

What's Shakin'?

Earthquakes, too, are noted in the Bible. Located near the fault of the Great Rift Valley, such scary and surprising events are not uncommon. Seismic events were sometimes interpreted as significant acts of God. In the New Testament, an earthquake occurs at the time of the death of Jesus and later, an earthquake shook open the doors of the prison where the missionary Paul was held captive.

Stormy Weather

Like anywhere, storms occurred from time to time, and the Bible notes several that occurred over water. In the story of Jonah, Jonah, who is trying to avoid a mission assigned to him by God, is purposefully thrown overboard in an attempt to calm rough seas. (See the next chapter to learn what happened to him!) In a dramatic New Testament story, Jesus slept soundly in a boat while a storm raged on the Sea of Galilee. His terrified disciples woke him up and Jesus miraculously calmed the tempest. In the twenty-seventh chapter of Acts, a lengthy storm batters a ship that ends up shipwrecked off the coast of the Mediterranean island of Malta.

> **Thus Saith**
>
> The Book of Matthew (27:51–54) reports the significance of Jesus' death with the story of an earthquake:
>
>> And behold, the curtain of the temple was torn in two, from top to bottom; and the earth shook, and the rocks were split; the tombs also were opened, and many bodies of the saints who had fallen asleep were raised, and coming out of the tombs after his resurrection they went into the holy city and appeared to many. When the centurion [a Roman guard] and those who were with him, keeping watch over Jesus, saw the earthquake and what took place, they were filled with awe, and said, "Truly this was the Son of God!"

Ancient Places

There are hundreds of place names in the Bible. Some are obvious geographical features while others remain elusive. We also know of a lot of ancient place names in Palestine from outside sources such as battle records and diplomatic correspondence in Egypt and Mesopotamia. Actually locating old towns and other sites can sometimes be a real puzzle. Still, a good number of places still retain some form of their ancient names.

When the famous British archaeologist Flinders Petrie excavated the site of Tel el-Hesi, for example, he thought he was excavating the famous fortified biblical city of Lachish and published his report as such. We now know that Lachish was actually located elsewhere and both it and Tel el-Hesi have since been well excavated.

The Least You Need to Know

- ◆ The Middle East and the Near East are essentially identical terms to describe the area encompassed by the Arab world along with Israel, Iran, and often Turkey.

- ◆ The Near East was home to some of the earliest and most sophisticated ancient civilizations, many of which played a role in biblical stories.

- ◆ The land of Palestine was at a strategic and cultural crossroad between some great civilizations such as Egypt and Mesopotamia.

- ◆ The geographical territory known as Palestine essentially encompassed the area of the modern-day state of Israel and some adjacent land to the east.

- ◆ Palestine is geographically diverse with seacoasts, lakes, rivers, plains, mountains, and valleys.

- ◆ The lay of the land and the climate play an important part in many biblical stories.

Chapter 4

Flora and Fauna

In This Chapter

- ◆ From trees to flowers: those versatile biblical plants!
- ◆ Mammals, birds, fish, and bugs
- ◆ Animal friends and foes
- ◆ Tales of strange and mysterious creatures

Plants and animals are important in the Bible from its very beginning. In the first book of the Bible, Genesis, God sets the stage for the appearance of humans by the creation of flora and fauna. The first couple, Adam and Eve, find themselves in a beautiful garden full of living creatures (see Chapter 5). Their pleasant existence there will be all too short after they break the rules and face the real world where you have to work to eat and where thorns can poke and animals can bite.

Dozens of plants and animals are mentioned in the Bible. Some play very practical roles like sources of food, building supplies, and beasts of burden, and some exceed these mere functional roles to serve in various symbolic ways. Let's take a brief look at some of those living things in the Bible.

What's What?

Although we have lots of names of plants and animals in the Bible, it can be problematic to figure out exactly what particular species is represented. Especially in the Old Testament, we are left with some words in Hebrew that no doubt made specific sense in their day but whose meanings have been clouded through the centuries. In such cases, it is necessary to make a best guess by description or context or by the use of similar words in other related languages.

It should be noted, too, that some early European translations of the Bible were produced without a sound knowledge of the flora and fauna of the Palestine region. So occasionally, European animals and plants found their way into the text as a result of the translator's own worldview. Most translations today are very careful to avoid this kind of interpretation.

> **Thus Saith**
>
> So out of the ground the Lord God formed every beast of the field and every bird of the air, and brought them to the man to see what he would call them; and whatever the man called every living creature, that was its name.
>
> —Genesis 2:19

The Big Plants

Plants, of course, come in all sizes. Let's start with the trees and then go for some of the smaller things.

Trees Bearing Fruit

The fruits of a number of trees played important roles in the lives of the inhabitants of the Palestine region. Perhaps first and foremost was the olive. The oil produced by olives could be used in cooking, as fuel for lamps, and as cosmetics. It also played a big part in Israelite religious rituals, including anointing. The tree also provides good wood for carving!

In the story of Noah and the Great Flood, a dove is sent out and returns with an olive branch in its mouth. It was a symbol of reconciliation between God and his creation, and today this image serves as a symbol of world peace. (Genesis 8:8–11) In Christianity, the dove also symbolizes the manifestation of God known as "The Holy Spirit."

Figs, mulberries, and apricots provided delicious fruit as did the sycamore fig or "fig mulberry." Figs are the first plant mentioned specifically by name in the Bible. In Genesis 3:7, Adam and Eve eat the forbidden fruit and "Then the eyes of both were opened, and they knew that they were naked; and they sewed fig leaves together and made themselves aprons."

The versatile olive tree was an important component of daily life in ancient Palestine.

(David Moyer collection)

The fruit of the pomegranate was sweet and its skin could be used for tanning leather. Almonds and pistachios were also enjoyed. Although sweet, the pods of carob trees were not the most desirable choice for human consumption and were more often used as animal fodder.

The date palm was an extremely valuable plant. Tall and long-lived, they are almost a symbol of the Near East. A cluster of palms in the desert was usually a sure sign of an oasis in the vicinity. Dates are tasty and nutritious and can be eaten both fresh and dried. They can also be processed into wine. The leaves of the versatile palm can be woven into sandals, baskets, and mats, and its fibers can be twisted into cordage for a multitude of uses.

> ### This and That
>
> Although the Hebrew word *tepuach* has been translated as "apple," apples were not native to Palestine. It's likely that the word means "apricot" or some other fruit.

Timber!

Several trees in the neighborhood of Palestine were useful to provide wood for the manufacture of everything from boats to doors. They could also be used, of course, as firewood. Several species of oak and pine flourished. One of the most notable is the huge Aleppo pine. Thorny acacia trees provided hard, durable wood. Much of the Hebrews' traveling tabernacle was made of this wood. Additionally, the plane tree and the terebinth could provide useful wood.

One of the most treasured resources of the Near East was wood from the fabled cedars of Lebanon. These majestic trees grew to an immense size and were prized for the beauty of their tough, strong wood (which also smelled nice!). Even the Egyptians went out of their way to obtain this special building material. Most notably, Solomon's Temple to God built in Jerusalem utilized a good bit of this wood. Not surprisingly, these beautiful trees would symbolize strength and endurance.

The wood of the cypress tree was desirable for similar reasons as was the hardwood of the box tree, both found in the forests of Lebanon. Exotic ebony and sandalwood were sometimes imported.

Down by the Water

Poplar trees and reeds were common near the streams and bodies of water. The famed bulrush deserves mention as the versatile papyrus plant that thrived along the Nile River in Egypt. Its stalks could be processed into writing paper, bundled to form boats, and used for many other purposes including making baskets. One such basket served as a little floating boat for the baby Moses in Exodus 2:3.

Grown for Food and Such

Although I'll discuss more about food in Chapter 16, it's worth mentioning a few here. Cultivated grains included wheat, barley, and millet. Flax was grown, its fibers were transformed into linen cloth, and its oil had many uses. Cucumbers, gourds, garlic, and onions were grown in gardens.

The King James Version of the Bible often mentions the word *corn*. This has confused a number of people who immediately think of tall green stalks, corncobs, and tortilla chips. But in fact, what we think of as corn did not grow in biblical lands. It's actually an old English term for wheat or grain. What grows in the New World is generally referred to as maize by the British.

Next to olives and perhaps figs, grapes were perhaps the most important edible plant in Bible times. When Moses sent a group of men out to investigate the resources of the Promised Land, they found it abundant in grapes. "And they came to the Valley of Eshcol, and cut down from there a branch with a single cluster of grapes, and they carried it on a pole between two of them ...." (Numbers 13:23) Wine was, and remains, a major commodity of the Palestine region, which is very well suited for the cultivation of grapes. Wine was regularly consumed and even exported. Grapes were also dried to produce the ever-popular raisins. It's interesting to note that after the Great Flood described in Genesis (see Chapter 6), Noah "was the first tiller of the soil. He planted a vineyard ...." (Genesis 9:20)

Flowers

There are many beautiful flowering plants in the Holy Land and they were admired for the same reasons we do today: They are pretty and often smell nice. Identifying them with the plants we know today has proved tricky. The term *lily of the field*, for example, might refer to anemones, while *lily of the valley* could be a hyacinth. The word *rose* can likewise be enigmatic and might refer to a kind of mountain tulip. We do know that narcissus, iris, and poppies also beautified the landscape.

Both myrtle and almond trees bloomed lovely flowers. The tall-growing mustard plant added a touch of yellow to the terrain. The tiny seeds of the latter were also a source of oil.

Ouch! Prickly Plants

Not all plants are friendly and desirable to people. Palestine had its share of potentially annoying species. In fact, a life that included "thorns and thistles" became the destiny of Adam and Eve and their descendents for disobeying God's warning in the Garden of Eden. Plants that we commonly characterize as "sticker bushes" were certainly known in ancient Palestine and can be found there today. Prickly plants translated as briers, nettles, and brambles are all well noted in the Bible, the latter probably being blackberry bushes. They are usually characterized as obnoxious and painful, and thorny weeds could torment many a farmer.

Is That So!

In the story of the trial and crucifixion of Jesus, a crown of thorns was placed on his head as a form of painful humiliation. (Matthew 27:29) The crown was likely made from the branches of a thorny tree, which even today is called the "crown of thorns" tree in reference to that event.

And a Couple More ...

The hyssop is a shrub that served a number of symbolic purposes including sacrifice and purification rituals. The mandrake plant has a root that resembles a human from about the chest down. It was thought to have fertility powers or was useful as an aphrodisiac.

Animals

Animals of all sizes and many habitats are mentioned in the Bible, some playing vital roles in different stories. Their creation is addressed in the first chapter of the first book, Genesis. Keep in mind that both the environment and fauna have changed in some startling ways over the last few thousand years! Let's start with the mammals and proceed to the birds and fish.

On All Fours

Most people probably don't think of deer and gazelles and antelope when they think about the Bible, yet the land of Palestine was home to several species of these agile creatures. Deer varieties included the fallow and roe deer, the latter being especially noted as "light of foot." The wild ibex can still be found in parts of the desert.

The word *unicorn* appears several times in the King James translation of the Bible. We think of a unicorn as a mythological creature, but in the Bible it probably refers to a species of straight-horned antelope.

Fierce Beasts

Lions in the Near East? Believe it or not, it was once so and they are mentioned many times in the Bible. The only place you'll find them there today, though, is in a zoo! They were likely eliminated by overhunting. Depictions of lion hunts, for example, have been found on the walls of an Assyrian palace, and we know the Romans captured them for use in their violent public arena shows. Bears, too, could be found, as well as wolves and possibly jackals and leopards, although their numbers are now quite few in most of the Near East. Matthew 7:15 contains a warning that is oft-quoted today: "Beware of false prophets, who come to you in sheep's clothing but inwardly are ravenous wolves."

Lions once roamed the ancient Near East as evidenced by this hunting scene from an Assyrian palace.

(David Moyer collection)

There are many disturbing stories in the Bible, and the following one probably rates near the top. I have also found that it seems to be one of the lesser-known incidents. The story involves the prophet Elisha, who apparently had both a thin skin and a harsh temper:

> He [Elisha] went up from there to Bethel; and while he was going up on the way, some small boys came out of the city and jeered at him, saying, "Go up, you baldhead! Go up, you baldhead!" And he turned around, and when he saw them, he cursed them in the name of the Lord. And two she-bears came out of the woods and tore forty-two of the boys. (2 Kings 2:23–24)

Thus Saith

In an example of highly poetic imagery, Isaiah 11:6 describes a future era of peace and harmony on earth in which "The wolf shall dwell with the lamb, and the leopard shall lie down with the kid, and the calf and the lion and the fatling together, and a little child shall lead them."

Apart from the story of bald-headed Elisha, there are a few other tales of animal attacks in the Bible. There were the insect plagues in Exodus and God sent hornets to drive away the Amorites. (Joshua 24:12) Samson was attacked by a lion (Judges 14:5–6) and Paul was bitten by a snake on the island of Malta. (Acts 28:3)

Domesticated Animals

A variety of animals were domesticated for the greater use of humans. Sheep and goats were herded to provide such things as meat, dairy products, wool, and leather.

Is That So!

Although camels are often routinely associated with Egypt, where many live today, these interesting creatures seemed to have played no major role in that ancient civilization.

Cattle could serve similar purposes, and sturdy oxen could be strapped to a plow and made to work hard for a living. Donkeys earned their keep as a form of transportation and beast of burden. They could also be hitched to a plow or wagon. Similarly, feisty camels are well-designed desert machines capable of traveling long distances carrying people and goods.

The camel is a strong and hardy creature of the desert.

Assorted Mammals

Some of the smaller-size mammals include the hares, mice, foxes, and dogs. Although in Europe and America today the dog is considered a household pet, they were often considered to be a household *pest* in Bible times. As is still the case today in places like Egypt, dogs are tolerated to the extent that they eat garbage and make a lot of noises when strangers enter the vicinity. Wild pigs and herded swine could be found here and there in ancient Palestine, although the Israelites' dietary code found them unfit as food.

People and Places

In the Bible, there are a number of Hebrew personal names that are those of animals; for example, *Deborah* means "bee," *Dorcas* means "antelope," *Tabitha* means "gazelle," and *Jonah* means "dove."

In the Air and the Sea

A wide variety of birds are noted in the Bible, including doves, pigeons, quails, sparrows, and swallows. Interestingly, a good listing of some of the birds is found in the books of Leviticus and Deuteronomy, where inedible animals are noted:

> And these you shall have in abomination among the birds, they shall not be eaten, they are an abomination: the eagle, the vulture, the osprey, the kite, the falcon according to its kind, every raven according to its kind, the ostrich, the nighthawk, the sea gull, the hawk according to its kind, the owl, the cormorant, the ibis, the water hen, the pelican, the carrion vulture, the stork, the heron according to its kind, the hoopoe, and the bat. (Leviticus 11:13–19)

"What's the bat doing in there?" is a question that is often asked. Keep in mind this is not a European scientific classification of creatures by genus, species, and so on. In this case, the bat is thrown in with "things that fly that aren't insects."

Although the inhabitants of the ancient land of Palestine were not particularly known as seafarers, they did enjoy their fish, both from the sea and freshwater sources. The Mediterranean was home to a wide variety of species and the freshwater Sea of Galilee was a popular place to bring them in.

Some early Christians used the symbol of the fish to identify each other as fellow believers. The letters of the Greek word for fish can stand for an acronym that translated into English means "Jesus Christ, God's Son, Savior."

Slithery, Scaly Things

Let's not forget the little fellers that played important roles! There were, and are, a lot of poisonous snakes in the Near East, including adders and vipers. Lizards are certainly common and large land and water monitor lizards were once found in Palestine. All reptiles were considered unfit to eat by the Israelites.

" " Thus Saith _____

A snake or serpent is a major character in the third chapter of Genesis. He tempted the first humans into breaking God's warning and thereafter was cursed "above all cattle, and above all wild animals; upon your belly you shall go, and dust you shall eat all the days of your life." (Genesis 3:14)

Don't Bug Me

There are thousands of insect species on this planet and Palestine and the Near East had its fair share. Some were considered quite useful, such as honeybees, and a few were even admired. Ants, for example, were a model of hard work and industriousness. Proverbs 6:6–8 says, "Go to the ant, O sluggard; consider her ways, and be wise. Without having any chief, officer or ruler, she prepares her food in summer, and gathers her sustenance in harvest."

On the other hand, we all know that many bugs can be real pests! Several of the plagues in the Exodus stories involved insects: flies, gnats, lice, and locusts. Locusts and grasshoppers can ravage crops, hornets can sting, and moths will eat your clothes and blankets. Surprisingly, given their numbers, spiders are barely mentioned in the Bible and its usually the fragility of their webs that is noted.

Interesting Animal Stories

Animals occasionally played a part in some fascinating biblical stories. Insects played a role in the plagues of the Exodus and Jesus caused fish to be caught and to multiply in order to feed the masses who came out to hear him speak. Quails were sent as food to the Israelites in the wilderness and God kept lions from eating the prophet Daniel. Here are a few of the more intriguing animal incidents and descriptions found in the Bible.

Balaam and the Talking Donkey (Numbers 22–24)

In the Exodus story, when the Israelites traveled from Egypt into new territory, they encountered various inhabitants who weren't always pleased with the huge number of newcomers. In one case, the elders of Moab and Midian paid a professional sooth-sayer named Balaam to put a curse on the Israelites. Balaam set out on his donkey to place the curse. An angel appeared blocking the path. Only the donkey could see him and the animal began to behave uncooperatively. Balaam beat the donkey and was quite startled when the animal talked back: "What have I done to you, that you have struck me these three times?"

Balaam, whom one might think would be utterly startled, answered that he felt like a fool, and the donkey continued to berate him: "Am I not your donkey, upon which you have ridden all your life long to this day? Was I ever accustomed to do so to you?" The angel then made himself appear and chastised the man, and ultimately, Balaam blessed the Israelites much to the consternation of those who hired him.

One Big Fish! (The Book of Jonah)

Like most people, I prefer to eat fish rather than be eaten by one. The story of Jonah tells the dramatic story of how a man survives for a few days inside a giant sea creature. Jonah was chosen by God for the task of preaching repentance to the mighty Assyrian city of Nineveh. Jonah didn't want to go, so he got on a ship and tried to leave town. God caused a big storm at sea. Ultimately, Jonah was tossed overboard and the sea was calmed.

"And the Lord appointed a great fish to swallow up Jonah; and Jonah was in the belly of the fish three days and three nights." After this ordeal, Jonah was released on a beach and headed for Nineveh where his missionary efforts were quite successful.

> **This and That**
>
> In the story of Jonah, the Hebrew words merely mention a "big fish." In the New Testament, Jesus actually uses the Greek word for "sea monster" in the retelling of the story.

Leviathan of the Sea (Job 41)

Genesis 1:21 mentions the creation of "great sea monsters." One of them, called Leviathan, is described in terrifying detail in Job 41:

> No one is so fierce that he dares to stir him up. Who can penetrate his double coat of mail? … Round about his teeth is terror. His back is made of rows of shields, shut up closely as with a seal … Out of his nostrils comes forth smoke, as from a boiling pot and burning rushes. … Though the sword reaches him, it does not avail; nor the spear, the dart, or the javelin. … Behind him he leaves a shining wake … Upon the earth there is not his like, a creature without fear.

Some have suggested that the description of this mighty beast is more like that of a crocodile than a creature of the sea. Even so, a crocodile is certainly quite worthy of awe and fear. On the other hand, perhaps it is some other symbolic or actual creature that is being described. There is another monster of the sea in the Old Testament, mentioned as a dragon named Rahab, but there is no detailed description.

River Behemoth (Job 40:15–24)

Behemoth is a strange animal that "eats grass like an ox" and lives in rivers "under the lotus plants … in the covert of the reeds and in the marsh." This sturdy beast's "bones are tubes of bronze, his limbs like bars of iron." It seems like none other than the hippopotamus is being described. Like the crocodile, the hippo is a fierce and dangerous creature that spends much of its time in the water.

Is That So!

Only a fraction of the world's oceans have been well explored. New species of sea life continue to be discovered and occasionally creatures thought to have been extinct for millions of years have been rediscovered in the oceans' depths. In addition, weird creatures still lurk beneath the seas. In 1977, a Japanese fishing vessel recovered the rotting carcass of an unidentifiable giant flippered animal. It was photographed and then tossed back into the ocean. Some say it was the remains of a huge basking shark; others are not so sure.

The Least You Need to Know

- ◆ Ancient Palestine was home to a wide variety of flora and fauna.

- ◆ Although the Bible refers to a lot of plants and animals, it's sometimes difficult to determine exactly which species is intended.

- ◆ Some of the biblical plants and animals are no longer found in the Holy Land.

- ◆ Many animals and plants served both functional and symbolic purposes.

- ◆ There are a few amazing animals mentioned in the Bible whose existence is truly mysterious.

Chapter 5

In the Beginning ...

In This Chapter

- ♦ God creates the earth
- ♦ Scientists present other options
- ♦ The debate between creationists and scientists
- ♦ The creation of Adam and Eve
- ♦ Life after paradise

The Bible begins with perhaps its most provocative book: Genesis. It sets the stage for all that follows including our own very existence! The book begins with the creation of the world in which we live and all that is in it. It then goes on to present stories to explain what it means to be human and where God fits into the picture. The book cannot necessarily be taken at face value; there are layers of meaning in most verses, some of which are truly enlightening.

In this chapter, we're going to look at a few of the earliest stories in the Bible, stories that address our greater world. They are not always easy to understand or accept, and the result is often controversy!

"Let There Be Light!"

The very opening lines of the first book of the Bible, Genesis, are some of the most provocative words ever written:

> In the beginning, God created the heavens and the earth …

It sounds simple enough, except for the following:

- ◆ It assigns the origins and existence of our world to a supernatural being: God.

- ◆ It causes some to ask the question: If the universe was indeed created by a Creator, then who, if anyone, created the Creator?

- ◆ The details that follow, such as issues of method and timing, tend to fly in the face of accepted scientific findings about how it might have all happened.

The Creation story continues with a sequence of six steps of creation over a period of six days: the earth, plants, animals, and a crowning achievement on the last day, humans. Then God took a break. The story is quite amazing. God speaks the universe into creation: "Let there be light! And there was light! And God saw that the light was good."

The opening verses of the Book of Genesis in the Hebrew Bible.

בְּרֵאשִׁית בָּרָא אֱלֹהִים אֵת הַשָּׁמַיִם וְאֵת הָאָרֶץ: וְהָאָרֶץ
הָיְתָה תֹהוּ וָבֹהוּ וְחֹשֶׁךְ עַל־פְּנֵי תְהוֹם וְרוּחַ אֱלֹהִים מְרַחֶפֶת
עַל־פְּנֵי הַמָּיִם: וַיֹּאמֶר אֱלֹהִים יְהִי אוֹר וַיְהִי־אוֹר: וַיַּרְא
אֱלֹהִים אֶת־הָאוֹר כִּי־טוֹב וַיַּבְדֵּל אֱלֹהִים בֵּין הָאוֹר וּבֵין
הַחֹשֶׁךְ: וַיִּקְרָא אֱלֹהִים ׀ לָאוֹר יוֹם וְלַחֹשֶׁךְ קָרָא לָיְלָה וַיְהִי־
עֶרֶב וַיְהִי־בֹקֶר יוֹם אֶחָד:

One Big Bang? Other Theories

Scientists studying the universe find it difficult to incorporate such metaphysical explanations into their theories of the origins of the universe and life. The distant beginnings are thought to have begun with an immense explosion, which has been given the name the "Big Bang." According to this theory, at one time, perhaps 15 billion years ago, a ball of matter and energy exploded to give birth to an expanding universe. Various chemical elements and material structures were formed as a result, including stars and the other features of the cosmos. In the right physical conditions, such as those found on earth, the chemical requirements for the simplest of life forms came together to ultimately develop through biological evolution into the living world we experience today. This theory, which in detail is quite complex, has received various modifications over the years as do many scientific theories.

Is That So!

Lurking in the background of scientific theories of origin are the questions: From where did original matter originate? What or who set the Big Bang into motion?

The Bible Tells Me So

Up until about 150 years ago or so, many people in Western countries (Europe and North America) weren't particularly interested in deep discussions about Big Bangs or human origins and such, as these sorts of matters were easily explained in the Bible. The age of the earth, for example, could be figured out by information available in the book of Genesis. Those who today believe in the literalistic truth of the biblical Creation story are called *creationists*.

And God said, "Let there be light."

(Illustration by Gustave Doré)

Using biblical information and theological ideas, Irish archbishop James Ussher (1581–1656) in 1654 calculated the date of the creation of the earth to the year 4004 B.C. For a long time, this was the accepted date from which to calculate the age of our planet. Although scientists today might add a few billion years to that age of the earth, we should be careful not to scoff at the archbishop, who arrived at a reasonable conclusion given the beliefs and tools of his time: the Bible and a trust in its literal truth.

What Mr. Darwin Says

The somewhat comfortable biblical explanation of the creation of life received an earth-shattering challenge with the publication in 1859 of *The Origin of Species* by Charles Darwin (1809–1882). The book provided an alternative theory to explain how various and diverse life forms came into being, including humans, without requiring the direct involvement of God. This latter part was particularly provocative as the theory suggested that humans were distantly related to apes and other primates. Modern evolutionary theory has since much further elaborated on Darwin's basic theme. Darwin is considered the founder of modern evolutionary theory, and *The Origin of Species* had a profound effect on science and religion.

> **" " Thus Saith**
>
> In my most extreme fluctuations I have never been an atheist in the sense of denying the existence of God.
>
> —Charles Darwin, *Life and Letters*, 1 (1887)

At Odds!

So what's the big deal? As I mentioned, Darwinian evolutionary theory doesn't require that God be directly involved in a one-time Creation or an ongoing creative process. (The thing about the ape-relatives is likewise annoying to some.) Because the most adamant of creationists argue that the Bible is the inerrant word of God, and what it says in there is how it happened, then you might think that there isn't much to defend, other than the integrity of the Bible. To such individuals, the Bible itself requires no defense as their faith is sufficient to justify that it is true. Scientists, however, perpetuate a lie, they claim, and their propaganda must be countered.

> **This and That**
>
> For some interesting, multi-dimensional discussions of the stories in Genesis, read *Genesis: A Living Conversation* by Bill Moyers (Doubleday, 1996).

A typical defense of creationists is to attack the weaknesses of evolutionary science, and this they do at times with great vigor! There are creationist institutes that make it their business to discover how the findings of scientists conform to the biblical notion of Creation, and to refute the data that doesn't. In a sense, though, this can be helpful. Pointing out weaknesses in science can lead to its correction no matter whether the results are favorable or not to creationist viewpoints. In most cases, scientists are quick to acknowledge their mistakes and move on. After all, they, like the rest of us, are fallible and science is an ever-evolving means of discovery and modification. Let me just say that the creationists versus scientists debate literature is vast and passionate.

There are a number of specific issues that receive the special attention of creationists:

♦ **The age of the earth.** Creationists might argue that the earth is only about 6,000 years old, certainly not the 4 billion or so years that geologists have claimed.

♦ **The inadequacy of the fossil record.** If evolution were true, than you might expect to find smooth transitions from one type of creature to another, but that's not usually the case. Where is the evidence of such transitions? Scientists respond by pointing out the fortuitous nature of the fossilization process and argue that evolution might have taken place in great bursts of change.

♦ **The coexistence of humans with extinct creatures such as the dinosaurs.** If the earth is indeed very young, then this would have to be the case. Most scientists will argue, though, that the fossil and geological data clearly demonstrate this could not have been the case, dinosaurs being extinct millions of years before the first evidence of humans.

Some Middle Ground?

There are many profoundly religious people who with clear conscience can accept both the existence of God and the approaches of science. There are many ways of looking at the Bible and stories such as Genesis. Rather than a literal six days of creation, could the story be more abstract than that? Could the process of evolution be God's tool for populating the planet with a diversity of life over a long period of time?

While there are those who insist that all was created in six 24-hour days, others point to the poetic description of God's time found in Psalm 90:4: "For a thousand years in thy sight are but as yesterday when it is past, or as a watch in the night."

In 1996, Pope John Paul II surprised many with his comments that "new knowledge has led to the recognition of the theory of evolution as more than a hypothesis." While such a statement seems to endorse scientific claims, the pope emphasized that evolution does not explain the spiritual nature of humans, nor did he discount a role in the process for the Creator.

Apples and Oranges

Another approach is to look at science and the Bible as being like apples and oranges—each viewpoint is equally valid, just different. Science cannot tell you what your purpose on earth is other than mating and perpetuating your genetic material. The Bible, however, can explain a higher purpose for your existence, and suggest the ultimate source for all things. Science can attempt to describe how and when it might have happened, religion can provide the whys.

Is That So!

Occasionally, the debate between science and creationists leaves the church halls and printed page to become a serious legal matter. In 1925, the famous Scopes trial tested a law banning the teaching of evolution in the classroom. The anti-evolutionists won but the case was later overturned. In 1999, the Kansas Board of Education ruled to give evolution a back seat in their public school curricula. Other states are likewise considering what stance to take on this volatile issue.

In God's Image: Adam and Eve

At the end of the Creation story, God creates two humans, one male and one female. The first man is created from dust, and God breathes life into him. The man is given the name "Adam," which is related to the Hebrew word *earth*, as he was taken out of the earth. He's then put under divine anesthesia and a female companion is created for him out of one of his ribs. Although the name is usually translated as Eve, the Bible's first woman is actually known as "Havah" in Hebrew.

I've heard a couple people speculate that men have one fewer rib in their skeleton then women. They get this idea, of course, from the story in Genesis. Not so! In fact, both men and women have the same number of bones in their body: 206 in the adult skeleton.

Paradise Found: The Garden of Eden

Some theologians will say that the story of Adam and Eve wonderfully illustrates human nature. For those seeking to understand why humans are the way they are, and why most of our lives aren't a free ride, the story has some profound insights.

Genesis tells us that Adam and Eve lived in a wonderful garden where they could frolic naked in a safe and worry-free environment. So where was this garden? The

Bible actually gives some geographical clues in Genesis 2:10: "A river flowed out of Eden to water the garden, and there it divided and became four rivers." And here are the names of those rivers:

- The Pishon, which flows around the land of Havilah where gold and other precious materials can be found

- The Gihon, which flows around Cush

- The Tigris, in Mesopotamia

- The Euphrates, also in Mesopotamia

This places the Garden of Eden somewhere in a fairly large area in the Middle East; some say right in the vicinity of modern-day Iraq. And what's left of this place today, you ask? Most likely nothing to speak of. The whole region is generally hot, dry, and occasionally troublesome. Frolic around naked like Adam and Eve there today and you'll either get the worst sunburn of your life or be thrown in jail for public indecency—or both!

Eve Meets Science

It would be fair to say that most scientists don't take the story of Adam and Eve as literal history. They might say, however, that at some point, there could be a female ancestor in common for all living members of the species *Homo sapiens*. By examining the mutations found in *mitochondrial DNA*, a type of DNA (the genetic code found in all human cells) transferred from mother to children, a scientific study announced that it had found that such a common ancestor existed in Africa around 200,000 years ago. Not surprisingly, this controversial idea has its critics, some of whom claim that it's difficult to make realistic time measurements of this sort with genetic mutations. Despite the theory's flaws, most evolutionary scientists agree that humans had their origins in Africa.

Logos

Mitochondrial DNA, or mtDNA, is a type of DNA found outside a cell's nucleus. This sort of DNA is thought to be inherited unmixed from one's maternal line and has given scientists hope for a means of tracking ancient relationships and migrations of people.

God Responds

Genesis relates the famous story of how the humans, created with free will, chose to disobey God. The first couple was welcome to enjoy all of the fruits of the Garden except for that of the "tree of the knowledge of good and evil," which God warned them not to sample. Eve was talked into taking a bite by a deceitful serpent and then she offered some to Adam.

Adam and Eve made their mistake and were apparently aware of it because they hid from God when he came to visit. Adam blamed the woman, of course, and Eve blamed the snake, and God imposed consequences for all three. Snakes were cursed and condemned to crawl along the ground. Childbirth would be unpleasant for Eve and her descendents. Adam's life on the gravy train was over. From now on, he'd have to work hard for a living! Not only that, they were kicked out of the Garden of Eden. And just in case they tried to sneak back in, an angel with a flaming sword was positioned at the entrance.

Paradise Lost

So Adam and Eve had to work for a living, but soon they would have some helpers when they had a couple kids. Cain was their firstborn and became a farmer. His brother was named Abel and raised sheep. Both made offerings to God. An argument arose between the two brothers and Cain killed Abel: the first murder of untold millions to follow. After the murder, God asked Cain where his brother might be, and Cain answered, "Am I my brother's keeper?" This question continues to be asked and discussed to this day. God punished Cain for his crime and exiled him to a miserable life.

Cain is mentioned to have gone out and built a city, which he named Enoch after his son. The stories of the Garden of Eden and Cain's building of a city are quite interesting from an anthropological point of view. In studying early civilizations, anthropologists have noted that the first human societies were hunters and gatherers who lived off the land and in a sort of harmony with nature. Similar societies in this way today seem to be egalitarian, share their resources, and have a lot more leisure time than you might expect. Out of some of these early hunting and gathering groups, about 10,000 years ago or so, the first villages arose and these were supported by agriculture and domesticated animals. Some argue that this change in lifestyle, although it had some benefits, encouraged some of the worst of human behavior including envy and theft of personal property, along with power inequities brought about by uneven wealth.

Thus Saith

God commanded Adam and Eve to "be fruitful and multiply." (Genesis 1:28) This is considered the first of the 613 commandments traditionally recognized by Jews in the Torah.

From some of these early agricultural societies would arise the first cities and civilizations. In a sense, the Genesis story shows a similar developmental sequence: Adam and Eve began in harmony with nature in the Garden of Eden. They were kicked out and began a much harder life, where bad things such as the murder of Abel occurred. Cain built the first city.

The Least You Need to Know

- The first few chapters of the first book of the Bible, Genesis, are both profound and provocative.

- The question of Creation is an incredibly controversial and complex subject.

- Creationists and some scientists are often at odds over the nature of our ultimate origins.

- Although both scientists and creationists often strongly disagree, it's also possible to see religion and science providing answers to different kinds of questions.

- The story of Adam and Eve illustrates that given free will, humans have the freedom to choose between good and evil.

- Life outside the Garden of Eden was no picnic.

Chapter 6

Mayhem and Confusion

In This Chapter

- ◆ God is disappointed
- ◆ Noah builds a boat
- ◆ The world's biggest flood
- ◆ Ark hunters, ancient and modern
- ◆ The tongue-twisting Tower of Babel
- ◆ God destroys a couple nasty cities

The marvelous Book of Genesis contains a few more stories that address the early world of the Bible, if not the entire planet itself. One is the story of a cataclysmic flood that required a repopulation of the earth in its aftermath. Another is a tale of God-less human ambition which also aims to explain the amazing diversity of human languages.

Let's examine these fascinating stories. I'll also throw in a little additional mayhem at the end of the chapter.

God Has Had Enough

In the clash between scientists and those who believe in a very literal interpretation of the Bible, the story of Noah and the Great Flood is nearly as volatile as that of Creation! Here's the story. In Genesis 6:5–6, it is written: "The Lord saw that the wickedness of man was great in the earth, and that every imagination of the thoughts of his heart was only evil continually. And the Lord was sorry that he had made man on the earth, and it grieved him in his heart. So the Lord said, 'I will blot out man whom I have created from the face of the ground, man and beast and creeping things and birds of the air, for I am sorry that I have made them.'" Verse 11 goes on to say that "the earth was corrupt in God's sight, and the earth was filled with violence."

Look what Adam and Eve started! Given free will, temptation, and bad choices, a habit of poor behavior is carried out in following generations. God decided it was time to start over. In Genesis 6:13 and 17 he said, "'I have determined to make an end of all flesh; for the earth is filled with violence through them; behold, I will destroy them with the earth ... I will bring a flood of waters upon the earth, to destroy all flesh which is the breath of life from under heaven; everything that is on the earth shall die.'" One man named Noah, however, was righteous and "walked with God," so he was chosen for a special job. He was instructed to build a boat that would save him and his wife along with their three sons and their wives.

> **People and Places**
>
> Noah is listed in the New Testament book of Hebrews as one of the giants of faith for taking God at his word and building the Ark.

That's One Big Boat!

God gave Noah specific instructions for building the boat:

- It was to be built of "gopher wood."
- It would be 300 "cubits" long, 50 cubits wide, and 30 cubits high.
- It would have three decks with rooms.
- It was to be covered with pitch inside and out.
- It would have a roof.
- There would be a door on one side.
- There was probably also a windowed area around the edge near the roof.

First, let's look at the building material. We really don't know what "gopher wood" is. It certainly has nothing to do with the modern rodent we call the gopher. The wood gets its name from the literal pronunciation of the Hebrew word as it appears in the Bible: *gopher*. It is a word that appears only in this story. It's possible that this wood is cypress.

To figure out the size of the boat, we need to know how big a cubit was. Traditionally, it was a distance from the elbow to the end of the fingers and was probably about 17½ to 20 inches. If we take 18 inches for our rough estimate, then Noah's boat would be 450 feet long, 75 feet wide, and 45 feet high! The tar on the walls inside and out would add waterproofing. There have been many attempts to reconstruct the boat based on the scant information provided in Genesis.

The boat is often depicted as a rectangular structure because of the three dimensions given in the text, but it's possible that it could have been wide in the middle like many wooden boats. It has even been suggested that "gopher wood" might be sturdy bundles of reeds, whose natural buoyancy might be further preserved with the coating of tar. Boats of papyrus and reeds were known to have been used in the region of the Bible lands so I suppose it's possible.

It had to be a roomy boat because not only would Noah's family be aboard, but male and female pairs of all animals that would be able to repopulate the earth after life is destroyed. In Genesis 6:19–21, God commanded Noah: "And of every living thing of all flesh, you shall bring two of every sort into the Ark, to keep them alive with you; they shall be male and female … two of every sort shall come in to you, to keep them alive. Also take with you every sort of food that is eaten, and store it up; and it shall serve as food for you and them." This certainly explains the need for all of the rooms to keep the various beasts separated as well as storage for their food!

> ### This and That
>
> Boats made of reeds are mentioned in Isaiah 18:1–2. In the late 1960s and 1970s, Norwegian explorer and scholar Thor Heyerdahl tested the seaworthiness of ancient reed boats by successfully crossing the Atlantic on a boat made of papyrus, and effectively traveling about the Persian Gulf region and beyond in another ship made of reeds. They do float!

"The Ark"

Noah's boat is traditionally called the *Ark*, but this word can be a bit confusing. It's an English translation of the Hebrew word *tevah*, which is also the same word used for the floating, tar-sealed basket in the story of Moses. The confusion comes when the word *ark* is also applied to another famous biblical artifact: the Ark of the Covenant, which is a special box that was likewise created with

> ### Logos
>
> Although the English word **ark** is used for two different famous biblical artifacts constructed under order from God, one is a boat, and the other is a very special box.

specific directions from God (see Chapter 15). The Hebrew word for this object, though, is *aron*. Like the Ark of the Covenant, Noah's Ark may have been rectangular and both are a kind of "vessel" used to carry things. Otherwise, in terms of size, history, and specific function, these two "arks" are extremely different. Today, the word *ark* is also used for the alcove in a synagogue that holds the Torah scrolls.

How Many Beasts?

So if the world was going to be destroyed, and a pair of each animal was needed to get things going again later, then that's a heck of a lot of animals even for a massive ship as large as Noah's! Furthermore, there's another description in the story that states that God wanted "seven pairs of all clean animals … and a pair of the animals that are not clean … and seven pairs of the birds of the air also." This immediately sounds like (1) a whole bunch of animals given the thousands of species that abound today, and (2) a conflict with the two-pairs story.

Is That So!

There was no need for big aquariums on the Ark. Apparently fish weren't affected by the flood.

Defenders of the story might argue that representative kinds of animals were placed aboard the boat, rather than a pair of each species. This idea, however, would require that there be some sort of evolutionary repopulation mechanism or a flood that wasn't worldwide. The seven pairs of clean animals might refer specifically to those species that were used in sacrifices because if you didn't have some extras around, you'd lose your species if you made a sacrifice.

The Great Flood

Noah, who at the time was 600 years old (he was a father, too, with three sons when he was 500), loaded up the Ark and the flood began. According to Genesis: "… all of the fountains of the great deep burst forth, and the windows of the heavens were opened. And it rained forty days and forty nights … the waters increased and prevailed and increased greatly upon the earth; and the Ark floated on the face of the waters. And the waters prevailed so mightily upon the earth that all the high mountains under the whole heaven were covered; the waters prevailed above the mountains, covering them fifteen cubits deep." The flooding continued for 150 days, and then the Ark came to rest on a mountain. Noah sent out a raven and then a dove multiple times in an effort to check for land. After being onboard for almost a year, Noah and company eventually left the Ark when things were sufficiently dry. He then built an altar and made a sacrifice to God.

Noah's boat at rest on a mountaintop.

(Illustration by Gustave Doré)

Now building a big boat is one thing, and Noah's age might raise a few scientific eyebrows, but a worldwide flood that destroys everything on the earth except the passengers of the Ark is a leading bone of contention between religious fundamentalists and many scientists. How could the entire earth be covered with water? Mount Everest, for example, is 29,028 feet tall! And where did all the water come from and where did it go afterward?

Yes, these are some troubling questions, but let's look at some of the answers of the literalist biblical apologists. The "fountains of the great deep," some say, was water trapped under pressure beneath the earth in the antediluvian (pre-flood) environment which may have been quite different from the shape of the world in the aftermath of the great flood. In those days, some claim, the atmosphere was quite different from the way it is now, and featured a "water vapor canopy" encircling the earth that provided the second source for the huge amounts of water necessary to flood the entire surface of the planet

> ### This and That
>
> The wettest spot on the face of the earth today is Mount Waialeale on Kauai in the Hawaiian islands. It rains there most of the time. And people in Seattle can certainly relate to what 40 days and 40 nights of rain is all about!

to great depth. Another theory suggests that a comet hit the earth, causing huge catastrophic effects including changes in the weather, radical alteration of the earth's surface, and massive flooding. Believers in a young Earth would have this happening about 5,000 years ago.

And where did the water go afterward? It constitutes the oceans, goes one theory, because along with and after the flood came a lot of reshaping of the earth's surface: rising ranges of mountains, big valleys and canyons, and deep ocean basins. Huge mountains like Everest were lifted up, and at the same time, drainage of the floodwaters to the deep areas below was enhanced.

As with Creation, the Bible was long used as a popular means of explaining various episodes of the distant past. The Great Flood provided the explanation for fossils of humans or other animals found in the ground, including the curious phenomenon of fossil seashells found in geological strata high up in the mountains. Modern geology, however, has quite a different story with the planet's present state being a result of various processes taking place over hundreds of millions, if not billions, of years.

Was There Really a Big Flood?

Although many geologists will dispute that there was ever was a worldwide flood, legends about big floods are common in many cultures around the world. In 1872, a dramatic announcement was made of the discovery of an ancient text that contains a story very much like the Genesis flood. The text was found on a clay tablet excavated from the site of Kuyunjik in Mesopotamia and is part of a popular tale known as *The Epic of Gilgamesh*. In this story an immortal man named Utnapishtim shares a story with Gilgamesh that is dramatically similar to that of Noah.

Logos

The Epic of Gilgamesh survives in several copies written on clay tablets in the Sumerian and Akkadian languages of Mesopotamia. The Epic describes the adventures of a demigod hero named Gilgamesh. At one point, Gilgamesh sought the survivor of the great flood, Utnapishtim, to try to find the secret of his immortality. Gilgamesh was unsuccessful in achieving a similar status.

Long ago, the gods were displeased with humans so they decided to destroy all living things on the earth. But one god gave his friend Utnapishtim advance warning so he could build a boat big enough for his family, belongings, and living creatures. A storm raged for seven days bringing massive flooding. The boat came to rest on a mountain and three birds were released to check for dry land. When it was safe to leave the boat, Utnapishtim built an altar and made a sacrifice to the gods. Is this independent confirmation of the biblical story in a distorted version? Did the author(s) of Genesis borrow from Gilgamesh? Or was the flood story part of a wider regional myth, legend, or historical memory?

Digging for Sediments

In the 1920s, while excavating at the site of Ur in Mesopotamia, British archaeologist Leonard Woolley found a very thick deposit of flood debris, which generated much excitement. Could this be archaeological evidence of the biblical flood? A big flood certainly had taken place at one time at Ur, but a check of other sites in the region didn't turn up the same evidence. Besides, the deposits found at Ur were much too late to have been related to the Great Flood. This flood had been more or less local, and in Mesopotamia, a flood plain in the midst of two rivers, it's not that surprising.

A More Limited Viewpoint

Is it possible that the flood that the Bible describes was not worldwide? The Hebrew word used in the Bible to describe what the flood covered is *eretz*, which also means "land." This being so, perhaps the flood was a more local event although some of the biblical literalists heartily reject this more easily explainable situation in favor of a global catastrophe. If the flood were immense and regional, then indeed it might appear to Noah that his entire world was inundated.

More Science

Is there any other evidence for large-scale flooding that might be reflected in the Genesis story? A recent theory has suggested that a real flood might be the result of a massive barrage of water crashing forth when the Mediterranean spilled into the waters of the Black Sea around 7,500 years ago. And relatively recently, in geological terms, the Ice Ages certainly had a profound effect upon the shaping of the earth. After the last period of glaciation, melting ice contributed to a global sea-level rise of about 300 feet! Large sections of land that were once exposed became submerged as a result. Could the story of Noah be an ancient memory related to these Earth phenomena?

Whether the details of the account of Noah and the flood are literal or a great tale that illustrates God's judgment and rescue, it is, nonetheless, a fascinating story that will continue to inspire Bible readers and Ark hunters. The end of the narrative is especially touching. God promised Noah that he would never again destroy the earth with a flood. As a reminder of his promise, God placed a bow in the sky as a sign: the rainbow that is seen in the sky when sun and mist come together.

Searching for the Ark

The Bible says that the Ark came to rest on the mountains of Ararat, so if we can identify this place, might we not be able to find the remains of the Ark itself? Finding

Noah's Ark would perhaps be the most important and amazing archaeological discovery of all time! But there are a couple things to consider first:

♦ We must first assume that what the Bible says in the story of Noah is literally true, and not a metaphor or some other literary device.

♦ We would have to assume that the Ark was deposited in an environment conducive to its long-term survival. This would be by no means necessarily guaranteed, especially being built of perishable materials such as wood.

With these conditions met, we might confidently go out looking for the big boat.

Which Mountain?

As the Bible says, it's the mountains, plural, of Ararat that are indicated and the likely region is that known as Urartu in ancient times, which is an area north of Mesopotamia. There one might expect to find the Ark firmly lodged on a tall mountain, and the all-time favorite candidate is a mountain in eastern Turkey called Agri Dagi or Ararat.

The Koran, the holy book of Islam, gives a different location for the Ark: a "Mt. Judi," which is usually identified with a mountain called Cudi Dagh in southern Turkey. Although not nearly as high as Agri Dagi, this mountain has what appears to be a much older tradition as the site of the Ark's resting place.

Ancient Reports

For *arkologists*, there are mentions of the boat's survival dating back a couple of thousand years. A Chaldean priest named Berossus (c. 275 B.C.) wrote that pieces of the Ark still survived and people could scrape pitch off of it for use on amulets. The first-century Jewish historian Josephus mentioned that others reported that the remains of the Ark were still in existence. Subsequent reports by Christian and Islamic writers continue to mention that Ark remains could be found on mountains that are named as, or fit the description of, Ararat or alternatively Judi.

Logos

Arkologists is a term used for those who are interested in locating the remains of Noah's Ark.

Modern Sightings and Expeditions

Several twentieth-century eyewitnesses have claimed to have actually seen the Ark on Mt. Ararat. A Turk named George Hagopian claimed that as a young boy he was taken by his uncle to the site of the Ark around the year 1905. It was located on a ledge at the edge of a cliff and was made of a rock-hard material. The boy thought the structure was stone until told otherwise by his uncle. The skeptic in me might suggest that maybe this was some sort of stone structure of undetermined origin that was believed by locals to be part of the Ark.

A fascinating report is that of a Russian pilot named Roskovitsky who allegedly flew his plane near Ararat in 1916 and spotted a boat at the edge of a frozen lake. The story goes on to say that a subsequent Russian expedition to investigate this report found the Ark and explored its interior, which contained hundreds of rooms of different sizes. A detailed description of the Ark is said to have been made along with photographs, but alas, all was lost in the Russian revolution in the following year.

An American serviceman, Ed Davis, reported being taken by locals high up on Ararat to visit a large fragment of the Ark. No pictures were taken. A Frenchman, Fernand Navarra, visited Ararat several times in the 1950s and 1960s and returned with some interesting samples of wood which he claimed were taken from a wooden structure embedded in ice high up on the mountain. When the wood was radiocarbon dated, however, most of it dated to between around A.D. 600 and 800.

The Ark has on other occasions been "spotted" from the air, but searches on the ground have yet to reveal anything substantial. A few years ago, another startling claim was made that the Ark had indeed been discovered but again the documentation was lacking. This time, it proved to be a complete hoax.

Is That So!

In the late 1950s, aerial photographs revealed an amazing site about 15 miles from the base of Mt. Ararat. A huge, boat-shape outline could be readily observed at a place known as Durpinar. Could this be the remains of the Ark, it having been carried by the forces of nature to the foot of the mountain? Despite the claims of a few arkologists that they could detect the remains of boat ribs and metal fittings, geologic studies of the Durpinar "Ark" have indicated that it is merely a geological feature. It's also too big to fit the biblical description unless you subscribe to the possibility of some sort of bigger "divine cubit."

The search for Noah's Ark continues, and sophisticated scientific equipment has been enlisted, including high-resolution infrared aerial photography, ice coring, and ground-penetrating radar. Occasionally, yet another Ark hunter will make a big announcement followed by a groan of disappointment when the weak or nonexistent evidence is presented. Perhaps the search has been in vain and many of the eyewitness reports are the result of hearsay, and misinterpretation of natural features, along with a few hoaxes.

The region of Mt. Ararat is at present a somewhat dangerous place. Kurdish nationalists in the vicinity aren't always pleased to have visitors, and kidnappings of arkologists have taken place. Some visitors, to the mountain have been given military escorts and only after a special permit from the Turkish government has been obtained.

Having somewhat explored this interesting subject, here are a couple comments from yours truly, who is both an archaeologist and a mountain climber:

♦ A lot of these expeditions seem very well intentioned and biblically inspired, but very weak on mountaineering skills. Injuries have not been uncommon and the glacial terrain that might be explored is hazardous and requires specialized skills to search some of the more dangerous places. So there is a need for good climbers to be involved. If need be, the Bible-guys can direct the climbing experts from a safe location.

♦ Even if a big wooden structure is found on a mountain such as Ararat, a careful scientist cannot alert the world that Noah's Ark has been indeed found until the object is thoroughly examined and subjected to tests, and a proper argument is developed. Holy mountains might attract the building of shrines high on their slopes.

♦ Most important, if you do find Noah's Ark and walk around in it and such, take some pictures, note the location as precisely as possible … and then hang on to your camera and don't lose the map! In short, show me the boat!

It seems that nearly every year, someone claims to have found Noah's Ark or knows exactly where to find it. Given a long history of little physical evidence, don't hold your breath until a sturdy case is made.

What Did You Say? The Tower of Babel

After the flood, the earth repopulated and in Genesis 11:1–9, a whole bunch of people were suddenly acting a bit arrogant. So arrogant, in fact, that they attempted to build a brick skyscraper so tall that it would reach heaven! This was a preposterous thing to do but it didn't stop them from trying. God didn't approve of this sort of activity and behavior so he messed up their building project in a very clever way. Instead of wrecking the place, he caused the workers to speak mutually unintelligible languages and scattered them over the face of the earth.

This story also serves as a kind of explanation for the multitude of languages found on the earth today. A lot of linguistic scholars see the real story as being a little more complicated than that, but perhaps at one time there was a single human language that originally diverged when groups became separated and their grammar and words evolved.

The Tower of Babel.

(Illustration by Gustave Doré)

The story of the Tower of Babel seems to have taken place in Babylon, an area and city in Mesopotamia, in the vicinity of modern-day Iraq (see Chapter 11). The ancient people of Mesopotamia were known to build tall temple platforms known as ziggurats, and the ruins of a number of these impressive structures survive. Nineteenth-century travelers through the region saw some of these remains and even went so far as to identify at least one as the remains of the famous Tower. Although a few are tall, there are no ziggurats to be found of sufficient size and height to identify with such a story, and even if there were, how could one identify it as the Tower of Babel? And if this story is meant as a parable, rather than as literal history, the chances of finding such a Tower are even more greatly diminished.

This and That

The number of the world's languages today is estimated to be around 4,000 to 5,000. Many of the smaller languages are dying out while English-speakers grow in numbers. One of the rarest languages is a biblical one, Aramaic, which is today spoken in only two villages in Syria.

Bringing Down Sodom and Gomorrah

While we're on the topic of destruction and confusion, in chapters 18 and 19 of Genesis we can find another story about how God dealt with some unruly humans. There were two cities with horrible reputations: Sodom and Gomorrah. The people were apparently engaging in all manner of depravity, and God had enough and told the biblical patriarch Abraham so. Abraham was a bit concerned because his nephew named Lot, a decent fellow, and his family were living in Sodom.

A couple angels were sent to warn Lot and a riot nearly broke out when the locals wanted to have a little fun with the divine visitors. Lot would have nothing of the sort. He even offered his two virgin daughters to the mob, but they insisted that he hand over the guys. The angels blinded some of these rioters as they attempted to beat the door down.

The angels warned Lot to remove his family from the city and the next day they escaped. The city of Sodom, along with Gomorrah, was destroyed in a "hail of fire and brimstone." Lot's family was told to leave the city and not look back. Lot's wife apparently couldn't resist and took a look at the city under destruction. The Bible says that she was transformed into a pillar of salt.

The old sites of Sodom and Gomorrah are usually thought to be near the Dead Sea. That area is interesting geologically and resembles a chemical waste-dump. There is even a rock formation that has been given the name Lot's Wife.

Recently, a couple geologists speculated that an earthquake may have swallowed up or submerged the cities as the shaking land liquefied. Others have suggested volcanic or geothermal activity contributed to the hail of fire and brimstone said to have demolished the cities. Or was it an earthquake followed by a natural gas explosion? Or was the story another biblical parable? The explanation remains unclear.

The Least You Need to Know

- According to the Bible, a disappointed God destroyed much of life on Earth with a great flood, but also reserved a remnant.

- Noah and his family, along with representatives of the different animal species, survived the flood in a huge boat and then repopulated the earth.

- Many scientists and biblical literalists are at odds when it comes to the idea of Noah's Ark and a worldwide flood.

- Despite numerous attempts to locate the Ark, there is no credible evidence that it has yet been found or even survives.

◆ The story of the Tower of Babel is a way of showing the arrogance of people, along with an explanation for the diversity of languages in the world and how humans spread across the earth.

◆ In the Old Testament, when God got mad or tired of human excesses, you'd better watch out. He destroyed the cities of Sodom and Gomorrah, for example.

Part 2

Residents of the Promised Land

In this part, we're going to look at the people who lived in and about ancient Palestine. These include some of the key players in the Bible. We're going to meet the Canaanites, some of the earliest inhabitants of the Holy Land, and then some of their neighbors such as the Philistines, Phoenicians, and Moabites. They all interacted with the Israelites, of course, and there's a chapter about the Israelites themselves. I think you'll find all of these people quite interesting!

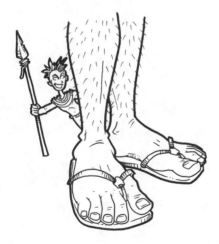

Chapter 7

Canaanites and Their Ancestors

In This Chapter

- Palestine as the crossroads of early man
- The shift from hunting to farming
- The development of "complex societies"
- Cultural complexity: the Bronze Age
- Canaanite cities and culture

Most events described in the Bible took place in the last 3,000 to 4,000 years and most of them in the Palestine region. In order to understand the context for those biblical events, a little background regarding human activity in the area is useful.

Although scholars have divided up ancient times into broad periods based on technology and lifestyles, keep in mind that such broad periods don't have sharp dividing lines. Many of the changes that archaeologists note are the result of gradual processes. The Neolithic period, for example, didn't appear overnight.

Caveman Crossroads

As I noted in Chapter 3, Palestine is situated at the crossroads of continents and thus was ideally situated for people coming and going, in peace or otherwise. Many scientists today believe that humans had their origin in Africa and spread out from there; Palestine is the obvious gateway to both Europe and Asia.

Scientists use the term *Paleolithic* to designate periods of time when early humans roamed about, making a living primarily from hunting animals and gathering nature's produce. The term means "Old Stone Age" because many tools in use during those times were made from stone. The Paleolithic era is divided up into four main stages:

- ◆ **Lower Paleolithic:** circa 1 million to 120,000 years ago
- ◆ **Middle Paleolithic:** circa 120,000 to 40,000 years ago
- ◆ **Upper Paleolithic:** circa 40,000 to 19,000 years ago
- ◆ **Epipaleolithic:** circa 19,000 years ago to 8000 B.C.

Stone tool styles changed through time and are the basis for some of the identification and dating of such sites. Lower Paleolithic sites, for example, usually feature big, clunky hand-axes, whereas the Upper Paleolithic is distinguished by more specialized and sophisticated tools. Archaeological sites representing all of these time periods can be found in Palestine.

> **This and That**
>
> Early humans no doubt used all kinds of materials to facilitate their lifestyles, but it's the durability of stone that survives the ages and allows archaeologists to study such ancient times hundreds of thousands of years later.

Paleolithic sites can often be found scattered out in the desert, sometimes in places where the environment was once very hospitable but is now quite desolate. Caves can make wonderful shelters for people, and Palestine is full of them. Several containing Paleolithic remains have been found. Caves up on Mt. Carmel near Haifa, Israel, for example, are famous for their stratified prehistoric remains. In Galilee, the skull of a man dating back 120,000 years was found in a cave!

A Change in Lifestyle

Around 8000 B.C., a major change in lifestyle took place for many people in Palestine. For reasons we don't fully understand, instead of hunting and gathering and living in small groups, they began to practice agriculture and the tending of domesticated animals. This was quite a change! Crops, including barley and wheat, required care but they also could produce a food surplus. This surplus allowed people to live together in permanent villages rather than as widespread foragers or nomads, and the population grew. Herds of goats and sheep were maintained and formerly wild cows were put to work plowing and providing milk. The time period when this lifestyle dominates is known as the Neolithic, or "New Stone Age." So radical a change is it that some scholars have referred to it as the "Neolithic Revolution."

Technology accompanied these changes and pretty soon another valuable tool for archaeologists appeared: pottery. Pottery has dozens of uses, of course, and was used to store and transport both solids and liquids. Some archaeologists have divided this time into the Pre-Pottery Neolithic and the Pottery Neolithic. When the use of copper metal appears on the scene, the time period is referred to as the Chalcolithic. Here's a basic time frame for these stages in Palestine:

- **Neolithic:** 8000 to 4500 B.C.

- **Early Chalcolithic:** 4500 to 3800 B.C.

- **Late Chalcolithic:** 3800 to 3300 B.C.

The Chalcolithic is one of the most interesting of these early periods. Many agricultural villages with mud-brick buildings began to appear. Religious sites from this period have been found, including what appears to be a rectangular stone temple near En Gedi, close to the Dead Sea. Another interesting practice from this was burial of the bones of some people in little ceramic houses.

People and Places

In 1961, one of the most magnificent discoveries ever in Palestine was found in a cave at Nahal Mishmar not far from En Gedi. The "Cave of the Treasures" contained a cache of 416 objects from Chalcolithic times. Many were masterfully manufactured from copper and appear to be ceremonial in nature, including scepters and what appears to be a crown. Some objects of hippopotamus and elephant ivory were also found in this amazing hoard. The exact function of these objects and why they were stored in the cave remains a mystery. Today these objects are displayed in the Israel Museum in Jerusalem.

One of the major questions of interest to archaeologists and anthropologists is why did the Neolithic phenomenon occur? Why after tens of thousands of years did people start settling down? This sort of lifestyle seems to have begun in the Near East, perhaps in the foothills of Iraq, and then spread from there to Palestine and elsewhere. There are many theories. The Neolithic lifestyle appears in the aftermath of the Ice Age at a time of great climate changes and it is possible that this was a major factor. However it happened, this kind of life would eventually change much of the world.

Yet Another Big Change!

Around 3000 B.C. in the Near East, profound things began to happen: the development of what anthropologists refer to as "complex societies." Some people use the term "civilizations" to describe this phenomenon and typical examples include the classic cultures of ancient Egypt and Mesopotamia. A complex society tends to have cities typically with religious and political structures such as temples and palaces for a ruler and priests. There are differences in wealth and status, and, as opposed to much simpler societies, there are lots of craft specialists. Writing tends to be an important component of such cultures as well.

This and That

There are six main areas where major complex societies developed in ancient times: Egypt, Mesopotamia, the Indus Valley, China, Mesoamerica, and Peru.

Why did this happen? Like the Neolithic, the development of complex societies is still a bit of a puzzle. Was civilization spread as ideas were shared between groups or did these cultures develop as they did independently? The one thing they seem to have in common, though, is that they have agriculture as a basic foundation. And given the relatively close proximity of cultures in the Near East, a lot of sharing was no doubt taking place.

The Bronze Age

The time when cities and cultural complexity began to appear and then thrived in Palestine is known to scholars as the Bronze Age. Scholars have divided up the Bronze Age into three periods, the Early, Middle, and Late. These periods, too, are subdivided up into smaller chronological sections such as Early Bronze II, Middle Bronze III, and so forth.

- ◆ **Early Bronze Age:** 3300 to 2000 B.C.
- ◆ **Middle Bronze Age:** 2000 to 1500 B.C.
- ◆ **Late Bronze Age:** 1500 to 1200 B.C.

During the Early Bronze Age, some villages began to transform into cities. At sites such as Arad, Taanach, and Megiddo, walled cities began to appear. The walls of the latter were 25 feet thick! The existence of such fortification gives a clue to the nature of the times during which there must have been a real need for defense. As we have no written texts from the Early Bronze Age, we must rely on the careful work of archaeologists to come up with some of the details of past events.

Many of the people associated with such cities were still involved in agriculture and pastoralism (herding) in outlying areas, but the city walls could provide for their safety in an emergency. These cities seemed to have served as little political entities of themselves, city-states, with a chief or ruler in charge. Their craft specialists produced everything from ceramic pots to jewelry. Trade relationships in the Bronze Age were extensive and involved import and export of goods from such places as Egypt, Anatolia (Turkey), Cyprus in the Mediterranean, and Mycenae in the Aegean.

> **This and That**
>
> Although the organization of Palestinian history refers to the "Early Bronze Age," the metal bronze (tin plus copper) isn't really very common until the Middle Bronze Age. Bronze was especially useful in producing weapons such as daggers, axes, and javelins.

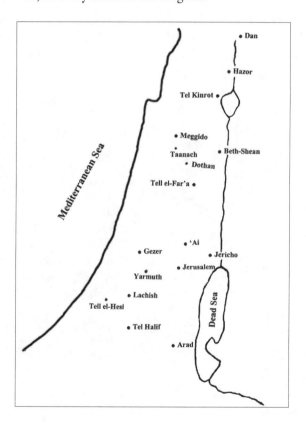

Map of some of the major Bronze Age cities in Palestine.

Downfall

Near the end of the Early Bronze Age, there was some sort of urban collapse. Some cities fell into ruin and others were abandoned. It could be that climatic events made it difficult to sustain cities, and some think that nomads may have overrun the land. Another idea suggests that commercial relationships between Egypt and the cities was so vital that when Egypt fell into temporary chaos about this time, the effect on the complicated system of the cities was catastrophic in Palestine.

Making a Comeback

During the Middle Bronze Age, we can start bringing in the Bible as a source of information along with other illuminating texts from the Near East. We can rightly now refer to the Palestinian area as Canaan and its regular inhabitants as Canaanites. Many of the old abandoned cities were reoccupied and some new ones were founded during this time. City walls were again big and thick! Several religious structures have been identified from this period.

The events portrayed in the biblical stories of the patriarchs Abraham, Isaac, Jacob, and Joseph seem to have occurred during this time. As we'll review in the next chapter, the people who would later become known as the Hebrew tribes/Israelites/Jews became established in Canaan and then migrated to Egypt before returning a few centuries later to take over the place!

This tomb painting from the Egyptian cemetery of Beni Hasan apparently depicts visiting Canaanites.

(David Moyer collection)

A little Egyptian history would be useful because Egypt was regularly involved in Canaan over the years. During what historians call the Middle Kingdom, Egypt was strong and thriving culturally. Foreigners from the east—the Hyksos—however, managed to capture the reins of authority over Egypt much to the resentment of the Egyptians themselves. Although we're not sure exactly who these Hyksos were, it's possible that they were some manner of Canaanites. The Hyksos managed to rule for about 150 years before being driven out, with the Egyptians following in hot pursuit thereby initiating their great Egyptian age of empire known in the historical framework as the New Kingdom.

Covering more than 200 acres, Hazor in Upper Galilee is one of the largest archaeological sites in Palestine. Much excavation has taken place there since 1928 and revealed the growth of this mighty city beginning in the Bronze Age.

(David Moyer collection)

As a result of this Egyptian expansion of power and influence during the latter part of the Middle Bronze Age, Palestine became a sort of Egyptian colony. Military outposts were established and tribute was demanded. Cities that cooperated were given protection from their feuding neighbors, but those who rebelled could expect the Egyptian army to visit. Egyptian pharaohs such as Tuthmosis III bragged about attacking Canaan and several of the large cities were seriously damaged.

Is That So!

Some of our knowledge of Canaanite cities and other places comes from what are called execration texts. In Egypt, the names of enemies were sometimes written on clay bowls and ceramic figurines, which were then smashed as a kind of ritual curse. Surviving examples have provided scholars with some great geographical information.

Rebuilding

During the Late Bronze Age, some of the previously damaged cities were rebuilt. The Egyptians still came in from time to time, and other groups with interests in Palestine occasionally competed with the Egyptians for strategic control. The remarkable discovery of letters written by Canaanite city chiefs to Egyptian rulers has given us wonderful insights into some of the events of the time. Written on almost 400 clay tablets in Mesopotamian cuneiform script, this collection of correspondence is known as the Amarna Tablets after the site in Egypt where they were found. Interestingly, many of the tablets are pleas for help to stop yet other invaders from harassing the Canaanite settlements! By the end of the Late Bronze Age, many of the cities of Canaan would be violently destroyed.

Meet the Canaanites

With a historical framework established, let's discuss some of the people themselves. As I mentioned in Chapter 3, the term *Canaan* can be applied to the general region of Palestine. The language and culture of the Canaanites extended well beyond these borders and far to the north through what is now Lebanon and much of Syria. The people whom we will later describe as the Phoenicians were essentially Canaanites who occupied coastal cities on the Lebanese coast and developed a wealthy maritime culture including far-flung colonies (see Chapter 9).

The Canaanites spoke a language that has been classified as belonging to the North-west Semitic family. Its close cousins include Hebrew, Phoenician, and Aramaic. It would be inaccurate to think of the land of Canaan as a country. Many, if not most, of the cities and other settlements in the area operated as little states of their own, with their own chiefs and rulers. There was no capital city for the region. Although there are variations among the different groups, they seemed to have shared a common religion and cultural features.

Play Baal!

Canaanite religion is of special interest to the student of the Bible. When the Israelite tribes invaded the land of Canaan, much of their cause was to cleanse the territory of paganism as ordered by God. The Canaanites were *polytheists*; that is, they believed in the existence of many gods. Some of the chief Canaanite gods are as follows:

- ◆ El, the wise and compassionate patriarch of the gods who lived on a mountaintop
- ◆ Asherah, El's consort and mother of the gods
- ◆ Baal, a powerful storm and fertility god
- ◆ Anat, the sister of Baal and the goddess of war and love
- ◆ Dagon, the god of grain
- ◆ Astarte, a fertility goddess

Other important deities include the sun goddess, Shemesh; Yarih, the moon god; Yam, the god of the sea; and Mot, the god of death. These gods could be worshipped in local temples or at "high places" on mountains or piles of stones.

Some of the Canaanite religious rituals involved blood sacrifices. Animals were slaughtered on altars by priests in attempts to appease the gods. In its most extreme and hopefully rare form, human children were sacrificed. This appalling practice is mentioned in the Bible. Deuteronomy 12:31 offers an opinion on Canaanite religious practices: "... every abominable thing which the Lord hates they have done for their gods; for they even burn their sons and their daughters in the fire to their gods."

Logos

Polytheism is the belief in many gods. A monotheist believes in only one god. Atheists deny the existence of God, and agnostics aren't sure.

And Some Thanks to the Ugarites

Written texts from Canaan are relatively rare and those that exist don't give us many details. Some of our most extensive knowledge of the Canaanite religion and belief system, however, comes from elsewhere: an interesting archaeological site called Ras Shamra in northern Syria. This is the site of the ancient city of Ugarit, which practiced Canaanite culture. What makes Ugarit special is that thousands of clay tablets survive, giving us a glimpse of many aspects of Ugaritic/Canaanite life.

From A to Z

While the Bible might present an unsavory picture of the Canaanites, we can be thankful for at least one of their inventions: the alphabet. Some of the major writing systems of the Near East were complicated and involved the learning of hundreds of symbols as utilized by professional scribes. The alphabet simplified things considerably and greatly improved the possibility of wider-scale literacy. The alphabet was spread by the Phoenicians (see Chapter 9) to the Greeks and the rest, as they say, is history. (See more about Near Eastern writing in Chapter 14.)

The Least You Need to Know

- ◆ For reasons not fully understood, the Paleolithic lifestyle of hunting and gathering gave way to the practice of agriculture and the tending of animals.

- ◆ Complex societies with cities began to appear in Palestine during the Bronze Age.

- ◆ Although sharing a common culture, the cities of Palestine pretty much operated as independent states with their own rulers.

◆ The people of Canaan both traded with and were at times dominated by the Egyptians.

◆ The Canaanites worshipped many gods and sacrifice was a major part of their worship.

◆ Texts found in such places as Egypt and Ugarit greatly enhanced our knowledge of the ancient Canaanite culture in Palestine.

Chapter 8

Children of God: The Israelites

In This Chapter

- Abraham makes a deal
- A people are founded
- Enslavement and deliverance from Egypt
- Conquering and ruling the Promised Land
- Archaeological evidence and dilemmas
- The rise and fall of the Israelite kingdoms

Apart from God, the central players in the Hebrew Bible/Old Testament are the Israelites, a people chosen by God to receive the divine Word and to live according to it. Who were these people whom the world now knows as their descendents, the Jews, and what was their origin?

In this chapter, we'll take a brief look at the intriguing course of events that characterize the history of these people. In later chapters, we'll view in more detail some of their specific beliefs and ways of life.

Big Daddy: Abraham of Ur

In the Book of Genesis, we meet a man named Abraham who was from the city of Ur in Mesopotamia. God instructed him to move to Canaan where he was promised, "I will multiply your descendants as the stars of heaven, and will give to your descendants all these lands; and by your descendants all the nations of the earth shall bless themselves." Many scholars suggest this move took place perhaps around 2000 B.C. Most profoundly, a contract or "covenant" was struck between Abraham and God. In return for exclusive worship as the one true God, and obedience, God would look after Abraham and his descendants. This belief system recognizing one Supreme Being, monotheism, would set these covenant-keepers apart from virtually all other cultures in ancient times.

Is That So! _____

Although Genesis notes that Abraham was from "Ur of the Chaldeans," the Chaldeans weren't in charge of that city at the time. The use of the term probably is a clue that this phrase in the Bible was first written down at a time much later than the events described. The Chaldeans who later controlled Ur were probably better known at that time so a reference would have made more specific sense to early readers.

It took a miracle for Abraham to become a father and ancestor of a great nation. God told Abraham and his wife Sarah that were going to have a son. They both laughed because Abraham was 100 years old and his wife was 90. But according to the story, it happened, and they named the child Isaac. Abraham would have another son by one of his maidservants. That child was named Ishmael and traditionally, he is considered the ancestor of the Arabs, whereas Isaac is that of the Jews.

Isaac is featured in one of the most disturbing stories found in the Bible. As a test, God ordered Abraham to take his beloved son Isaac up to a mountain, build an altar, and sacrifice the boy. Abraham was just about to do the deed when he was told to stop and a ram was found nearby to be sacrificed instead. This troubling story has confounded theologians for decades.

Jacob and His Many Sons

Isaac grew up and had twin boys, Jacob and Esau, by his wife Rebekah. The two brothers were extremely competitive and Jacob ended up cheating his brother out of his inheritance. Jacob's life story is quite amazing. At one point, he wrestled with either God or an angel all night long. Afterward, he was given another name, Israel, meaning "struggles with God." Anyway, Jacob had a number of sons—12, to be exact—and he favored one in particular named Joseph. This, of course, was bound to promote sibling rivalry. One day Joseph's brothers threw him into a pit and told their aging father that animals had eaten the boy. Actually, they sold him as a slave and Joseph ended up in Egypt.

Joseph's sparkling personality got him a nice job with an Egyptian official but when he turned down the naughty advances of his employer's scheming wife, he ended up in jail. There, he was brought to the attention of the pharaoh, the ruler of Egypt, due to his ability to interpret dreams as predictions of the future. Joseph was rewarded with a job as one of the highest officials in Egypt.

Meanwhile, there was a dry spell in Palestine, and Joseph's brothers traveled to Egypt to stock up on food. After a few dramatic encounters with his clueless brothers, Joseph revealed himself and it was reunion time. The whole family, including Jacob, and their households emigrated to Egypt. This interesting story of Joseph can be found in Genesis chapters 37–50.

> **This and That**
>
> Omens and dreams were taken very seriously in many Near Eastern cultures. Rulers often took the advice of astrologers and other prognosticators in attempts to learn the future or engage in effective planning. Dream interpreters with credible track records were likely considered valuable commodities!

A National Epic: The Exodus

The Hebrew-speaking descendents of Jacob and his sons settled in and can be referred to now as the "Hebrews" (referring to the Hebrew-speaking descendants of Jacob's 12 sons, who would themselves become the patriarchs of twelve tribes), the "children of Israel" (referring to Jacob's nickname), or as the "Israelites." (The term *Jews* refers to the same people as well, but was not in use until much later.) In a story generally referred to as "the Exodus," God made good on his promise of looking after Abraham's descendents and delivered them from slavery, leading them to the Promised Land of Canaan.

The Exodus story began in Egypt 430 years later, after the Hebrews settled in Egypt. The situation had become not so nice for the Israelites. They were enslaved by the Egyptians and there were so many of them that the Egyptians feared a revolt. An order was given to exterminate all newborn Hebrew boys. One mother saved her son by putting him in a waterproofed basket where he was discovered by a bathing princess. The boy was given the name Moses and was raised in the royal household.

Moses later killed a brutal foreman over some slave abuse and went into exile. When Moses reached the age of 80, God contacted him through an amazing talking burning bush. God ordered the fugitive to go back to Egypt to save his people who were still enslaved. Moses was understandably reluctant but with assurances that God would help, he set out and confronted the pharaoh. A new pharaoh was in place since he left, but the memory of Moses was still alive in Egypt. The pharaoh scoffed at Moses' insistence that he set free the Hebrew slaves, then the miracles began.

Pain, Suffering, and Deliverance

Moses and his brother Aaron confronted the pharaoh with their outrageous demands to free the Hebrew slaves. As a demonstration of the might of his God, Moses, occasionally with Aaron, attempted to bend the will of the king by invoking a series of 10 miserable plagues. (For more details, see Chapter 12.) The pharaoh finally relented and the Hebrews were free to go, although not without one desperate attempt by the Egyptians to pursue their former captives. In one of the most dramatic episodes in the Bible, the miraculous parting of waters at the Sea of Reeds allowed the Hebrews to escape but drowned the Egyptian army.

Under the leadership of Moses, the Hebrew tribes wandered for years in the wilderness—40, the Bible says—but the highlight of the experience occurred at a place called Mount Sinai. Here at this high desert mountain, God called Moses to receive the rules that would govern the behavior of his people.

People and Places

Where is Mt. Sinai? There have been a good number of proposals. A favorite location is Jebel Mousa, which is located in the Sinai Peninsula of Egypt. The mountain was identified as the sacred one in A.D. 327 by Helena, the mother of the Roman emperor Constantine. A chapel was built at the base, and today a large, beautiful Greek Orthodox monastery named St. Katherine's can be found there. While Jebel Mousa receives the bulk of tourists, other obscure sites have been proposed based on various ideas about the route of the Exodus and the wanderings of the Israelites. These include other mountains on the Sinai Peninsula and sites located in present-day Saudi Arabia, Israel's Negev desert, and Jordan.

A Curious Lack of Evidence

Given the epic proportions of the Exodus story, one might think that there would be a lot of evidence of it. Archaeologically, though, this is a real problem. One would think that a wandering group of hundreds of thousands of people for 40 years would leave quite an impact on the landscape. Under the right conditions, a single stone campfire circle can remain intact for many thousands of years, but there is as yet no physical trace of the Exodus.

It's possible that the forces of nature have altered or destroyed the evidence, or that it lies buried. It's also possible that the route of the journey is genuinely unknown and unexamined and the true site of Sinai remains to be found.

According to some of the biblical minimalists, it's a waste of time to be looking for such places and evidence, as they believe the whole story never happened. It's not real history, they say, but along with the conquest of the Promised Land that followed, it is part of a national origins myth that was put down in writing perhaps in the fifth century B.C. But then again, who would construct a story in which their ancestors were slaves and after being delivered by God, continually misbehaved? There is also a reasonable amount of knowledge about Egypt in the book that lends an air of authenticity.

Ultimately, the meaning of the Exodus story, a tale of God's deliverance and the giving of the law, is what is of lasting importance. Wherever and whenever it might have happened, the fact remains that its impact, much of it positive, continues to persist into modern times.

After the giving of the laws at Sinai, the wandering Israelites eventually prepared to enter the land of Canaan, a land promised to them by God. The Israelites' great leader Moses would not be joining them. He died before that, but not before he caught a glimpse of the land from a high peak, Mt. Nebo in modern Jordan.

> **Thus Saith**
>
> According to Deuteronomy 34:5–6, God buried Moses in the land of Moab (modern Jordan) "but no man knows the place of his burial to this day."

Coming to Conquer

The book of Numbers gives specific instructions about conquering and dividing up Canaan:

> … then you shall drive out all the inhabitants of the land from before you, and destroy all their figured stones, and destroy all their molten images, and demolish all their high places; and you shall take possession of the land and settle in it, for I have given the land to you to possess it. You shall inherit the land by lot according to your families; to a large tribe you shall give a large inheritance, and to a small tribe you shall give a small inheritance; wherever the lot falls to any man, that shall be his; according to the tribes of your fathers you shall inherit. But if you do not drive out the inhabitants of the land from before you, then those of them whom you let remain shall be as pricks in your eyes and thorns in your sides, and they shall trouble you in the land where you dwell. (Numbers 33:52–55)

Poised at the border of Canaan, the Israelites sent out spies to check it out. The spies returned with some good news and bad news. The good news was that Canaan was a bountiful "land of milk and honey." The bad news was that they were going to have to confront some very intimidating people who would include various groups of Canaanites and the Philistines.

Jericho Falls

Under the command of a new leader, Joshua, the attacks began, accompanied by more miracles. Separating the Israelites from their first goal of conquest was the Jordan River. In an episode reminiscent of the Sea of Reeds, a dry place appeared in the river and the Israelite army was able to attack the city of Jericho on the opposite side.

The walled city of Jericho was not captured in the traditional fashion. Instead, the Israelite army marched around its wall six times blowing trumpets over a period of six days. Then on the seventh, they did seven laps, blew some trumpets and yelled, and the Bible says that the walls came tumbling down. The Israelite army then went in and completely demolished the place.

On God's Side

After Jericho, Joshua and his army continued their program of conquest and cities continued to fall. During an attack against the Amorites, the Bible records two more amazing miracles. As the enemy army was fleeing from the Israelites, "the Lord threw down great stones from heaven upon them ... and they died; there were more who died because of the hailstones than the men of Israel killed with the sword." (Joshua 10:11, RSV)

Is That So!

The books of Joshua and Judges both describe the conquest of much of the Promised Land. Joshua's description describes a relatively fast attack on major cities, whereas Judges suggests a much more gradual process. Both lend interesting perspectives to the situation.

What happened next, though, is truly mind-boggling. Apparently running out of daylight to finish the work, Joshua commanded the sun and the moon to stay still, "And the sun stood still, and the moon stayed, until the nation took vengeance on their enemies ... The sun stayed in the midst of heaven and did not hasten to go down for about a whole day. There has been no day like it before or since, when the Lord hearkened to the voice of a man; for the Lord fought for Israel." (Joshua 10:13–14, RSV)

Jugs and Houses: The Iron Age

Many scholars believe that the entry of the Israelites into Palestine began at the end of the Late Bronze Age, and evidence for people moving into the hill country of the region is readily apparent around the beginning of the Iron Age, 1200 B.C. Many sites have been found there of this date with distinct home architecture and artifacts which appear to be associated with the newcomers. A distinctive kind of large pottery storage vessel, or "collared-rim store jar," for example, was likely manufactured by the Israelites. And a notable style of house is also found in such sites from that time. These four-room houses, with a covered court with three adjacent chambers, can be likewise linked to the Israelites.

We've already dealt with the chronological periods known as the Stone Age(s) and the Bronze Age during our discussion of early Palestine. Archaeologists and historians follow the Bronze Age with the Iron Age beginning at 1200 B.C. Again, these terms are helpful for organizing time and in the case of the Iron Age in Palestine, profound things are happening at its beginning and end! As we'll see in the next chapter, both the Israelites and the Philistines seem to appear about the same time near the beginning of the Iron Age and that time period ends with the brutal destruction of Jerusalem by the Babylonians in 586 B.C. As was the case with the Bronze Age, the Iron Age can be subdivided as follows:

- ◆ **Iron Age I:** 1200 to 926 B.C.
- ◆ **Iron Age II:** 926 to 586 B.C.

These two periods themselves are often subdivided, for example, Iron Ia and Iron IIc. Iron Age I ends when the Israelite kingdom divides (see the following section) and Iron Age II ends with the capture of Jerusalem by the Babylonians.

Fact or Fiction?

Although the Bible goes into considerable detail about the conquering of the Promised Land, there is great debate among some scholars about how much of this story is real. Take the site of Jericho, which apart from its role in the Bible, has the reputation of being one of the world's oldest cities. People had been living there since at least circa 8500 B.C. The city was walled during much of its history, and the evidence indicates that it was abandoned and later expanded and rebuilt several times.

The ruins of the ancient city of Jericho.

(David Moyer collection)

The site of Jericho was excavated most notably by John Garstang (1876–1956) from 1930 to 1936 and Kathleen Kenyon (1906–1978) from 1952 to 1958. They did find collapsed walls, but even so, it is not possible to prove who or what is to blame. Furthermore, some strongly argue that the timing is all wrong for the biblical destruction and that Jericho was already wrecked and abandoned by the time the Israelites got there. On the other hand, there is suspicious destruction at sites such as the cities of Lachish and Hazor at the end of the Late Bronze Age. But who did it? Was it the work of the Israelites? Or could their rivals, the Philistines, have been involved?

People and Places

British archaeologist Kathleen Kenyon was one of the most prominent female excavators ever. Along with her mentor Sir Mortimer Wheeler, Kenyon devised methods of excavating difficult sites that would be adopted extensively in Near Eastern archaeology. She is most well known for her excavations at the site of Jericho and in the city of Jerusalem. She was a tough and persistent leader, and apart from digging, she served as a lecturer in Palestinian archaeology at University College in London.

There are a number of biblical minimalists who strongly advocate that the conquest of the Promised Land never even happened. It's foolish to look for physical evidence of these events, they say, because they simply didn't happen. The archaeological evidence just doesn't support it. Along with the Exodus, it's part of a national epic saga, like Homer's *Iliad*, that provides a heroic history for the Hebrew people. Like the Exodus, perhaps it received its final form in the 500s B.C.

But what would account for the fact that at least one Egyptian text mentions a people called Israel (see Chapter 12) and that there is plenty of physical evidence of Israelites to be found in the Palestine region? The minimalists will answer that yes, the people were there, but they came not out of Egypt, but probably from within Canaan. Some have suggested that the emergence of Israel was some sort of peaceful immigration or perhaps even a civil revolt. Small settlements began to appear on less desirable land on the hilltops of Canaan at that time and perhaps even a population crisis could have caused a split.

On the other hand, some of these hard questions might be resolved if these scholars gave some historical credence to the biblical stories. There have been all kinds of proposals for the whos, whens, and wheres of the Exodus, and perhaps a different date for that story or a reinterpretation of the evidence might make some of the dates in Palestine, such as the destruction of Jericho, fall more in line with what the Bible says.

We Three Kings

According to the Bible, the conquered land was divided among the Hebrew tribes who were ruled by "judges" before a united monarchy was established around 1030 B.C. The first king, Saul, was appointed by Samuel the priest. He in turn was followed by David, who established the official Hebrew capital at Jerusalem around 1005 B.C., and then by Solomon. Each of these kings had distinct personalities, and each was very human with plenty of personal flaws.

Although the Bible provides us with many details about the lives and times of Saul, David, and Solomon, physical evidence of their existence is rare. A few critics have gone as far as equating King David with the mythical King Arthur, in the sense that their historical reality is in question, and they both serve as cultural icons. That theory has recently suffered a major blow.

This and That

All the tribes received land in the Promised Land except for the Levites. They were destined to be servants of the Holy Temple, but were allocated separate cities to live in.

Map showing Canaan and its division among the Hebrew tribes.

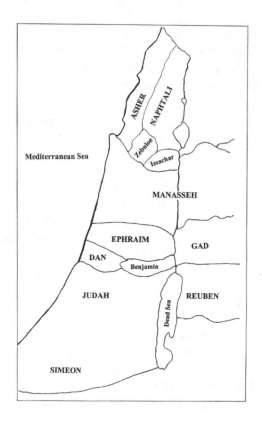

Written in Stone

In 1993, at the site of Tel Dan in Israel, a fragment of stone was uncovered with an ancient inscription referring to "the House of David." This is some of the first tangible evidence of King David's existence and it is still controversial. Some have called it a fake, whereas other skeptics maintain that the name "David," being written without vowels in Hebrew, could actually mean a couple other things, such as the word *beloved*, thus "House of the Beloved." Nevertheless, the potential remains that more and more clues will be found in the future. That's one reason why archaeologists continue to dig.

Is That So!

In tracing the Israelites through archaeology, ceramics once again provides a means of following their comings and goings. A special type of red glossy pottery appears at the time of David and is found in likely areas of Israelite settlement at least through the time of Solomon.

Solomon Was Here

The Bible describes King Solomon as a great builder and mentions that he was active in fortifying several notable cities. Evidence of such activities at the appropriate age is found at such sites as Megiddo, Gezer, and Hazor. There, large walls featuring gates with four entryways can be found of similar style and date.

The ancient city of Megiddo was greatly enhanced by the building activities of King Solomon.

(David Moyer collection)

The Great Split

Not long after the death of Solomon, the central monarchy dissolved and the Israelites broke into two kingdoms. This marks the beginning of Iron II according to our historical framework. In the south, centered at Jerusalem, were the two tribes of Judah and Benjamin (usually referred to collectively as "Judah") and the other ten tribes of Israel were confederated in the north. The Bible records the names and activities of these various rulers on each side, some of whom were very short-lived. A good many of them were miserable fellows who took to worshipping pagan gods and behaved rather dishonorably. Interestingly, more evidence exists for some of these individuals than for some of the earlier, more famous kings.

The ten northern tribes of Israel "disappeared," so to speak, when the Assyrians invaded Palestine around 721 B.C. Although it is likely that many of them were marched back to Mesopotamia and incorporated into Assyrian society, there has been plenty of wild speculation about what else might have happened.

The "Ten Lost Tribes of Israel" has been a source of great and often misguided speculation. Some early explorers of the New World, for example, refused to believe that the Indians they encountered were capable of building such things as the huge artificial mounds found in parts of North America. Could some of the people found there be descendants of the "Lost Tribes," they asked? Most unlikely, concur most modern archaeologists. Other speculators have suggested that all or individual tribes may have ended up in such places as Ireland, Nigeria, Kenya, Persia, North Africa, Ethiopia, Yemen, Sweden, India, and the Netherlands.

The Evidence Increases

Although there isn't a great amount of concrete, objective physical proof for the accuracy of biblical history through the reign of Solomon, evidence started accumulating after the time of the united monarchy. Names of rulers of the divided kingdom began to appear in foreign texts as did events reported in the Bible. A good example is that of the Assyrian attack on the fortified Israelite city of Lachish.

When the Assyrian king Sennacherib attacked Palestine, fortified Lachish was one of the cities he assaulted in 701 B.C. This is noted in the Old Testament, and most remarkably, the attack is featured on sculptured reliefs in the palace of Sennacherib in the Assyrian capital of Nineveh. The reliefs show the Assyrian use of siege machines against the city and the carrying away of booty. When the tell was excavated, archaeologists found plenty of evidence of this event.

Perhaps even more interesting than foreign collaborative reports of biblical events and personages are some discoveries made in the Promised Land itself. In the last few decades, clay seals called bullae have been found which actually record the names of specific individuals noted in the Bible. The seals, which date to the appropriate biblical time periods, were stamped in clay, typically as official signatures on such things as sealed papyrus scrolls or letters.

A bulla with the name of Baruch the Scribe, an individual mentioned in the Bible as the scribe to the prophet Jeremiah. The inscription dates to the late seventh century B.C.

(After: P. Kyle McCarter, Ancient Inscriptions, 1996, p. 149)

A Long Tortured History

After fighting so hard for the Promised Land, the Israelites would lose their grip, regain it, and lose it again. The ten northern tribes disappeared at the hands of the Assyrians. After the Babylonians put the Assyrians out of business, they, too, turned their eyes to Palestine and attacked Judah. Their success in this endeavor was crowned by the capture and destruction of Jerusalem in 586 B.C.

Many members of the two surviving tribes, Judah and Benjamin located in the south, would be led away by the Babylonians, only to be allowed to return home when the Persians became the latest winners of ancient Near Eastern musical chairs of power in 539 B.C.

The Greeks would follow and rule and fight over Palestine. The Jews would again emerge as an independent entity, but only temporarily until the Romans became the dominant regional power. You'll be reading more about them later in this book. Arabs, Crusaders, Turks, and the British are just some of the others who would control the Promised Land. It wasn't until A.D. 1948 that the Jewish people would once again be formally reinstated to the land of their ancient heritage in the modern state of Israel.

The Least You Need to Know

- Abraham's covenant with one God was a dramatic departure from the polytheistic cultures of his day.

- The 12 sons of Abraham's grandson Jacob (a.k.a. "Israel") served as the patriarchs of the twelve Hebrew tribes.

- The story of the deliverance from Egyptian slavery, the Exodus, is a demonstration of God's promise to look after the descendents of Abraham.

- The evidence for the conquest of Canaan is archaeologically controversial.

- The Israelites eventually established a monarchy under kings Saul, David, and Solomon, but then split into two kingdoms, Israel in the north and Judah in the south.

- The kingdom of Israel dissolved under Assyrian attack. Judah would be conquered later by the Babylonians, and later return to Palestine under Persian rule.

Chapter 9

The Coast Peoples

In This Chapter

- The mysterious people of the sea
- Philistine culture
- The Philistines' tussles with Samson and Saul
- Those enterprising Phoenicians: sailors and traders

Apart from groups of Canaanites, others in Palestine and its immediate vicinity had a big impact on the Israelites. The Philistines, for one, are quite famous for giving the Israelites a rough time. As you'll see, they've got some interesting origins and they're not as crude as their modern reputation would have them.

The Canaanites on the Lebanese coast who would become known as the Phoenicians had an impact not only on Palestine, but on much of the rest of the ancient world. As master seafarers and merchants, they could really get around!

Trouble Abroad

Around 1200 B.C., something happened in the northeastern region of the Mediterranean. Lots of people started moving out of parts of Greece and

This and That

The funerary temple of Rameses III records battles with the Sea Peoples in both words and pictures. Some of these inscriptions actually show foreigners identified as Philistines with their battle gear!

elsewhere in the Aegean looking for other places to live. The reasons are not clear. Perhaps it was over-population, bad economies, or natural disasters. Whatever the cause, the impact was certainly felt in areas such as Egypt, Palestine, and Syria. Prominent among these migrating peoples were several groups that have been given the name "Sea Peoples." The Sea Peoples were fierce warriors and the Philistines were one of these groups.

A good bit of our knowledge about the Sea Peoples comes from Egyptian sources. During the reign of Rameses III, in particular, they attacked Egypt by land and sea. Although Rameses III brags about soundly defeating them, he merely drove many of them off. One group mentioned in Egyptian texts has been identified as the Philistines and we know that they would establish themselves on the southern coastal plain and foothills of Palestine about 1200 B.C. There they would prove to be a major factor for perhaps the next 600 years.

The Book of Genesis mentions the Philistines, although most scholars think there couldn't have been very many of them around at the time as this would have been hundreds of years before they invaded the coast. One story tells of Isaac who during a time of famine went to Gerar, a land in Palestine ruled by a Philistine king named Abimelech. While there, he pulled a stunt that his father Abraham was known for: trying to pass his wife off as his sister to save his own life. When his ruse was discovered, Abimelech promised that neither he nor his wife would be harmed. Isaac went to work and his fields and herds were so wildly successful that the Philistines kicked him out, saying, "Go away from us; for you are much mightier than we." (Genesis 26:16)

The Philistine Pentapolis

Most of the dramatic biblical action with the Philistines, though, doesn't begin until the Israelites enter Canaan. Before we consider some of that, let's take a look at the Philistines themselves.

The Philistines as Sea Peoples established themselves on the southern coastal plain and foothills around 1200 B.C. They no doubt had to fight and conquer groups of Canaanites in the process and they took over some cities and established a few new settlements as well. Their territory was dominated by five important cities, each ruled by a king/army commander. These famous cities were as follows:

◆ Gaza

◆ Ashkelon

- Ashdod

- Ekron

- Gath

Like many of the great cities in the region, those of the Philistines were walled for defense.

Much of our information about the cultural lives of the Philistines is derived from biblical information. Interestingly, the Philistines seem to have adopted many Canaanite traditions. Their principal god, for example, was Dagon, right out of Canaanite mythology, as were Baal-zebul and Ashtoreh, who were likewise worshipped. The Philistines set up temples to their gods. At least some of them had pillars to hold up their ceilings and featured large clay or wooden images of the god worshipped. Warriors also carried smaller images with them to battle in hopes of divine assistance.

An interesting story found in 1 Samuel tells how during a battle, the Philistines captured the Israelites' proud possession, the famed Ark of the Covenant. They set it down in their temple to Dagon in Ashdod and the next day, they found that the statue of Dagon had toppled over. It happened a second time, this time seriously damaging the statue. A plague of tumors broke out, as did infestations of mice, and the Ark was passed on to other Philistine cities with similar results. The Philistine "soothsayers" correctly attributed the calamities to their possessing the Ark. The Ark was sent on its way on an unmanned cart towed by two oxen. The oxen found their way back to the Israelites, and the biblical story once again emphasizes the power of the one God of the Hebrew people over the belief in pagan entities.

> **Is That So!**
>
> When the Philistines sent the Ark away, they sent with it golden models of mice and tumors, that is, things that afflicted them, as a kind of "guilt" offering. There were five of each, representing the five primary Philistine cities.

Not So Crude: The Philistine Culture

In modern times, the term *Philistine* is often used in reference to someone who is coarse, brutish, or otherwise ill-mannered. Much of this seems to come from the way these people were portrayed in the Bible, as the enemy of God's people, the Israelites. When we look at the archaeological evidence, we find that the Philistines were actually rather sophisticated.

Pretty Pots

As militaristic as they seem to have been, the Philistines were creative and artistic. Excavations at their cities demonstrate that they engaged in a wide range of crafts. Some of the most beautiful and intriguing pottery (in my opinion) in all of the ancient Near East was made by the Philistines. A wide variety of pot shapes and sizes were often decorated with black and red designs over a whitened surface. The painted designs very much resemble those found in the Aegean region of the northeastern Mediterranean and seem to be motifs brought from their homeland. Such motifs include birds, fish, spirals, and checkered patterns.

This example of a Philistine pot demonstrates some of their characteristic beautiful designs.

(*After: Trude Dothan*, The Philistines and Their Material Culture, *1982, p. 101*)

Men of Metal

The Philistines were apparently quite adept in their use of metal, iron in particular. This no doubt gave them a military advantage from time to time, iron being much harder and more durable than the common bronze. The Bible suggests that the Philistines may have even had a monopoly on the production of iron implements. 1 Samuel 13:19 seems to indicate this: "Now there was no smith to be found throughout all the land of Israel; for the Philistines said, "Lest the Hebrews make themselves swords or spears …"

Philistine Funerary Arts

Although excavations at the great Philistine cities have yet to reveal cemeteries, Philistine graves have been found. Some are rock-cut tombs like those found in the Aegean while others are burials in large ceramic coffins. These artistic pottery sarcophagi are very reminiscent of Egyptian coffins complete with modeled human face and the concept was probably adapted from Egyptian style.

Farming Philistines

The Philistines controlled some choice agricultural terrain and grew a lot of their own food. Not only that, but they apparently operated a sophisticated olive oil industry, the remains of which have been found at such sites as Ekron.

> **People and Places**
>
> Two of the largest digs in Israel in the last few decades have been at Philistine sites. The work of archaeologists Seymour Gitin and Trude Dothan at Tel Miqne (Ekron) has revealed much about Philistine daily life. The excavations directed by Lawrence Stager at the complicated site of Ashkelon began in 1985 and continue still.

Fighting Philistines

The Philistines knew how to tussle. Egyptian inscriptions show them with their weapons and feathered headdresses. There seems to have been a military hierarchy led by city-kings and their officers. The Philistine military included foot soldiers, cavalry, archers, and chariots. Being Sea Peoples, they could attack from the water as well.

One of the most famous of all biblical stories is the confrontation between David, the Israelite shepherd boy (and future king) and a giant Philistine named Goliath. An interesting challenge to a duel was offered by Goliath, complete with obnoxious scoffing. Some of Goliath's taunts to the Israelites included "Am I a dog, that you come to me with sticks?" and "Come to me, and I will give your flesh to the birds of the air and to the beasts of the field." (1 Samuel 17:43–44) Only the lowly David was brave enough to confront the terrifying Goliath, and he knocked the giant out with a sling-thrown stone and then cut his head off. The Philistines then fled.

One particularly interesting aspect about the David and Goliath story is the description of Goliath's armor and weaponry:

> He had a helmet of bronze on his head, and he was armed with a coat of mail, and the weight of the coat was five thousand shekels of bronze. And he had greaves of bronze upon his legs, and a javelin of bronze slung between his shoulders. And the shaft of his spear was like a weaver's beam, and his spear's head weighed six hundred shekels of iron; and his shield-bearer went before him. (1 Samuel 17:5–7)

With 50 shekels being the equivalent of about 1.25 pounds, Goliath's equipment was heavy indeed!

Samson Gets Rough

One of the most colorful characters in the Bible is Samson, a Nazarite and a major Israelite opponent of the Philistines. Nazarites either took special vows of holiness to God, or their parents made vows on their behalf. The Nazarites were not to do three things if they wanted to retain their status: partake of the "fruit of the vine" (including grapes, wine, grape juice, and raisins) or other intoxicants, touch dead people, or cut their hair. In the case of Samson, his long hair seemed to be the source of his mighty strength, which he put to use against the Philistines. Among some of his anti-Philistine antics:

♦ He killed 30 men in the city of Ashkelon to get their nice clothes and pay back a bet.

♦ He caught 300 foxes, tied their tails together, and let them loose with torches to burn down the Philistines' fields and trees.

♦ He killed a thousand Philistine warriors with the jawbone of a donkey.

♦ He uprooted the city gates of Gaza and carried them off.

The Philistines were, of course, interested in knowing the secret of his power, and they used a woman named Delilah to woo him as his girlfriend. When Samson gave up his secret to her, he woke up one morning with his hair gone. The Philistines poked out his eyes and threw him in jail. Meanwhile, his hair was growing back …

The Philistines were so happy to have subdued Samson that they decided to have a big celebration. They brought Samson out and tied him between two pillars holding up the party house. With all the Philistine officials there and 3,000 people on the roof, the teasing must have been ruthless.

Pleading with God for strength, Samson got an answer to his prayers, and he was able to press against the pillars, causing the building to collapse. Samson was killed, along with a whole lot of others. According to the story, "the dead whom he slew at his death were more than those whom he had slain during his life." That's a lot of people!

Saul's Demise

The first king of the Israelites, Saul, met his doom during a battle with the Philistines on Mt. Gilboa. Heavily wounded and with three sons killed, he fell on his own sword. The Philistines cut off Saul's head and hung his body from a city wall and placed his battle armor in their temple of Ashtaroth. That's harsh!

Samson brings down the house.

(Illustration by Gustave Doré)

Remaining Mysteries

Although archaeology and the Bible have revealed many interesting things about the Philistines, several mysteries remain. From where, exactly, did they come? What language did they speak? Did they have their own writing system, and if so, do archives exist that remain to be discovered? What happened to them? Regarding the last question, it seems likely that the Philistines were eventually culturally absorbed into the Canaanite population. By around 600 B.C., there's not much trace of them as a distinct culture.

Those Fabulous Phoenicians

Up north, on the Lebanese coast, lived a group of people that the Greeks (and now us) referred to as the "Phoenicians" and the area where they dwelt, *Phoenicia*. The Phoenicians were basically Canaanites who settled around natural harbors and in the territory between the sea and the Lebanese mountains.

Logos

The word *Phoenicia* is thought by some to be related to the Greek word for "purple," referring to the beautifully colored cloth that was exported from this area.

How this culture developed from its Canaanite roots is somewhat controversial. Some say that their access to natural harbors stimulated the development of their somewhat unique culture with manufacturing and export, trading, and seafaring at its core. Others suggest that perhaps the coming of the Sea Peoples to the region played an instrumental role. However it happened, by the onset of the Iron Age, we can safely identify the culture there as Phoenician.

Map showing Philistine and Phoenician territories, including major cities.

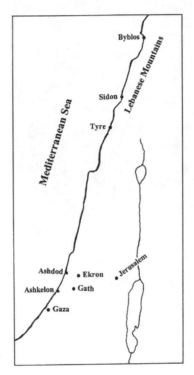

City-States

Like so many groups in the region, the Phoenicians were not unified as a nation, but operated as independent city-states typically with separate rulers but a similar underlying culture. They often competed with each other, sometimes aggressively. The most famous Phoenician cities were the following:

- Tyre
- Sidon
- Byblos

With their noted seafaring abilities, the Phoenicians established colonies in various places around the Mediterranean beginning around 750 B.C. These colonies assisted in the procurement of natural resources for trade and manufacture, and for the facilitation of mercantile enterprises. Phoenician presence could be found in such places as the islands of Cyprus, Sicily, Sardinia, Malta, and on the coasts of North Africa and even Spain.

The most famous colony is that of Carthage on the North African coast in what is modern-day Tunisia. While their Phoenician brethren at home were being domineered by the likes of the Assyrians, Babylonians, and Greeks, the Carthaginians were relatively free to carry on the world of business. When the Romans were in the process of building their huge empire in the first few centuries B.C., the Carthaginians were considered to be a threat and competitor and the result was a series of "Punic" wars. The Carthaginians under the great general Hannibal even invaded Italy with war elephants, but that's another story. Eventually, the Romans won and burned Carthage to the ground in 146 B.C.

The Phoenicians and Carthaginians were also known as great explorers. The Greek historian Herodotus reports that a Phoenician ship was commissioned by an Egyptian pharaoh named Necho to navigate around the African continent around circa 600 B.C. Apparently the explorers were successful, and accomplished the trip from the Red Sea around Africa to the Mediterranean in a period of three years.

Meanwhile, Back in Phoenicia ...

As mercantile folk, the Phoenicians were well known for several products. Up in the mountains were the famous Cedars of Lebanon, a source of wood that was highly valued in the Near East. The Egyptians imported this wood, and it was a key material in the building of Solomon's temple in Jerusalem.

Purple or reddish-colored cloth was also a famous export. The dye for the cloth was derived from the *Murex* mollusk, which thrived in the coastal waters. The Phoenicians also manufactured many items for trade, including jewelry and glass bottles.

 Thus Saith

And Hiram king of Tyre sent messengers to [King] David, and cedar trees, also carpenters and masons who built David a house.
—2 Samuel 2:14

Minions of Melqart

The Phoenicians worshipped many of the usual Canaanite gods, for example, Astarte, plus a few of their own. The major cities each had a favored god. For Tyre, it was Melqart; for Sidon, it was Baal-Sidon; and in Byblos, Baalat Gubla was held in special esteem.

An interesting story can be found in the Book of 1 Kings. There it says that King Solomon "loved many foreign women" and had "seven hundred wives, princesses, and three hundred concubines … from the nations concerning which the Lord had said to the people of Israel, 'You shall not enter into marriage with them, neither shall they with you, for surely they will turn away your heart after their gods.'" As predicted, Solomon turned away from God and among other deities, took to the worship of Ashtoreth of Sidon. A later king, Josiah, tore down Solomon's shrine to the goddess.

Ahab, a king of Israel, married a princess of Sidon named Jezebel, who also encouraged the worship of foreign gods, Baal and Asherah. When the Israelite prophet Elijah challenged 450 prophets of Baal to a competition between gods, Baal lost to God and the pagan prophets were executed.

> **Is That So!**
>
> One of the more disturbing facets of Phoenician culture is the possibility that they practiced child sacrifice. In Carthage, a cemetery was uncovered containing around 20,000 cremation urns with the remains of children. The Bible condemns such ritual offerings, which were apparently practiced in times of desperation or during other times when it was felt desirable to appease the gods.

Where'd They Go?

Like many cultures in the region, the Phoenicians took beatings from several of the great Near Eastern civilizations. The Assyrians held sway for a while, of course, and demanded their tribute, as did the Babylonians. The more lenient Persians actually made Sidon a provincial capital. With the coming of the Greeks, however, it would not be long before Phoenician culture was essentially absorbed into obscurity.

The Least You Need to Know

- The Philistines were a group of Sea Peoples whose origins in the northeastern region of the Mediterranean remain obscure.

- Settling in Palestine/Canaan around 1200 B.C., the Philistines became a major foe of the invading Israelites.

- Despite their reputations as brutes, the culture of the Philistines was actually quite sophisticated.

- The Phoenicians were Canaanites who developed a maritime mercantile culture along the Lebanese coast.

- Cedar wood, dyed cloth, and glass were among the Phoenician specialties, some of which were incorporated in Israelite royal and religious structures.

- The Phoenicians established colonies in many Mediterranean areas including Spain and North Africa. Their most famous colony, Carthage, became a power on its own.

Chapter 10

The Other -Ites

In This Chapter

- ◆ A look at the lesser-known groups in the Bible
- ◆ Ammonites stir up trouble
- ◆ Residents of Moab
- ◆ Those mischievous Edomites
- ◆ Desert nomads: the Midianites and the Amalekites
- ◆ The Arameans leave their mark

In the last few chapters, we've looked at some of the principal biblical players residing in Palestine. The Canaanites and Philistines, to name a couple, played huge roles in many stories. Apart from the great Near Eastern powers like Egypt and those in Mesopotamia, which we will be looking at in the next few chapters, a lot of other groups in the vicinity make their appearance in the Bible from time to time.

Some of these people we know little about. Can anyone, for example, tell me much about the Perizzites? Others, like the Arameans, left lasting cultural influences. In this chapter, we're going to look at a few of these groups.

Big Groups, Little Groups

It's almost a cliché that the Bible is full of *-ites*. Look at Genesis 15:19–21. It refers to "the land of the Kenites, the Kenizzites, the Kadmonites, the Hittites, the Perizzites, the Rephaim, the Amorites, the Canaanites, the Girgashites, and the Jebusites." The Hittites, whom I'll discuss in Chapter 13, were a major civilization about whom much has been learned in the last 100 years. The Jebusites, however, were some sort of ethnic group principally known as the residents of Jerusalem before its Israelite conquest, and we know little of the details of their history.

Logos

The suffix **-ite** can be attached to all manner of groups big and small. The Israelites were the descendents of Jacob/Israel while the Jebusites were the old residents of Jerusalem. It can also be used to name groups with unique characteristics such as the Nazarites, who took special vows, or the Zadokites, who were the upper echelon of the Jewish priesthood.

Here are a few of the interesting but lesser-known groups mentioned in the Bible:

- **Cherithites and Pelethites:** Apparently Sea Peoples or Philistines who served in David's personal army

- **Girgashites:** A Canaanite tribe whose specific territory is unknown

- **Kadmonites:** Desert nomads in the area of Syria

- **Kenites:** A nomadic tribe of metal smiths

While relatively obscure ethnic groups are to be found here and there in the world of the Bible, there are a few that are becoming slightly better known. And three of these groups can be found on the eastern side of the Jordan River: the Ammonites, Moabites, and Edomites. (See the map in Chapter 3.) The Israelites had to pass through that region before entering Canaan, and these folks, too, gave them lots of trouble from time to time.

The Ammonites

The culture known as the Ammonites occupied the central Transjordanian plateau from at least the Late Bronze Age until the end of the Iron Age. Their capital was called Rabbah-ammon and was located at the site of the modern Jordanian capital of Amman. It's difficult to find evidence of their origins. According to Genesis, though, the Ammonites were the descendents of Lot (Abraham's nephew) and his younger daughter.

Archaeologists have located a number of Ammonite sites and have determined that they were probably, at least in the beginning, self-sufficient herders. Settlements increased during the first part of the Iron Age, and in Iron II curious stone structures were built in the countryside. Some have suggested that these were defensive towers.

A couple hundred short Ammonite inscriptions survive that don't tell us a whole lot. They do demonstrate, however, that their language is related to their Canaanite neighbors across the river. The Bible confirms that their principle god was named "Milcom."

Leave Them Alone

In Deuteronomy, the Israelites were instructed not to harass the Ammonites when they came to their territory on the way to the Promised Land. The land is described as having been formerly occupied by the Rephaim, otherwise known as the Zamzummim. These people are described as giants and were wiped out and succeeded by the Ammonites.

Deuteronomy notes a King Og, a ruler of the land of Bashan north of Ammon and the last surviving member of the giant Rephaim. His huge iron bed, 9 cubits in length and 5 cubits in width (about 13½ by 6 feet), was apparently kept in the Ammonite capital as a curious souvenir.

Ganging Up on Israel

Much of what we know about the Ammonites comes from the Bible. In 1 Samuel, for example, we learn that they were ruled by a king, in this case, a fellow named Nahash. Nahash conquered the city of Jabesh-Gilead and struck some tough terms for a peace treaty with its residents: "On this condition I will make a treaty with you, that I gouge out all your right eyes, and thus put disgrace upon all Israel." Upon hearing this, the soon-to-be king Saul was infuriated, gathered a mighty army, and "cut down the Ammonites until the heat of the day; and those who survived were scattered, so that no two of them were left together." (1 Samuel 11:1–11)

This same Nahash apparently did future king David some sort of favor, perhaps hiding him from Saul. When Nahash died, David sent servants to offer condolences to the king's son Hanun. Hanun became suspicious that the servants were spies so he humiliated them and sent them home. In the resulting confrontation, the Ammonites fled before the battle took place.

Is That So!

Hanun intentionally humiliated David's servants when he "shaved off half the beard of each, and cut off their garments in the middle, at their hips ...." (2 Samuel 10:4) To spare them public embarrassment, David told them to wait in Jericho until their beards grew back.

David later conquered the Ammonite capital: "And he took the crown of their king from his head; the weight of it was a talent of gold, and in it was a precious stone; and it was placed on David's head. And he brought forth the spoil of the city, a very great amount. And he brought forth the people who were in it, and set them to labor with saws and iron picks and iron axes, and made them toil at the brick kilns; and thus he did to all the cities of the Ammonites." (2 Samuel 12:30–31)

The Moabites

South of Ammon was the territory of Moab, a land well suited for grazing and agriculture, set between the eastern cliffs of the Dead Sea and the Syrian desert. The Bible indicates that the Moabites were the descendents of Lot and his older daughter and that in olden days, Moab, too, played host to that race of giants, the Rephaim.

Settlements in Moab date back at least to the early Bronze Age. As is the case with the Ammonites, we have spotty information about these people. Interestingly, they are mentioned a couple of times in Egyptian texts. At the temple of Karnak, Moab is mentioned twice in texts describing the warrior pharaoh Rameses II's conquests.

As with the Ammonites, the Israelites were told to leave the Moabites alone on the way to Canaan. The Book of Numbers tells how the Moabites were afraid of the numerous Israelites passing through their land so Balak, their king, paid a diviner named Balaam to curse them. That's when the story of the talking donkey took place that was mentioned in Chapter 4 of this book.

People and Places

The Moabite king Eglon was assassinated by "Ehud, the son of Gera, the Benjaminite, a left-handed man" who was sent to bring tribute. Along with the tribute, he apparently brought a sharp sword.

The Moabites caused plenty of trouble for the Israelites. One of their kings, Eglon, oppressed them for 18 years until he was assassinated. The Israelites then attacked the Moabites, who were apparently subdued for a number of decades thereafter.

A Rare Find

In 1868, one of the most important artifacts relevant to the Bible was found in Jordan. It's called the Moabite stone or Mesha stele. This stone, inscribed with 34 lines of alphabetic text, was commissioned by Mesha, a Moabite king. It praises

Chemosh, the chief Moabite god, and brags about a victory over the Israelites. It also mentions the Israelite king Omri and the name of the Hebrew God. The Bible records its own side of the story and mentions that after years of paying tribute, Mesha staged a rebellion under Omri's grandson Jehoram. The resulting conflict resulted in heavy Moabite losses.

The famous Moabite Stone.

(David Moyer collection)

Apart from the Bible, the Moabite stone provides scholars with insights about the Moabite people. It is written in the old Phoenician alphabet with language almost identical to biblical Hebrew. It is the longest inscription known from the region. Sadly, the stone was broken up into pieces not long after it was discovered. Fortunately, copies were made of the inscription. What's left of it can be seen in the Louvre Museum in Paris.

Like just about everyone else in the region, the Moabites became Assyrian vassals. The eighth-century B.C. prophet Amos prophesized a nasty fate and condemned the land of Moab: "So I will send a fire upon Moab, and it shall devour the strongholds of Kerioth, and Moab shall die amid uproar, amid shouting and the sound of the trumpet." (Amos 2:1–3) Like many others in the region, the Moabites seem to have lost their independence for good with the invasion of the Babylonians in the sixth century B.C.

People and Places

The Book of Ruth begins with the story of an Israelite couple with two sons who moved to Moab during a time of famine. Both sons married Moabite women, including one named Ruth. Ruth is the star of the story as she travels back to Israel with her mother-in-law after all the menfolk die. Despite the regular bad relations between Moab and Israel, the story seems to indicate that they must have tolerated each other on occasion.

Banned for Being Bad

Because they were inhospitable to the Israelites when they came out of Egypt, both the Ammonites and Moabites are banned from ever entering "the assembly of the Lord; even to the tenth generation none belonging to them shall enter the assembly of the Lord for ever." (Deuteronomy 23:3–4) And that whole curse thing with Balaam was cited as another reason. When Saul became king, he fought them both along with another Transjordanian culture, the Edomites.

This and That

The Moabite women earned a reputation as enticers. In the book of Numbers, the "daughters of Moab" are noted as seducing some of the Israelite men into worshipping foreign gods.

---

2 Chronicles 20:1–29 records a story from the time of the Judean king Jehoshaphat. The Moabites, Ammonites, and Edomites (see the next section) gathered together for a big attack. Jehoshaphat prayed for help and God told him not to worry. The Judeans came out to the battlefield praising God, and God went to work confusing the enemy. The Moabites and Ammonites first slaughtered their Edomite allies before turning on each other. The Jews walked away with the massive spoils.

The Edomites

Yet another major Transjordanian group occupied the craggy mountainous region south of Moab. These were the Edomites, and their land stretched south to the Red Sea. The Bible traces their ancestors back to Esau, the brother of Jacob, who lived there. According to Genesis 25:30, Esau returned hungry from a hunting trip and met his brother cooking soup. This was a turning point in an important story as Esau traded his birthright to his brother for some stew: "And Esau said to Jacob, 'Let me eat some of that red pottage, for I am famished!' (Therefore, his name was called Edom.)" *Edom* means "red," thus the land became known as Edom and its inhabitants Edomites. (Esau also was covered with red hair.)

Egyptian texts refer to them as nomads and it is also known that they worked the sources of copper in the region. There are few Edomite inscriptions and we really don't know that much about them. The Bible notes that they joined in the harassment of the Israelites and that David put garrisons in Edom to control the troublemakers.

We know that the Edomites had at least one urban center called Bozrah, were ruled by a king, and that their chief god went by the name of Qos. The amazing ruins of the ancient city of Petra, known as Sela in the Bible, are found in Edomite territory. The site is known for its immense carved façades, which grace narrow canyons. The ruins of Petra are considered some of the most beautiful and enchanting in the world and have inspired a number of poets and artists. Alas, the most spectacular of these remains were created not by the Biblical Edomites, but by a non-Biblical group called the Nabateans probably from northeast Arabia. They moved into the area about 300 B.C. and probably drove out the Edomites.

People and Places

It was not unusual for Near Eastern kings to marry foreign princesses as a political gesture, and King Solomon was no exception. And they occasionally convinced him to stray from his God. "Now King Solomon loved many foreign women: the daughter of Pharaoh, and Moabite, Ammonite, Edomite, Sidonian, and Hittite women." (1 Kings 11:1) He even "built a high place for Chemosh the abomination of Moab, and for Molech the abomination of the Ammonites, on the mountain east of Jerusalem." (1 Kings 11:7)

Desert Wanderers

A couple other groups are certainly worthy of mention. Both the Midianites and the Amalekites roamed the desert as shepherds and traders. The Midianites seemed to be primarily based in the Sinai region, while the Amalekites seemed to be spread across several desert areas including the Negev and the Sinai.

Traders and Fighters

The Midianites make an appearance in the story of Jacob's favorite son, Joseph (see Chapter 8). Joseph's jealous brothers threw him in a pit and sold him to passing Midianite traders. The traders in turn sold him to a group of "Ishmaelites" for 20 shekels of silver. Moses lived with the Midianites and his father-in-law was a priest of Midian named Jethro. On the way to the Promised Land, the Israelites under the leadership of Moses ferociously attacked the Midianites, killed many of them, and took their belongings.

During the time of the judges, before the Hebrew monarchy in Palestine, the Bible tells how the Midianites harassed the Israelites for several years:

> The people of Israel did what was evil in the sight of the Lord; and the Lord gave them into the hand of Midian seven years. And the hand of Midian prevailed over Israel; and because of Midian the people of Israel made for themselves the dens which are in the mountains, and the caves and the strongholds. For whenever the Israelites put in seed the Midianites and the Amalekites and the people of the East would come up and attack them; they would encamp against them and destroy the produce of the land, as far as the neighborhood of Gaza, and leave no sustenance in Israel, and no sheep or ox or ass. For they would come up with their cattle and their tents, coming like locusts for number; both they and their camels could not be counted; so that they wasted the land as they came in. (Judges 6:1–5)

The Israelite leader Gideon, however, was able to subdue the Midianites.

Yet More Conflict

The Amalekites seem to be related to the Edomites. They attacked the Israelites coming out of Egypt and opposed their entry into Canaan. Here's a good story: While traveling through the desert wilderness, the Israelites, under the leadership of Moses, battled with the Amalekites. Moses held a staff in his hand and when it was raised high, the Israelites prevailed, and when it was lowered, the Amalekites gained advantage. To keep things going the right way, his brother and brother-in-law held up his hands when Moses got tired.

> **Thus Saith**
>
> The obstructive behavior of the Amalekites was never to be forgotten. They battled with the Israelites and even followed them and killed their stragglers. In Exodus 17:14–16, God instructs Moses to "Write this as a memorial in a book and recite it in the ears of Joshua, that I will utterly blot out the remembrance of Amalek from under heaven."

The Amalekites continued to pester the Israelites after the latter entered Canaan, sometimes even joining up with the Midianites to do so. One of the first things Saul did when he became king was to go out and ravage the Amalekites on God's orders. He didn't complete the job and David had to deal with some of them later. At one point, the Amalekites conducted a raid and kidnapped his two wives, Ahinoam and Abigail. Needless to say, David tracked them down, rescued his wives, and killed many Amalekites except for four hundred of them who got away on their camels.

They Left Their Mark

No discussion of the various groups in the Bible would be complete without mentioning the Arameans. They were widespread in Syria and in parts of Mesopotamia. Some were nomads while others were known to settle in villages, towns, and cities. One powerful Amarean city-state was known as Aram, or Aram-Damascus. It, too, was involved in war with ancient Israel and eventually fell under Assyrian domination.

So many Arameans ended up in Mesopotamia via immigration, forced or otherwise, that their language, Aramaic, gradually became the dominant spoken language. It spread far and wide and during the time of the Persian Empire, and it was essentially the official international language of the Near East. In Palestine, it was the common language during the first century A.D. and was spoken by Jesus of Nazareth.

The Aramean language was also written with an alphabetic script borrowed from the Phoenician. It developed into the square script that is the ancestor of the common Hebrew writing system. The Hebrew Bible was translated into Aramaic, and Aramaic became the language of the Talmud, the Jewish discourse on law.

The Hebrew Bible includes a few sections written in Aramaic. These can be found within the books of Daniel and Ezra. Some of the words Jesus spoke on the cross during his crucifixion were in Aramaic and are recorded in the New Testament.

The Least You Need to Know

- The Bible mentions many ethnic, geographical, and other groups, some of which we know little about.

- The territories on the east side of the Jordan River were home to several major ethnic groups including the Ammonites, Moabites, and Edomites, all of whom battled with the Israelites.

- Desert cultures such as the Midianites and Amalekites were both traders and fierce warriors.

- The ethnic group known as the Arameans left a lasting impact on the Near East when the Aramaic language and script was widely adopted.

Part 3

The Empires Nearby

The Near East was home to some of the earliest and most powerful civilizations the world has ever known. Mesopotamia was home to the Sumerians, Babylonians, and Assyrians, and the splendor of old Egypt continues to fascinate. Palestine was a desired piece of land and lay smack in between these great powers which played important roles in biblical history. And it wasn't just the neighboring big civilizations that were influential, but empire-builders such as the Persians and the Greeks who also left their marks. In the next few chapters, we're going to learn about these significant players in the world of the Bible—a little culture, a little history, and some archaeology—and some the biblical stories where they played a major part.

We're going to wrap up this part of the book with some information about what one can easily argue was the greatest invention of all time: writing. It's an intriguing subject and our ability to read some of the previously undeciphered scripts of the ancient Near East has contributed a lot to our knowledge of the biblical world.

11

Mesopotamia: Land Between the Rivers

In This Chapter

- ◆ Early civilizations in Iraq
- ◆ Those ever-so-creative Sumerians
- ◆ Babylonians: the Old and the New
- ◆ Assyrians and Babylonians on the rampage
- ◆ The deportation of Jews to Babylon

A ways to the east of Palestine lies a region that was home to some of the earliest and mightiest of ancient civilizations. Their impact was widespread and they played a major part in the world of the Bible. Abraham, the great patriarch of Israelites, came from this region, then later, armies from this area rolled through Palestine causing great calamity. The region is generally known as Mesopotamia.

Mesopotamia is located in an area that encompasses much of modern-day Iraq and stretches south to the Persian Gulf. There we have some of the earliest evidence of the first domestication of plants and animals. Early on, small villages there developed into large towns and eventually cities. It is no wonder that this region has often been called "the cradle of civilization."

Who's in Charge: Early Civilizations in Iraq

Mesopotamia means "the land between the rivers," and the rivers in question are the Tigris and Euphrates, which flow south to drain into the Persian Gulf. Irrigation and the rich soil of the rivers' flood plains provided the basis for the population growth that fueled the development of big cities.

Map of Mesopotamia.

The history of Mesopotamia is an interesting and exceedingly complicated one. Before going into some specifics about its various civilizations, let's take a look at who came and went, to help put things in order. Keep in mind that no single group ruled in Mesopotamia indefinitely and that there were different cultures and powers that co-existed in the same region with different rulers so it's not as straightforward as, say, a single continuous group of rulers. Its history is more a matter of one group being more dominant, followed by another. Here is a simplified scenario.

The first major civilization in the area was that of the Sumerians, who later came under the control of the Akkadians. The Sumerians made a brief comeback, and were eventually absorbed by the Old Babylonians (Amorites) and after a while the Kassites (Middle Babylonians) dominated for a time and then the Assyrians had their turn. The latter succumbed to the Neo-Babylonians, who were conquered by the Persians, who were vanquished by the Greeks, to be eventually incorporated into the Roman Empire. That's not the end of it, but it's enough for our purposes.

Here's a very basic timeline:

- **Early Dynastic Period (Sumerian):** 3000 to 2350 B.C.

- **Akkadian Period:** 2350 to 2150 B.C.

- **Dynasty of Ur (Sumerian):** 2150 to 2000 B.C.

- **Old Assyrian Period:** 2000 to 1300 B.C.

- **Old Babylonian Period (Amorites):** 1900 to 1595 B.C.

- **Middle Babylonian Period (Kassites):** 1595 to 1000 B.C.

- **Middle Assyrian Period:** 1300 to 1000 B.C.

- **Late Assyrian Period:** 1000 to 612 B.C.

- **Late Babylonian Period:** 1000 to 539 B.C.

- **Neo-Babylonians:** 625 to 539 B.C.

Unlike some other civilizations in the region, Mesopotamia generally lacked stone, and there wasn't a huge supply of wood to be had. Living along the two rivers, however, they were assured of plenty of one thing—mud—which could be used to build not only houses, but also elaborate palaces and temples.

Unfortunately, mud brick doesn't have the lasting power of stone, and many of Mesopotamia's mightiest monuments now are ruined and melted piles of dirt. Many of these ruins are now stranded out in the middle of the desert, abandoned after they were pillaged, or perhaps when the rivers changed course or the surrounding agricultural soil became poor. Scholars who specialize in ancient Mesopotamia are called *Assyriologists*, and they have their hands full sorting out all these remains!

Logos

The study of ancient Mesopotamia is called **Assyriology,** practiced by Assyriologists (after one of the dominant groups, the Assyrians). They are interested in all aspects of the civilizations of Mesopotamia and are usually trained in reading the difficult ancient scripts of the region. A specialist in ancient Sumer is called a **Sumerologist.**

The Sumerians: Creative Types

By 3500 B.C., there were large towns in much of Mesopotamia, and not long after, we find the first evidence of the Sumerians in the southern part of the region just north of the Persian Gulf. Determining the origins of these people is problematic. Some say that they came into Mesopotamia from elsewhere and became the dominant culture; others suggest that perhaps they were indigenous to the region. It really is a puzzle, especially because their language is like no other known, ancient or modern. Surrounded by groups who speak languages belonging to either the Semitic or Indo-European families, Sumerian is an isolated orphan with no known relatives.

The achievements of the Sumerians are many and impressive. There were so many, in fact, that it prompted the eminent *Sumerologist* Samuel Noah Kramer (1897–1990) to write a book called *History Begins at Sumer* (1959). Because Sumer is the first known civilization, it's not surprising that we find in it early evidence for all sorts of new things, including the wheel, metal casting, and architectural innovations such as the arch and dome.

The Sumerians aren't mentioned in the Bible. Explorers digging in Mesopotamia for biblical cities such as Babylon and Assyria were surprised to find a sophisticated culture that predated the others. The Sumerians, though, had a profound influence on all that followed, providing a sophisticated cultural foundation for their successors.

> **People and Places**
>
> American scholar Samuel Noah Kramer was perhaps the world's foremost expert on ancient Sumer. His careful translations of difficult Sumerian texts are widely known, and his autobiography, *In the World of Sumer* (1986), gives a fascinating glimpse of the amazing career of a professional Sumerologist.

> **Is That So!**
>
> Did you ever wonder why a minute is divided into 60 seconds? Or why a circle has 360 degrees? Couldn't we have 100 shorter seconds or 500 degrees in a circle? Blame it on our Mesopotamian friends, who established the base-60 system in use today.

Writing It Down

Perhaps the greatest invention of all time first appears among the Sumerians: writing. The writing system, with its characteristic wedge-shape script known as *cuneiform*, was adopted and adapted by other peoples in the region for writing their own languages. Additional information about Sumerian and other Mesopotamian writing can be found in Chapter 14. For now, it will suffice to say that the scribes of Mesopotamia wrote primarily on clay tablets (and occasionally on stone).

Life in Ancient Sumer

A good deal of our knowledge about ancient Sumer and other Mesopotamian civilizations comes directly from the surviving cuneiform texts. There are thousands of economic, legal, religious, and personal documents on clay tablets that provide an interesting picture of daily life. Archaeology, though, has done much to fill in the blanks or to verify the accuracy of some of the texts.

When we talk about the Sumerian culture, we can't think of it as if it were a modern country or nation. The Sumerians organized themselves into city-states. Each city had its own government or ruler and maintained a population of up to 50,000 people, and sometimes more. At the heart of each city was a temple dedicated to a favorite deity. Nanna, the moon god, for example, was especially worshiped in Ur and the goddess Inanna was popular in Uruk. These temples were often situated on raised platforms that would develop into one of the characteristic components of ancient Mesopotamian civilization: the ziggurat.

Ziggurats were built with up to seven stacked platforms, with a temple area on top. They shouldn't be confused with the early Egyptian step pyramids. Ziggurats were not tombs, and pyramids did not have stairs leading to a religious structure on top. Unfortunately, most unrestored ziggurats today look like dirty mountains in the sand. Some were quite huge, and those that have been studied show a tremendous amount of creativity with the use of mud bricks. Buttresses and recesses could be added for architectural interest, and walls could be decorated with friezes and colored tiles or cones.

The partially reconstructed massive ziggurat of Ur.

(David Moyer collection)

The most spectacular discovery from ancient Sumer occurred during the excavations of Sir Leonard Woolley (1880–1960) at the ancient city of Ur in the 1920s and 1930s. There he uncovered around 2,500 graves of various sorts, including 16 royal burials. They showed that the elite of Ur not only were buried with an impressive quantity of precious goods, but also took along members of their household.

In one "death pit," Woolley uncovered 6 male and 68 female servants, many dressed up for the big day. They probably killed themselves or were sacrificed to be buried with the boss. Although the whole concept is disturbing to us today, to archaeologists the whole ghastly scenario, with its many artifacts and human remains, has provided an incredible wealth of information about the ancient Sumerians.

> **People and Places**
>
> Sir Leonard Woolley excavated in many lands, including Nubia, Syria, Palestine, and Egypt. He is best known for his work at the Mesopotamian site of Ur. Woolley published a number of archaeological reports and some popular books as well, including *Digging Up the Past* (1930) and *Dead Towns and Living Men* (1920).

From Akkad to Babylon

You might think that with a common culture and language, the Sumerians could get along peacefully. Not always. The city-states used to battle with one another from time to time. This lack of unity didn't always work in their favor, and in fact probably weakened them for the likes of mighty Sargon of Akkad.

> **Logos**
>
> A **Semite** is someone who speaks a Semitic language as his or her native tongue, including Akkadian, Arabic, and Hebrew. It is a common misunderstanding among Westerners that everyone in the Near East is Semitic. Iranians (Persians) are not Semites, and neither are the Turks. Their languages belong to the Indo-European family.

Sargon was perhaps the first warlord in ancient history; around 2370 B.C., he conquered Sumer and parts thereabouts. He and his Akkadian-speaking colleagues ruled the Sumerians for the next 150 years.

Speaking of Akkadian, this would become the dominant language of Mesopotamia. It is a *Semitic* language and is in the same family as Hebrew and Arabic. The Akkadians lived in an area north of Sumer, and when Sargon of Akkad conquered his southern neighbor around 2370 B.C., he adopted much of their culture and borrowed their script to write his own language. Later rulers of Mesopotamia, such as the Babylonians and the Assyrians, would likewise speak dialects of Akkadian.

Not long after the Akkadians' power waned, the Sumerians reestablished themselves in the Third Dynasty of Ur, named for their principal city. It's possible that it was from this city and time that Abraham stepped forth to settle in Canaan. This brief and creative period would not last long. Around 2000 B.C., a group of Akkadian-speaking people known as the Amorites invaded Sumer and established their own capital at Babylon, becoming known as the Babylonians. Much of southern Mesopotamia comprised the land of Babylonia.

One of best-known individuals from this period was the sixth king of Babylon, Hammurabi (ruled 1792–1750 B.C.), who unified much of Mesopotamia. Hammurabi was known for his outstanding administrative skills. Most famous of all is his code of law, which has survived for us to study. The 282 laws are typically in two parts: a set of conditions and the resulting penalties. Here are some examples:

♦ If a man accuses another of murder and cannot prove it, the accuser dies.

♦ If a man passes a burning house and loots it, he will be thrown into the fire.

♦ If a son strikes his father, the son's hand shall be cut off.

♦ If a noble puts out the eye of another noble, he shall lose one of his own eyes. However, if he puts out the eye of a commoner, he shall pay a set penalty; and if it is a slave who is injured, the noble will pay the owner half his value.

♦ If a builder constructs a house and it collapses and kills the owner, the builder will be killed. If the house kills the son of the owner, the builder's son will be killed.

> ### This and That
>
> Hammurabi's laws were carved on a pillar of black diorite about 7 feet tall, which was later (probably around 1200 B.C.) carried off from Babylon by the Elamites as a war trophy. In the winter of 1901 and 1902, French archaeologists discovered the pillar at Susa, the ancient capital of the Elamites and later the Persians. It can now be seen at the Louvre in Paris.

There are plenty of harsh penalties, and responsibility for the quality of workmanship and services is emphasized. I imagine that there probably wasn't a lot of crime or too many shoddy goods after those laws were issued! The laws not only give us numerous important insights into ancient Babylonian society, but also show the characteristics of a complex society. The laws mention lots of different occupations and differences between the classes, and they didn't apply evenly to everyone.

The Mesopotamian law codes have often been compared with those in the Bible. Both seem to address many similar problems and emphasize a sense of justice. The biblical rules, though, have a very different spirit about them. They prioritize moral behavior over class distinctions and seem more concerned that the punishment fit the crime. And unlike the last example in the list, an offender's son would not be put to death for the crimes of his parent nor vice versa. The Hebrew law codes also have a distinct monotheistic tone to them and forbid a lot of the things that were regularly practiced in such places as Mesopotamia and Egypt, including consulting oracles and engaging in idolatry.

The Old Babylonians succumbed to outsiders and were eventually taken over by a group called the Kassites. Meanwhile, a province in northern Mesopotamia was beginning to stir, and the ancient Near East was in for a nasty surprise.

The Assyrians: Bad Boys of Mesopotamia

The Akkadian-speaking Assyrians had been up in the region of northern Mesopotamia for a long time, and were usually dominated by someone else. They get their name from their chief god, Ashur. There were at least four major cities: Ashur, a religious center; Nineveh, which became the capital; Nimrud; and Khorsabad. The Assyrians made their livings in the usual ways of complex societies and their land was agriculturally productive. Eventually, they would become very wealthy as they began to expand their power and influence over others in the region.

Beginning around 1300 B.C., the Assyrians started to secure their borders and then made forays to the south. They even managed to temporarily capture Babylon around 1100 B.C. Two hundred years later, they really struck out and began to conquer the Near East, destroying and demanding tribute nearly everywhere they went.

Assyrian king Tiglath-pilaser III became ruler of Babylon in 728 B.C., and his successor, Shalmaneser V, subdued much of Palestine. Sargon II deported the ten tribes of Israel in 721 B.C. and extended Assyrian dominance all the way to the border of Egypt. His successor, Sennacherib, continued the conquests, attacking Jerusalem and ravaging many Judean cities. The next king, Essarhadon, managed to conquer Egypt in 671 B.C.

Is That So!

A black stone obelisk was found at the Assyrian site of Nimrud in 1846. The obelisk is carved with texts and illustrations including a depiction of Jehu, one of the Israelite kings, presenting tribute to the Assyrian king Shalmaneser III.

Under his son and successor, Ashurbanipal, the Assyrian empire reached its greatest extent, and not long after began to fall apart. Egypt was lost in 660 B.C. It then took the combined forces of several different Near Eastern groups, including the Medes and the Babylonians, to shut down the Assyrian war machine. Their capital, Nineveh, was destroyed in 612 B.C.

The War Machine

The Assyrian military machine was an amazingly well-organized force, complete with iron weapons, cavalry, and chariots. The army traveled with a variety of specialists, including interpreters, spies, engineers, and even accountants to tally the booty. The Assyrians had a reputation as real terrorists, and word that they were coming was probably sufficient to send many a village fleeing.

Big walled cities were apparently not much of an obstacle either, as Assyrian engineers built large siege machines that could attack the walls while diggers tunneled underneath. Needless to say, the homeland received the benefits of the conquests, and lots of fine goods and captured people were sent back to Assyria.

The Assyrian ruler Sennacherib visually recorded his 701 B.C. attack on the Judean city of Lachish in stone reliefs on his palace walls in Nineveh. The reliefs show the Assyrian war machine in action, complete with battering rams and ladders to scale the walls.

Digging Up the Assyrians

Major excavations of ancient Assyrian sites began with the French diplomat Paul Emile Botta (1802–1870), who excavated Sargon II's palace at Khorsabad in 1843. The site would produce an amazing quantity of carved stone reliefs that would prove typical of Assyrian palaces. Most striking were the huge sculptures of human-headed winged lions and bulls. Tons of sculptures from the site were loaded up on rafts to be floated down the Tigris, where they would eventually be loaded onto ships for the long journey to France. They are now displayed in the Louvre.

The most famous excavator of Assyrian sites was Austen Henry Layard (1817–1894), who notably dug up the Assyrian capital of Nineveh, which was well known from the Bible. Layard estimated that he found almost two miles of sculptured reliefs. He also discovered the library of King Ashurbanipal, with well over 20,000 clay tablets. Many of his discoveries can today be seen in the British Museum in London.

The Neo-Babylonians

When the Assyrians were effectively put out of action, part of the power vacuum was filled by a new dynasty of rulers from a group known as the Chaldeans, who took over the throne of Babylon. We call these folks the Neo-Babylonians so as not to confuse them with the Old Babylonians of Hammurabi's day or others. This new establishment would accomplish quite a bit in its short 70 years or so, but would never achieve the extent of the Assyrian empire.

Nebuchadrezzar of Biblical Fame

Nebuchadrezzar II (ruled 605–562 B.C.) is the most famous king of the Neo-Babylonians. He is notorious in the Bible for attacking Jerusalem in 597 and destroying it in 586 B.C. and exiling many of the Jews to Babylon. Back at home, Nebuchadrezzar (also known as "Nebuchadnezzar") engaged in spectacular building projects that would amaze the German excavator Robert Koldeway (1855–1925), who between 1899 and 1917 uncovered Babylon's huge walls and city gates and its temples and palaces. Many were beautifully decorated with glazed tiles.

A Little Babylonian Culture

The Neo-Babylonians had much culturally in common with their predecessors. They spoke Akkadian, wrote on clay tablets, and had a good sense of astronomy, science, and mathematics. Their chief god was named Marduk, but most of their other deities would be well familiar to Assyrians and others in the region. In fact, many Babylonian gods were the same as those of the Sumerians, albeit often with different names. Here's a sample (the Sumerian name is in parentheses):

♦ **Anu (An):** God of heaven

♦ **Enlil (Enlil):** God of winds

♦ **Ea (Enki):** God of magic and wisdom

♦ **Shamash (Utu):** The sun

Is That So! _____

Perhaps the most famous example of ancient Mesopotamian literature is "The Epic of Gilgamesh," which tells of the dramatic adventures of Gilgamesh, who was half-man and half-god. Although of Sumerian origin, its popularity is demonstrated by copies written in Akkadian.

In terms of actually ruling the place, most Mesopotamian civilizations practiced father-to-son kingship. Unlike in Egypt, where the kings were actually considered to be living gods on Earth, the Mesopotamian rulers were considered to be mortal representatives of the gods. Part of their responsibilities was to make sure that the proper respect and rituals were performed by the appropriate priests. The gods of Mesopotamia themselves, though, behaved like mortals. They reproduced, fought, and were capable of acting both foolishly and wisely.

The reconstructed Gate of Ishtar at Babylon gives a hint of the splendor of that ancient city.

(David Moyer collection)

The Hanging Gardens

The Babylon of this time is also known as the site of one of the Seven Wonders of the Ancient World, the famous Hanging Gardens of Babylon. (The list of the seven wonders was compiled by Greeks in a later day.) The Gardens were rumored to be a magnificent tiered structure built by Nebuchadrezzar for the pleasure of his foreign wife, who missed her forested homeland. Excavator Robert Koldeway thought he might have found the actual site of the Gardens, but it's quite hard to prove.

Captives in Babylon

Many Jews, especially the political and religious elites, along with wealthy landowners, were deported to Babylon beginning in 597 B.C. Many more were hauled away during the Babylonian destruction of Jerusalem in 586 B.C. The Babylonians also looted Jerusalem and carried away the precious items from the Holy Temple they destroyed. The Jewish community established itself in Babylon as best it could; for many in the community, it would be decades before they could return to Palestine.

The Book of Daniel provides some fascinating stories from the time of Babylonian captivity. A couple of these tales show Daniel and his companions' steadfast devotion to the One God, even to the threat of death. On one occasion, three of Daniel's friends were sentenced to death for their beliefs and placed in a hot furnace. They miraculously survived unscathed. In another incident, Daniel himself kept the faith and was thrown to hungry lions and survived.

Another intriguing story is told in the fifth chapter of Daniel. During a royal Babylonian party during which captured sacred vessels from the Hebrew temple were being used as wine cups, a spooky hand appeared and wrote a mysterious message on the wall: "Mene, Mene, Tekel and Parsin."

 " " **Thus Saith**

The Jewish prophet Jeremiah prophesized a bad end to the Neo-Babylonians:

Thus says the Lord: "Behold, I will stir up the spirit of a destroyer against Babylon, against the inhabitants of Chaldea; and I will send to Babylon winnowers, and they shall winnow her, and they shall empty her land, when they come against her from every side on the day of trouble. Let not the archer bend his bow, and let him not stand up in his coat of mail. Spare not her young men; utterly destroy all her host. They shall fall down slain in the land of the Chaldeans, and wounded in her streets. For Israel and Judah have not been forsaken by their God, the Lord of hosts; but the land of the Chaldeans is full of guilt against the Holy One of Israel." (Jeremiah 51:1–5)

Daniel, who could interpret dreams with God's help, translated the inscription to the frightened Babylonian ruler. "Mene, God has numbered the days of your kingdom and brought it to an end; Tekel, you have been weighed in the balances and found wanting; Peres, your kingdom is divided and given to the Medes and Persians." That night, the ruler was slain and the prophecy came true.

Time for a Change

The successor of Nebuchadrezzar II, Nabonidus, was unpopular with his own people. This made it even easier for the Persians under Cyrus the Great to conquer Babylon in 539 B.C. (We'll meet the Persians in Chapter 13.) From then on, the people of Mesopotamia would be under the thumb of various foreign powers until the twentieth century A.D.

The Least You Need to Know

- ◆ Complex societies, a.k.a. civilizations, probably first emerged in the region of Mesopotamia.

- ◆ We find the first evidence of writing in the ancient civilization of the Sumerians, among many other innovations that were passed on to subsequent cultures in Mesopotamia.

- ◆ The history of Mesopotamia is the story of a succession of groups dominating each other.

- ◆ The Assyrian war machine wreaked havoc in Palestine as they built their empire, eliminating the northern kingdom of Israel and attacking Judah.

- ◆ The Neo-Babylonians succeeded in destroying Jerusalem and leading many Jewish captives to Babylon.

Chapter 12

Egypt: Land of the Pharaohs

In This Chapter

◆ Land of many gods

◆ An overview of Egyptian history

◆ Plagues and wonders

◆ Egyptians in Palestine

◆ Baby Jesus visits the Nile

When it comes to ancient history and archaeology, Egypt is perhaps the most popular old civilization of them all. Its reputation as an exotic land and the often startling surviving remains of its past have an immense appeal. Egypt played an important role in the world of the Bible and is mentioned hundreds of times. Let's take a brief look at the civilization of ancient Egypt and then at a few of those biblical stories.

To facilitate our study of ancient Egypt, we need to be able to know a bit about how things are arranged in time and space, so first we need to look at a little geography. And after that, we'll see how ancient Egyptian history is organized within that space.

Egypt on the Map

The area we know as Egypt is found in the northeast corner of the African continent. If you look at a modern map or globe, you'll see some straight lines on the south and west and the Mediterranean and Red Sea on the north and east. These are modern political boundaries. Don't confuse them with the area of ancient Egypt; they aren't the same. The civilization of ancient Egypt grew up around the Nile River. In concept, it's better to look at the land of Egypt in a way much different than the modern map. Think of it as looking like a beautiful lotus flower, with the Nile River forming its stem, and the river's broad Delta as its bloom!

Egypt was dependent on the Nile River for its very existence. As one Greek historian put it: "Egypt is the gift of the Nile." It is the Nile River and its natural cycle that allowed the Egyptian civilization to develop and thrive. Every year, the river would go through a flood stage. In doing so, it would leave a nutrient-rich deposit of silt, which would renew the agricultural farmland annually. With this natural cycle, along with extensive irrigation, Egypt was typically a veritable breadbasket!

Because of the dark, fertile soil along the Nile, the Egyptians called Egypt *Kemet*, which translates as the "Black Land." *Kemet* could also be contrasted with "the Red Land," referring to adjacent desert regions.

Is That So!

For a good overview of the subject of ancient Egypt, take a look at my book *The Complete Idiot's Guide to Ancient Egypt* (Alpha Books, 2002).

This and That

Because the Nile River flows from south to north, the Nile Valley was referred to as Upper Egypt (upstream) and the Delta as Lower Egypt (downstream). The unification of these areas was constantly reinforced in the titles and regalia of the ruler.

The land of ancient Egypt can be readily divided into two geographically distinct areas: the generally narrow Nile Valley in the south and the broad Nile Delta in the north. The Egyptians themselves were very aware of this distinction, which they referred to as the Two Lands, and the unification of both territories became a major concept in their notion of political unity and stability. One of the ancient capitals of Egypt, known by its Greek name Memphis, was located near the junction of the two lands, as is the city of Cairo, the capital of modern Egypt.

Egypt's position at the northeast edges of the African continent was strategic for interaction with the cultures of West Asia including those in Palestine, Mesopotamia, and Persia. These interactions could involve peaceful trade or domination and invasion, coming from both sides. The Mediterranean was an active place in ancient times and provided access to and from the land of Egypt, as it continues to do today.

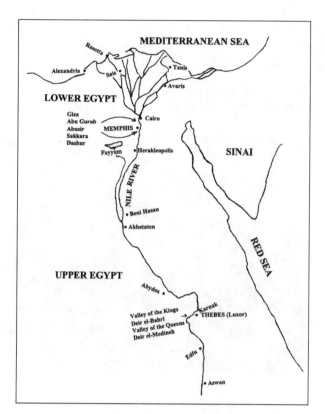

Map of Egypt featuring important sites from ancient times.

Cultural and Historical Highlights

There are several characteristics of Egyptian civilization that are worth knowing:

♦ Egypt was ruled by a king ("pharaoh") who was considered to be a living god. His authority was administered by an elaborate hierarchy of secular and religious bureaucrats.

♦ The Egyptians worshipped numerous gods who were often depicted in animal or human forms or a combination of both. They believed that many of these gods had to be appeased to maintain order in the universe.

♦ Egypt was primarily an agricultural society, although there were numerous craft specialists from wood carvers to jewelry makers.

♦ Egypt had access to great natural resources and wealth including quarries of beautiful stone and gold mines.

◆ Although the Egyptians believed in an afterlife, they were not obsessed with religion and death. The fact that their temples and tombs built of stone have survived the ages has given that false impression to many.

◆ The Egyptians had a hieroglyphic writing system that has allowed us to learn many details of their daily life and beliefs.

The immense temple complex of Karnak at Thebes is an amazing example of Egyptian religious devotion and architectural skills.

There are some easy ways to remember how Egyptian history is organized. Think of the Archaic Period as the old and formative time in the development of Egyptian civilization. Then there are the kingdoms (Old, Middle, and New), which are time periods when Egypt was generally unified, strong, and wealthy. These are each followed by an "intermediate period" that designates times when the central rulership of Egypt is in dispute or Egypt is being ruled by foreigners. The Late Period is the prelude to the coming of the Greeks and Romans. Here are names and dates:

Is That So!

The discovery in 1922 of the virtually intact tomb of the Egyptian pharaoh Tutankhamun remains perhaps the greatest archaeological discovery of all time. Many don't realize that Tut was a relatively obscure character in Egyptian history and it was the chance survival of his tomb that brought him everlasting fame!

◆ **Archaic or Early Dynastic Period:** Dynasties 1 and 2 (c. 3000–2686 B.C.). The formative period of Egyptian civilization.

◆ **Old Kingdom:** Dynasties 3 through 6 (2686–2181 B.C.). The age of building the great stone pyramids.

◆ **First Intermediate Period:** Dynasties 7 through 11 (2181–2055 B.C.). A period of civil chaos.

◆ **Middle Kingdom:** Dynasties 11 through 13 (2055–1650 B.C.). Egypt once again unified, strong, and enterprising!

- **Second Intermediate Period:** Dynasties 14 through 17 (1650–1550 B.C.). Foreign invaders from the east temporarily control most of Egypt.

- **New Kingdom:** Dynasties 18 through 20 (1550–1069 B.C.). The great age of empire. The likely time period for the Bible's Exodus story.

- **Third Intermediate Period:** Dynasties 21 through 24 (1069–644 B.C.). More civil confusion.

- **Late Period:** Dynasties 25 through 31 (664–332 B.C.). Foreign rulers including Nubians, Assyrians, and Persians.

- Although not within the traditional system, we can also add the **Graeco-Roman Period** when the Greeks and Romans ruled Egypt (332 B.C.–A.D. 395).

Floods, Famines, and Pharaohs

Mention of Egypt occurs in the very first book of the Bible, Genesis. After the Great Flood, the sons of Noah and their wives began to repopulate the land. Genesis 10:6 names Noah's son, Ham, as the great ancestor of the Egyptian people.

Genesis also tells how the great biblical patriarch Abraham ventured into Egypt during a time of famine. His wife, Sarah, was so beautiful that the pharaoh found her particularly attractive. Abraham, fearing for his life, passed her off as his sister. The ruse was exposed and he and Sarah were deported.

And then there is the story of Joseph, of course, which I discussed in Chapter 8 along with a sketch of the Exodus story. As you recall, the Joseph story explains how the Hebrew people ended up in Egypt, where they were eventually enslaved. The story features a Hebrew raised in the Egyptian royal household who flees his land to return years later to demand the freedom of his people—with God's help, of course! Let's take a closer look at some of the details of the Exodus story in its Egyptian context, starting with the plagues that occurred as Moses attempted to convince the pharaoh to allow the Hebrew people to leave Egypt.

This and That
The name Moses was common in Egypt. Several kings had the name Tuthmosis and Rameses; the mosis/moses part meaning "born of," in these cases, the Egyptian gods Thoth and Ra.

Joseph interpreting Pharaoh's dream.

(Illustration by Gustave Doré)

Ten Terrible Traumas

First, the water of the Nile River was turned to blood, making the water undrinkable and killing all the fish. Next came frogs, followed by gnats, flies, some sort of cattle disease, boils, hail, locusts, and a bit of scary darkness. The Book of Exodus makes it clear that God was offering an awesome demonstration of power over the Egyptian gods to the point of ridicule.

Egypt's pharaoh proved very stubborn despite these nine utterly nasty plagues. One more would be needed to sway the king to release the Hebrew slaves: The first-born sons of all the Egyptians would die. The Hebrews were instructed to kill an unblemished lamb and smear its blood on the doorposts and lintels of their homes. This would serve as a sign to pass over the homes of the Hebrews when the Angel of Death was on his way to deal with the Egyptians.

> **People and Places**
>
> A few speculators have tried to equate Moses with the curious pharaoh Akhenaten of the Egyptian eighteenth dynasty. Akhenaten upset the religious establishment by advocating the worship of a supreme god in the form of the sun disk. This, however, was not Hebrew monotheism. Akhenaten himself was worshipped as a living god among a host of other lesser gods.

This final horrible plague had the proper effect. The Hebrews quickly packed up and left with Pharaoh's permission. (When they exited Egypt, they also took with them a mummy: the bones of Joseph.) The Hebrews were miraculously guided in their journey by a cloud during the day and by a pillar of fire at night. All went well until Pharaoh decided to give chase while the Hebrews approached a body of water known as the Sea of Reeds. Here, one of the most magnificent miracles of Exodus occurred. With his people trapped between the water and the marauding Egyptian army, complete with chariots, God caused the waters to part, allowing the Hebrews to safely cross. The waters then crashed down again, drowning the Egyptians. From there, the Hebrews wandered for years in the wilderness of Sinai before entering the promised land of Canaan in the Palestine region.

Natural Explanations

There has been lots of speculation about the many interesting events in the Exodus story, particularly because most of these incidents seem to be the kinds of things that can occur on their own in nature. It has, for example, been suggested that many of the plagues might have been a chain reaction to a temporarily polluted Nile. Frogs get out and die, flies abound, animals and humans get sick. Hail is known to be very damaging, and in Egypt every year there is the "khamseen" season, which is a time when sandstorms are prevalent. And some of these storms can radically affect visibility and perhaps explain the darkness.

Defenders of the Bible, of course, will point out that the timing and the intensity of these events are a demonstration of God's power. The story also tells how the Hebrew slaves were spared all of these things. The last plague, the death of the first-born Egyptians, does not follow any known natural phenomena.

Is That So!

There have been attempts in recent years to explain the guiding cloud and pillar of fire along with the parting of the waters as effects of the eruption of a Mediterranean volcano named Thera around 1629 B.C. Perhaps the escaping Hebrews were viewing the massive volcanic plume of the erupting Thera and could likewise see its fireworks by night. The parting of the sea might be a result of a huge tidal wave or tsunami that would cause the water to withdraw before closing. Then again, these just might be miracles!

Not the Red Sea

The body of water that parted, allowing the Hebrews to cross, has often been called the Red Sea. The words in the Hebrew Bible are actually *"yam suf"* or Sea of Reeds. This suggests a marshy area such as those found in the northeastern Delta region of Egypt. It would be a lot shallower and perhaps a shorter distance, depending on where the crossing took place. On the other hand, there are those who insist that indeed the *yam suf* is the great body of water known as the Red Sea, and the Hebrews might have crossed in the narrows of its westernmost arm before entering the Sinai peninsula.

Who's That Bad Man?

The Exodus tale talks about two pharaohs: One is popularly referred to as the Pharaoh of the Oppression and the other as the Pharaoh of the Exodus. The former is the fellow in charge when the Book of Exodus begins, and the latter is the one who dealt with Moses and the plagues. A tremendous amount of discussion has been leveled at trying to figure out who these pharaohs might be, and thus tie the Exodus firmly into historical chronology.

Is That So! _____

Despite what might be depicted in the movies, Hebrew slaves had nothing to do with building the pyramids of Egypt. The Great Pyramid of Egypt, for example, was probably already more than a thousand years old when the Hebrews were enslaved!

Rameses the Great

After years and years of discussion, there is still no consensus, but here are a couple clues. The Bible mentions that the Hebrew slaves were working on the twin store-cities of Pithom and Pi-Ramses, both of which have been located up in the Nile Delta area of Egypt in the vicinity where the Hebrews were likely settled. The name "Ramses" is the big tip-off, as there were several kings by that name who ruled in the Egyptian nineteenth and twentieth dynasties (c. 1307–1070 B.C.). As a great builder and a formidable military leader, Rameses II is a real favorite candidate for the pharaoh of the Exodus.

Read the Fine Print

There is but one mention of the Israelite people in Egyptian texts. It is found on a large inscribed stone table, or *stele*, dating to the reign of the successor of Rameses II, Merneptah. Merneptah's stele gives a list of names of cities conquered by the Egyptians in Palestine. Along with these cities is the name Israel, and it is written differently than the other names. Rather than using the special hieroglyph at the end of the word which would indicate that it is the name of a city, the word Israel uses the glyphs that indicate a people, rather than some sort of settlement. This is fascinating, but it indicates that the Hebrews were already established by that time in the region of Palestine. For some with a literalist approach to biblical history, this causes some serious chronological problems, as there wouldn't have been enough time for all of the events leading up to their presence there.

The name of Israel as it appears on Merneptah's stele.

A modern portrait of Pharaoh Rameses II by Winifred Brunton. Was he the pharaoh of the Exodus?

Interestingly, in the last few years it has been noted that there might also be a picture of the Israelites on an Egyptian temple! The picture is part of a damaged inscription of Merneptah that seems to report the successes recorded on his stele but with the addition of illustrations. There's a good argument for this being the case, but it's hard to prove. Even so, it's the closest thing to a picture of the ancient Hebrews that we might have.

Where's the Proof?

Critics might point to a lack of Egyptian evidence for the details of the Exodus, but then again, the Egyptians were not known for admitting their mistakes. Would a grandiose pharaoh such as Rameses II brag anywhere that his army was defeated by a ragged group of slaves? Hardly. Even when the Egyptians won a battle, they tended to exaggerate their success in very boastful terms.

The miraculous and wonderful story of the Exodus is precious in Judaism. It tells how God indeed looked after his people and delivered them from slavery in Egypt. The story is commemorated every year in the Jewish observance of Pesach, or Passover.

Egypt in Palestine

By now you're aware that Palestine was in the path of all sorts of marauders and empire-builders, including the Babylonians, Assyrians, Persians, Greeks, Romans, and the Egyptians, of course. The Egyptians passed through the area many times, subjugating towns, demanding tribute, and fighting battles against their enemies on foreign turf. It wasn't all mayhem. One of the early Jewish kings, Solomon, was said to have had a pharaoh as a father-in-law in a marriage alliance!

Raiding the Temple

The Bible tells of the attack by an Egyptian pharaoh on Jerusalem during which the Holy Temple and the palace were looted:

> In the fifth year of [the Jewish] King Rehoboam, Shishak king of Egypt came up against Jerusalem; he took away the treasure of the house of the Lord and treasures of the king's house; he took away everything. He also took away all of the shields of gold which Solomon made. (1 Kings 14:25–26)

"Shishak" is usually identified with the twenty-second dynasty pharaoh Sheshonq I. Chapter 12 of 2 Chronicles provides more details, including some military details and mentions the employment of "… twelve hundred chariots and sixty thousand horsemen. And the people were without number who came with him from Egypt—Libyans, Sku-ki-im, and Ethiopians." And God through a prophet explained to the Jewish rulers why this was allowed to happen to his people: "You abandoned me, so I have abandoned you to the hand of Shishak."

This and That
Goods from Palestine have been found in Egypt for most of its ancient history and vice versa. Wine from Canaan was a particularly favorite import.

Foul Play

In the Book of 2 Kings (23:29), it is noted that an Egyptian king actually killed his Hebrew counterpart, King Josiah:

> In his days Pharaoh Neco king of Egypt went up to the king of Assyria to the river Euphrates. King Josiah went to meet him; and Pharaoh Neco slew him at Megiddo, when he saw him.

Egypt Be Cursed!

Elsewhere in the Old Testament, Egypt, along with other pagan lands, is offered dire futures because of their pagan and wicked ways. Here is a small sample courtesy of the prophet Isaiah:

> An oracle concerning Egypt. Behold, the Lord is riding on a swift cloud and comes to Egypt; and the idols of Egypt will tremble at his presence, and the heart of the Egyptians will melt within them. And I will stir up Egyptians against Egyptians, and they will fight, every man against his brother and every man against his neighbor, city against city, kingdom against kingdom … And the waters of the Nile will be dried up, and the river will be parched and dry; and its canals will become foul, and the branches of Egypt's Nile will diminish and dry up, reeds and rushes will rot away. (Isaiah 19:1–2, 5–6)

Given the disintegration of the ancient Egyptian civilization, and the environmental changes that have occurred since, one can't help but wonder if some of these things indeed came to pass!

Is That So!

The Bible notes that the wisdom of the Jewish King Solomon surpassed that of "all the people of the east, and all the wisdom of Egypt." (1 Kings 4:30) There are several examples of surviving Egyptian "wisdom texts," and some scholars have pointed out amazing parallels between these and such biblical works as the Book of Proverbs. Are they somehow related? Did one group borrow wise advice from another, or was this sort of information part of the great Near Eastern culture?

Hiding Out in Egypt with Jesus

Egypt also plays a role in the life of Jesus. In the Gospel of Matthew, three wise men from the east set out in the direction of Palestine in search of a miraculous baby. The wise men approached Herod, a Jewish king ruling under the permission and bidding of the Romans, and asked him where they might locate the newborn king of the Jews. This, of course, immediately riled the egotistical and homicidal Herod, who decided to locate the baby Jesus and have him killed. He asked the wise men to let him know where this special baby would be found. Warned in a dream, they presented their gifts to Jesus and left without informing Herod. Herod, determined to have the baby destroyed, went on a killing rampage of all male children two years or younger in the vicinity of Bethlehem.

An angel appeared to Joseph, the husband of Mary the mother of Jesus, in a dream telling him to take his family and escape to Egypt. The details of their travels are not described in the Bible. In Egypt, however, there are rich traditions that trace the path of the Holy Family on a journey that may have lasted up to three years. There are lots of interesting stories about the baby performing a variety of miracles including healing people, calming wild animals, and producing springs of fresh water. On at least a couple of occasions, the legends say, he was able to cause trees to bend over so that their delicious fruit could be picked.

Today, one can find churches located up and down the Nile and elsewhere in Egypt built at places where Jesus and his family were thought to have spent time or where miracles occurred.

The Least You Need to Know

- The Nile and its natural cycle allowed for an Egyptian civilization to flourish.

- Egypt was ruled by a divine king and practiced the worship of many gods.

- Egypt plays an important role in the Bible.

- Egyptian archaeology is relatively silent regarding many of the biblical stories.

- Egypt continued to play a role in the lives of the Hebrew people even after they established themselves in the Promised Land.

- Jesus journeyed to Egypt as an infant and stories of this visit persist today among Egyptian Christians.

Chapter 13

Hittites, Persians, and Greeks

In This Chapter

- ◆ Hittites from Hebron and Hattusha
- ◆ Persians build an empire
- ◆ The Jews get to go home
- ◆ Alexander brings the Greeks to Palestine
- ◆ A revolt against abuse and oppression
- ◆ The origins of Hanukkah

In this chapter, we're going to look at three more big powers who had an impact on the world of the Bible. Two of them, Persia and Greece, developed massive empires in which Palestine became incorporated. As you'll see, their attitudes and policies toward the Jews were quite different.

The third is a group called the Hittites, whose physical existence as a people was not known outside their mention in the Bible until about a hundred years ago. Let's start with them.

How About Those Hittites?

The Hittites are mentioned sporadically in the Old Testament. Here's a sample:

> **People and Places**
>
> The cave that Abraham bought from Ephron the Hittite for the burial of his wife Sarah is called Machpelah. Abraham, Isaac, Rebecca, Jacob, and Leah were also interred there. Several commemorative monuments have been built on the site that is located in Hebron.

- A Hittite named Ephron sold a cave on his property in Canaan to Abraham for the burial of Sarah.

- Esau, the brother of Jacob, is said to have had two Hittite wives.

- Although they generally seemed pretty civil to Abraham, the Hittites were included in the list of peoples to be conquered in Canaan by the invading Israelites.

- Solomon is said to have exported horses and chariots to the Hittites, and a Hittite woman was among his many wives.

Map of the ancient Near East showing Hittite territory, Persia, Mesopotamia, and Palestine.

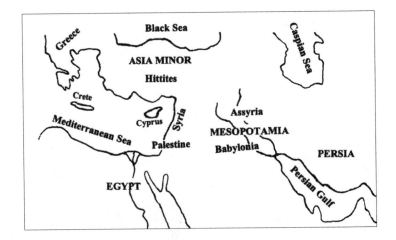

David Does Wrong!

King David is one of the most admired people in the Bible, but one incident in his life is utterly despicable. One day, he noticed a beautiful woman named Bathsheba bathing. Bathsheba was the wife of a mercenary Hittite soldier named Uriah, who fought with the Israelites. David impregnated her and in order to have her to himself (and to also no doubt avoid the wrath of Uriah), he organized a sinister plan. During a siege of the Ammonite capital of Rabbah-Ammon, he sent orders to his commander to "[s]et Uriah in the forefront of the hardest fighting, and then draw back from him, that he may be struck down, and die." (2 Samuel 11:15) As planned, Uriah was killed and David married the pregnant widow. Needless to say, God was very displeased!

The Hittites Rediscovered

Very little was known about the Hittites until about a hundred years ago, when some of their sites were excavated. Their capital was called Hattusha, and was located in Asia Minor at the site of Bogazkoy, in what is now central Turkey. The Hittite Kingdom was established around 1750 B.C.

The Hittites and their "Kingdom of Hatti" became serious players in the Near East. They established their own moderate-size empire and even vigorously competed with the Egyptians for influence in the Syro-Palestinian area. And yes, there are even scholars who specialize in the study of the Hittites, and they are called *Hittitologists*.

Logos

Hittitology is the study of the Hittites. A **Hittitologist** is a scholar specializing in this study.

They actually fought and essentially defeated the Egyptians during a battle for control at Kadesh in Syria around 1274 B.C. (The Egyptians bragged about how they themselves were victorious, but that was a familiar pattern.) After the battle of Kadesh, a peace treaty was made between the Hittites and the Egyptians, and Pharaoh Rameses II took two Hittite princesses as wives.

The Hittite kings were hard bargainers and included rulers with great names like Suppiluliumas and Hattusilis III. Eventually, the Hittites had to fight off the Assyrians in the East and were weakened. The capital of Hattusha was devastated by invaders around 1200 B.C., effectively putting an end to the great Hittite civilization.

Some of what is left of Hattusha, the capital of the Hittites.

(David Moyer collection)

The Palestinian Hittite Mystery

Given our knowledge of the great Hittite civilization in Asia Minor, the biblical mention of Hittites in Canaan is somewhat of a mystery. Perhaps they were a group who settled there sometime before the time of Abraham. Most seem to have Semitic rather than Hittite names, so they probably assimilated with the local population. They must have kept some sense of ethnic identity, however, in order to be identified as Hittites during the time of the Israelite monarchy and thereafter.

Empire-Building with the Persians

Ancient Persia, one of the best known of the ancient Near Eastern states, was located in the area presently occupied by the state of Iran. The Persian civilization reached its height during what is called the Achaemenid Dynasty, under which the Persians had a truly international impact. The first king of this dynasty, Cyrus II, or Cyrus the Great (ruled 559–530 B.C.), conquered his neighbors, including the Medes and the Lydians, and began to build a huge empire, the size of which had never been seen in the Near East.

Cyrus next turned his attention to Babylon, which he successfully conquered in 539 B.C. Important for our interest is the fact that Cyrus allowed the Jews held in Babylonian captivity to return home to Palestine. (More on that a little later in this chapter.) Before his death, Cyrus managed to put the Persians in control of much of Asia Minor and Afghanistan, and took over the territory of the Babylonian empire. At its greatest, the Persian Empire would eventually span from the Indus River to the Nile and to the very edge of Greece.

Cyrus's successor, Cambyses II (ruled 530–522 B.C.), added Egypt and parts of North Africa to the Persian pie. The expansion of the Empire continued under Darius I (521–486 B.C.), who conquered parts of India and a number of Greek colonies and islands along the coast of what is now Turkey.

The Persians were quite clever in their attempts to maintain their empire. They divided their territory into governed regions that were connected with a massive system of roads to facilitate communication and the movement of troops, trade, and booty. Compared to some of the other empire-builders in the region, the Persians were relatively gentle to the peoples they conquered, allowing them to retain much of their cultural independence.

Is That So! ___

One intriguing aspect of old Persian culture is the appearance around 600 B.C. of a prophet named Zoroaster. A religion called Zoroastrianism grew up around his teachings, which promoted a belief in a conflict between good and evil. The supreme god of the religion is named Ahura Mazda.

Darius I moved the Persian capital of Susa to Persepolis, where he built an utterly spectacular city. Although it was destroyed in 330 B.C. by a vengeful Alexander the Great, many of its incredible columned buildings and carved stone reliefs have survived, and Persepolis today is truly a magnificent archaeological site.

The remains of the magnificent Persian capital of Persepolis can only hint at its former glory.

(David Moyer collection)

A Return to Palestine

With the coming of the Persians, the Jews were able to leave Babylon and return to Palestine. Cyrus even encouraged them to rebuild the Holy Temple and made sure the Jews were given back their sacred treasures which the Babylonians had removed from the Temple as booty! The return to Palestine took place in stages and the books of Ezra and Nehemiah list the names of many of the people involved.

Thus Saith

The edict allowing the Jews to return to Palestine was recognized as so remarkable that it is recorded in the book of Ezra:

> Thus says Cyrus king of Persia: The Lord, the God of heaven, has given me all the kingdoms of the earth, and he has charged me to build him a house at Jerusalem, which is in Judah. Whoever is among you of all his people, may his God be with him, and let him go up to Jerusalem, which is in Judah, and rebuild the house of the Lord, the God of Israel—he is the God who is in Jerusalem; and let each survivor, in whatever place he sojourns, be assisted by the men of his place with silver and gold, with goods and with beasts, besides freewill offerings for the house of God which is in Jerusalem. (Ezra 1:2–4)

Problems in the Homeland

The Book of Ezra describes the trials and tribulations of rebuilding the Temple. Some of the people who had moved into Jerusalem in the previous decades were obstructing progress. After the work was halted, an appeal was made to Persian king Darius I to search his archives in order to find the original decree of Cyrus, which authorized the construction. The document was found and the Temple was allowed to be rebuilt with the support of Darius.

Around 458 B.C., during the reign of Persian king Artaxerxes (ruled 464–424 B.C.), the Jewish scribe Ezra was sent from Persia to Palestine to see that his people were following the law of God. What he found when he arrived was disappointing. Some of the returnees, for example, were marrying local women and falling well short of their traditional laws. Ezra insisted that the Jews divorce their foreign wives and the book of Ezra lists some of the names of the offenders who participated in this reform.

Jerusalem Restored

When reports reached Persia that the city of Jerusalem was in poor shape, a Jew named Nehemiah, an employee of Artaxerxes, was also sent from Persia to see that things were set right. He, too, met local resistance when he tried to rebuild the damaged walls of the city of Jerusalem. Nehemiah persisted and the walls were built.

The Book of Nehemiah also describes an event in which Jewish law was reintroduced to the returnees:

> And all the people gathered as one man into the square … and they told Ezra the scribe to bring the book of the law of Moses which the Lord had given to Israel. And Ezra the priest brought the law before the assembly, both men and women and all who could hear with understanding, on the first day of the seventh month. And he read from it facing the square … from early morning until midday, in the presence of the men and the women and those who could understand; and the ears of all the people were attentive to the book of the law … And Ezra blessed the Lord, the great God; and all the people answered, "Amen, Amen," lifting up their hands; and they bowed their heads and worshiped the Lord with their faces to the ground … And they read from the book, from the law of God, clearly; and they gave the sense, so that the people understood the reading. (Nehemiah 8:1–8)

Thereafter, vows were made to keep the Sabbath and other religious obligations.

Troubles with the Greeks

While the Jews reestablished themselves in Palestine—albeit under foreign rule—the Persians continued to build their empire. With a widespread empire made up of a large number of people of different cultures, it's not surprising that the Persians would often be called upon to quell various rebellions. Their squashing of such an uprising in the Greek colonies resulted in some of the most famous episodes of Persian history. To punish the Greek city-state of Athens for assisting in the uprising, Darius decided to invade Greece in 490 B.C. He lost.

His son, Xerxes (ruled 486–465 B.C.), however, put together a massive land and sea force and invaded Greece again in 480 to 479 B.C. Despite initial successes, the Persians were again defeated, but not until they had inflicted significant damage, including the burning of Athens. The Persian Empire continued to prosper despite this defeat, until it was finally conquered by Alexander the Great, who battled the forces of Darius III (336–331 B.C.) between 334 and 331 B.C.

Meet the Greeks

By now, you're well aware that the ancient Near East was an important source of "civilized influence" for the modern world. The Greeks, though, seem to command a lot of attention themselves for the same thing. Although they benefited greatly from certain Near Eastern inventions such as writing, the Greeks themselves were great innovators. For Western civilization, at least, much of how we think, conduct politics, and look at art and beauty, for example, has roots in ancient Greek culture. Let's take a look at these people who also left their mark on the world of the Bible.

The Land of the Greeks

The area known as Greece is essentially a big peninsula that juts out of eastern Europe into the north Mediterranean. In Greece itself, a peninsula called the Peloponnese splits off to the south. To its east, between the Greek mainland and Asia Minor, is the

Aegean Sea, in which are found many islands that were inhabited by the ancient Greeks. And farther to the south, in the Mediterranean, lies a linear island, Crete, which was home to a truly unique civilization.

The geography of Greece in many ways shaped the nature of its civilization. Areas like Mesopotamia were broad and relatively accessible and thus conducive to control and invasion. Large kingdoms and empires could be established by invading armies. Greece, on the other hand, is mostly composed of narrow valleys and small plains, and much of the region is bordered or surrounded by water. Here in these little pockets independent Greek city-states developed that, although sharing much of a common culture, were mostly independent political entities.

History Fast and Furious

You want some fast history? Hang on, here it comes. Agriculture spread to Greece about 7000 B.C., and bronze appeared around 2800 B.C. Around 2000 B.C., Greek-speaking people moved into the area and began to dominate. A rich civilization called the Mycenaeans (after its biggest city, Mycenae) developed and flourished, especially between 1600 and 1100 B.C., after which the area seems to have been overrun by a new people, traditionally thought to have been a group of Greek-speakers called the Dorians—but who knows for sure?

> **People and Places**
>
> Athens and Sparta demonstrate some of the variety found amongst the Greek city-states. Athens was located near the sea, was heavily involved in trade, had a well-developed navy, and practiced a form of democracy. Sparta, on the other hand, was landlocked, strove to be self-sufficient and austere, was ruled by two kings, and maintained a formidable army.

The next 300 or 400 years are referred to as the Dark Ages, because little is known of them, but then the lights came on. Around 700 B.C., Greek colonies started appearing around the borders of the Mediterranean, and Greek city-states, including the famous Athens and Sparta, began to develop and bloom.

What might be called the Classical Age began around 500 B.C. (The study of ancient Greece and Rome is called Classics, and its practitioners are classicists.) This is the era most people probably think about in connection with ancient Greece. It is a time when the arts flourished and many of the city-states thrived. It was also a time of wars.

War and Peace

There were the two wars with the Persians, and later, alliances of city-states fought each other during the series of skirmishes known as the Peloponnesian Wars (431–404 B.C.), which essentially pitted Sparta and its allies against Athens and its allies. All this discord weakened the Greek city-states, thus preparing them to be invaded, beginning in the fourth century B.C., by an old Greek kingdom in the north, Macedon, ruled by King Philip II (382–336 B.C.) and then his son, Alexander III (356–323 B.C.), popularly known as Alexander the Great.

While the Greek city-states fought in the south, the kingdom of Macedon watched in the north, and finally made a move. King Philip II began a campaign to conquer the Greek city-states, a project that was only temporarily cut short by his assassination, because his successor and son, Alexander, would finish the job and then some! Alexander III had quite an upbringing. The Greek philosopher Aristotle was his personal tutor, and when his father Philip went to war, Alexander was left in charge of Macedon at the tender age of 16.

> **This and That**
>
> Some of Athens's greatest architectural achievements were accomplished during their so-called Golden Age, circa 450 to 430 B.C. The Athenians were greatly aided by their looting of the war-chest established by a group of city-states to finance any future wars with the Persians.

With the death of Philip II, his son Alexander III was not merely content to consolidate the Greek city-states within his domain; he first and foremost wanted to go after the Persians, who had more than a hundred years before invaded Greece and burned Athens, and who still posed a threat. Alexander attacked Persia with a vengeance, burned Persepolis in 331 B.C., and took over the mighty Persian Empire, including Egypt. In Egypt he was made pharaoh and established a city named after himself, Alexandria. He was more than happy to accept the various ruling titles as he pressed east all the way to India over a period of a dozen years.

Alexander wanted to keep going, but his troops were tired and wanted to go home. On the way back, the mighty Alexander died of a fever, and his vast empire was divided among a few of his generals, who set up ruling dynasties in their various territories. The most important among these generals were Seleucus, who took over the territory of the old Persian Empire, and Ptolemy, whose prize was Egypt. Palestine was caught in the middle and was eventually controlled by the descendents of Seleucus.

Spreading the Greek Culture

In each conquered land, Greek culture was introduced as Greek colonists flocked to set up settlements and towns. Greek became the universal language in these regions, and the arts would again flourish, often in new ways influenced by local traditions. Many people adapted and were assimilated into the Greek culture, including many Jews.

This time is known as the Hellenistic period—from the Greek word *Hellas*, which means "Greece." Hellenization is the process of spreading Greek culture. It was a policy regularly practiced by the Greek rulers of the territories conquered by Alexander the Great. Alexandria in Egypt became an international capital of this Hellenistic world, and a major economic and cultural center. Its cosmopolitan atmosphere was home to a number of diverse cultures, including a large number of Jews.

> ### People and Places
>
> Among the numerous notable features of the new Egyptian capital of Alexandria was a great library that would eventually hold most of the written works of the areas dominated by the Greeks. The library grew through time into a huge facility with perhaps more than half a million papyrus documents. A professional staff of librarians and copyists were employed, and scholars were put to work editing such texts as the works of Homer. The Hebrew Bible was even translated into Greek there, a translation known as the "Septuagint." The library was eventually burned to the ground—an immense loss to civilization.

True to the Faith

In Hellenistic Palestine, many Jews remained true to their faith and refused to succumb to the new culture. The numerous gods of the Greeks (Zeus, Athena, and others) did not conform to their belief in one God, but at least the early Greek rulers didn't seem to pursue the issue much. Things changed, though, under the reign of the Hellenistic monarch Antiochus IV which began in 175 B.C.

With the goal of homogenizing the people living in his territories, Antiochus forbade many of the essential Jewish customs, including circumcision, observance of the Sabbath, and the use of the Temple for Jewish worship and offerings. Just to be nasty, pigs were sacrificed on ceremonial altars and a statue of Zeus was erected in the Temple. Jews were forced to give up their religious practices and perform profane acts under penalty of death.

The Mighty Maccabees

Given this intolerable situation, it's not surprising that there was a strong reaction. A Jewish rebellion began under the leadership of a man named Mattathias of the Hasmonean (or Maccabees) family. His son, Judah Maccabeus, would prove to be a great general. The rebels engaged the Greek enemy on many occasions, using guerilla tactics in difficult terrain and hiding in the inhospitable desert. Several great battles were fought, and the Jewish army, with God's help, according to the Bible, was ultimately successful.

When officers of Antiochus approached Mattathias and asked him to serve as an example to others and engage in pagan worship, the Jewish leader was steadfast in his refusal:

> And Mattathias answered and said in a loud voice: "Even if all the nations that live under the rule of the king obey him, and have chosen to do his command-ments, departing each one from the religion of his fathers, yet I and my sons and my brothers will live by the covenant of our fathers. Far be it from us to desert the law and the ordinances. We will not obey the king's words by turning aside from our religion to the right hand or the left." (1 Maccabees 2:19–22)

(By the way, the story of the Maccabees are found in the two apocryphal books called 1 Maccabees and 2 Maccabees, which are not included in all Bibles.)

Festival of Lights: The Origin of Hanukkah

When Judas Maccabeus and his men finally liberated Jerusalem, they found that the Temple had been greatly desecrated and badly damaged. They set about cleaning up the mess and made repairs, including building a new altar. There were eight days of celebration and thanksgiving when the Temple was rededicated.

The Jewish holiday of Ha-nukkah is often called the "Festival of Lights." As part of the tradition, candles on a menorah are lit over a period of eight nights.

As part of the rededication, a perpetually burning flame in the Temple was relit, but there was only enough untainted kosher oil remaining to last one day. According to Jewish tradition, a miracle occurred when this limited amount of oil burned and provided light for eight days.

Is That So!

Technically, Hanukkah is considered to be a minor Jewish holiday. Yet at least in the Western world, it has become one of the best known, because it occurs annually during December, the month of the Christian Christmas celebration. As a result, it has taken on more public recognition, and, like Christmas, has suffered from a good bit of commercialization.

The story of this rebellion against oppression is celebrated annually in the Jewish holiday of Hanukkah. The story of Antiochus IV and Judas Maccabeus is retold, and the liberation of the Jewish people and the Temple is remembered by the symbolic lighting of a candelabra called a "menorah"; eight candles are burned over eight nights to represent the miracle of the Temple oil.

Along with special food, gifts, and music, there is a game played with a spinning top called a dreidel. On each of the four sides are Hebrew letters, which together stand for the phrase "a great miracle happened there," referring to the lamp oil.

To Each Their Turn

We have seen how the Egyptians played their part in Palestine, how the Assyrians incorporated that region into their empire followed by the Babylonians, how the Persians defeated the Babylonians only to be defeated in turn themselves. Empires come and go, and that of Alexander, too, would pass. To the west of Greece, an empire based in Rome was steadily growing and accumulating territories in the western Mediterranean and Europe. They would begin to hammer away at the Greeks and it would be their turn next to rule over Palestine. We'll deal with those Romans when we start talking about the times of Jesus in Chapter 19.

The Least You Need to Know

- Although the Hittite homeland was in the area of modern Turkey, some of these people apparently lived in Palestine during Old Testament times.

- The Neo-Babylonian Empire was defeated by the Persian ruler Cyrus the Great. Cyrus allowed the Jews to return home to Palestine and facilitated the building of the Second Temple.

- Despite obstruction, returnees to Jerusalem were able to restore their city and its Temple and culture through the leadership of the likes of Ezra and Nehemiah.

◆ Alexander the Great defeated the Persians and produced a massive empire of his own that included Palestine. Everywhere the Greeks went, they actively spread their language and culture.

◆ Groups of steadfast Jews in Palestine were able to resist forced attempts by some of the Hellenistic Greek rulers to destroy their faith.

◆ The Jewish tradition of Hanukkah tells the story of rebellion against oppression.

Chapter 14

The Greatest Invention Ever!

In This Chapter

- ◆ The evolution of writing
- ◆ Wedges on clay tablets
- ◆ Deciphering Egyptian
- ◆ The alphabetic achievement
- ◆ Ancient manuscripts

Writing could very well be considered the greatest invention ever. It allows us to record, share, and remember information across time and space. It's a truly marvelous thing and it developed in the Near East, the Bible lands.

For our present purposes, it allowed the Bible to be transmitted to us down through the ages and for scholars to continually study it and write about it. Let's take a look at this great invention as it appeared and developed in the Near East.

The Writing Phenomenon

Writing was not invented all at once, but rather was an evolving process. We don't know exactly what happened but here's the currently favored theory. In early Mesopotamia, little clay tokens were used to keep track of how many of something people might possess. For example, an ox might be represented by a token in the shape of an ox. These tokens could be sealed in a sort of clay "envelope" for safe accounting purposes.

Later, it became more common to draw a picture of the object, let's say an ox, on a flat piece of clay with some sort of tally marks next to it—for example, three marks, three oxen. At this point, we could call this drawing a pictograph; not yet real writing. Writing can be defined as language in visible form. Although the ox and the tally marks might convey a message, these symbols are technically not writing until they are used to represent sounds in a language.

The next big step to writing would be when that ox picture stood not just for an ox, but became a sound symbol that could be used to construct other words. So if the Sumerian word for "ox" was *gu*, the ox symbol might be used as a syllable and combined with other symbols to spell other words that have the *gu* sound in them. Such a symbol could be applied to other languages such as Akkadian, which borrowed the script, and had a completely different word for ox.

The classic example often used to describe this uses the two words *bee* and *leaf*. If we want to express those two things, we can draw a bee and a leaf and, provided that the drawing is good, we can convey a message. The symbols really become writing, though, when they stand for sounds and can be combined to write other words (such as "belief"), or be used in any other word containing those sounds. In fact, the ancient Sumerian script was written in such syllables, with additional symbolic signs to aid in understanding. It first appeared in Mesopotamia around 3100 B.C.

Wedge-Script

Over the next couple thousand years, the original pictographs behind the sound signs evolved until they were barely recognizable. It became standard in Mesopotamia to write on little tablets of clay, and a reed stylus was used to produce wedge-shape impressions in the tablets. This type of script is known as *cuneiform*, which means, literally, "wedge-shape." Hundreds of thousands of clay tablets bearing this writing system have survived, allowing us some often detailed glimpses of ancient life and times in the Near East.

Logos

Cuneiform is the wedge-shape script, typically impressed into clay, which was used to write such languages as Sumerian, Akkadian, and Old Persian.

The pillaging of an ancient Mesopotamian town was no doubt an unpleasant experience for its inhabitants, especially when fire was used. For the archaeologist, however, a little fire in the right places brings a happy result: It bakes clay writing tablets hard, so their chance of survival is much greater.

The development through time of the cuneiform symbol representing the sound gu *from its Sumerian roots to its Late Assyrian form.*

(After: R. Labat and F. Malbran-Labat, Manuel d'épigraphie Akkadienne *[Paris: Geuthner, 1995], pp. 138–39)*

The Sumerian cuneiform script was borrowed, adapted, and applied to other languages in the region, such as Akkadian—the language of the Akkadians, Babylonians, and Assyrians—and Old Persian. Just as we have adapted the Latin alphabet to write such languages as English, German, Spanish, and even Hawaiian, so could the wedges be used for non-Sumerian.

A clay tablet bearing Sumerian cuneiform script.

(David Moyer collection)

Clever Decipherments

The decipherment of cuneiform script and the Akkadian language was an interesting process. Around 1802, Georg Grotefend (1775–1853) studied drawings that had been made of ancient Persian inscriptions using the script—inscriptions that were apparently written in three languages. Using some shrewd deductions, he was able to figure out that one of the scripts was Old Persian, and so was able to read some of the words, which proved to be royal inscriptions.

The key to translating Akkadian would ultimately be found primarily through the dogged efforts of a bold man, Henry Rawlinson (1810–1895), an English military officer and diplomat. While posted in Persia, Rawlinson heard of inscriptions carved into a huge rock cliff near the town of Behistun. There he found more than 1,000 lines of cuneiform inscriptions, written in three languages and located more than 300 feet above the ground.

Over the next several years, Rawlinson risked his life many times to make copies of the texts. After much comparative study, he published his translations in 1846. He concluded that apart from Old Persian, one of the languages was Babylonian (Akkadian), and thus the door was opened to further study the many thousands of texts that would be recovered from Mesopotamia.

At this point, the existence of the Sumerians was a bit of a surprise. Although the Babylonians and the Assyrians were known from the Bible, the older civilization was long forgotten. The idiosyncrasies of the Akkadian script, however, suggested that it had been borrowed, and the discovery of cuneiform inscriptions in a language other than Akkadian gave a clue that some other group was involved. Bilingual inscriptions, Sumerian words borrowed by Akkadian, and a study of the origins of the signs eventually allowed this unique language to be likewise translated.

The ancient Egyptian language was not written with wedge-shape symbols as was cuneiform, but with hundreds of pictorial signs. As the Egyptian civilization transformed, knowledge of the old writing system was lost probably sometime in the first several centuries A.D. To Europeans with an interest in ancient monuments, the hieroglyphs took on an air of mystery with much speculation as to their ultimate meaning. Were these symbols a form of visual storytelling? Might they perhaps embody mystical philosophical teachings?

Meet the Rosetta Stone

The age of speculation would eventually come to an end as a byproduct of Napoleon's invasion of Egypt. In 1799, one of his soldiers discovered a large chunk of black granite at a town called Rosetta. One face of the stone was completely covered with three kinds of ancient writing displayed in three groups. The top portion contained an inscription in the mysterious hieroglyphs; the middle, an undeciphered cursive script known as Demotic; and the bottom, Greek. The French recognized the potential importance of the stone and sent it off to Cairo.

The Greek inscription on the stone could be read, as the knowledge of that ancient language had never been lost and there were plenty of European scholars capable of reading it. The Greek inscription indicated that the stone was a decree dating to 196 B.C. during the reign of Ptolemy V. The actual historical context of the inscription is not itself of profound importance. The key could lie in the possibility that the Rosetta Stone might contain an identical inscription written in multiple languages and scripts, including the hieroglyphs! Copies of the stone were made and sent to scholars in Europe, who got busy comparing the Greek text to the undeciphered scripts above. Meanwhile, the Rosetta Stone was confiscated from the French by the British, who still retain it. It can be found today in the British Museum in London, where it is a major attraction.

> ### This and That
>
> The irregularly shaped Rosetta Stone is 3 feet 9 inches tall, 2 feet 4 inches wide, and 11 inches thick. It weighs just under 1,500 pounds. In its complete form as a standing stone stele or tablet, it probably stood between five and six feet tall.

The Rosetta Stone.

(Courtesy of the British Museum)

The decipherment took a couple of decades. There were a number of small steps made by different scholars who contributed to a final conclusion. It had been proposed, for example, that a series of hieroglyphs specially enclosed in an oval symbol, or cartouche, were the names of the royalty mentioned in the Greek text. This would prove to be correct. Others made a surprising bit of progress with the cursive inscription.

After several years of study, a young French prodigy named Jean-François Champollion (1790–1832) proclaimed in 1822 that he had solved the puzzle: The hieroglyphs were basically phonetic in nature. By comparing the alphabetic Greek royal names with the individual hieroglyphs found in the cartouches, he was actually able to identify several phonetic signs. From there, rapid progress was made in further decipherment and Champollion himself went on to write, among other things, a grammar and dictionary of ancient Egyptian.

People and Places

Jean-François Champollion was a French scholar credited with the decipherment of Egyptian hieroglyphs in 1822. He was a master of many languages and even as a child he had studied Hebrew, Arabic, Coptic, and Chinese. In 1826, he was made conservator general of the Egyptian antiquities in the Musée du Louvre in Paris and he led a scholarly expedition to Egypt in 1827. He accomplished much in his relatively short life and is generally considered one of the founding figures in Egyptology.

An Egyptian hieroglyphic text telling how King Tuthmosis III ordered the dredging of a clogged canal. His name is found in the oval or "cartouche."

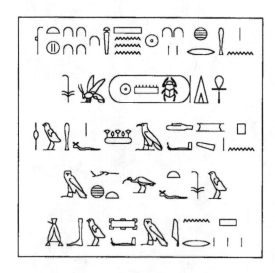

No Easy Task!

Although the cuneiform and hieroglyphic writing systems were each quite capable of expressing the languages in which they were used, they were extremely cumbersome. Without getting into the great complexities of each system, it will suffice to say that they consisted of hundreds of signs, a good many of which represented syllables or combinations of consonants. This being so, it was a considerable task to learn how to read and write these scripts, just as it is today. The literacy rate in the ancient Near East was very low and professional scribes made their living writing and reading letters. Many people probably learned the Bible through listening and memorization.

It's easy to imagine what a real breakthrough it was when a far more simple form of writing was developed: the alphabet. An alphabet is a system of writing in which each sound of the language is represented by a single symbol. This greatly simplifies both the writing and the learning process.

An Amazing Breakthrough: Alphabetic Script

The earliest inklings of an alphabetic script appeared perhaps around 1700 B.C. in the areas of Egypt, Sinai, and Palestine. A small number of Egyptianlike characters were used as sound-signs to write a few simple Canaanite inscriptions. By around 1000 B.C., a functional alphabet with 22 characters was in use in Phoenicia for writing such related Semitic languages as Phoenician, Hebrew, Canaanite, Moabite, and so on.

The idea of the alphabet caught on and spread. Scripts that developed from the Phoenician included Aramaic and Greek. Later, a modification of Greek script was used by the Romans and a version of the Roman alphabet is essentially what you're using to read this book! The Greek alphabet was also modified to form the basis of the Cyrillic script used to write such languages as Russian, and it was adapted to write Coptic, the last phase of the Egyptian language.

A version of the Phoenician script that was used to write the earliest inscriptions and texts in that language was eventually replaced with the Aramaic alphabet. The Aramaic alphabet served as the basis of the Hebrew "block-script," which is still used today for writing and printing the Hebrew Bible and the modern Hebrew language.

Is That So!

The ancient people of Ugarit had an alphabet that utilized a limited set of cuneiform symbols. The study of numerous clay tablets in this script has greatly aided our knowledge of Canaanite cultural practices.

The ancient Phoenician alphabet (top) inspired the Aramaic script that forms the basis of the modern Hebrew script (bottom).

𐤉𐤔𐤅𐤒𐤐𐤑𐤏𐤎𐤌𐤋𐤊𐤉𐤈𐤇𐤆𐤅𐤄𐤃𐤂𐤁𐤀

א ב ג ד ה ו ז ח ט י כ ל מ נ ס ע פ צ ק ר ש ת

(Courtesy of Robert Fradkin)

It may seem strange that some scripts, such as Hebrew, Arabic, and Ancient Egyptian routinely don't represent their vowels. For example, CN Y RD THS SNTNC? If you know the language, either patterns in the words or the context of a sentence usually make it clear which vowel is appropriate. And for those of you who find that concept difficult, unlike European languages, these languages are typically written from right to left.

The Phoenician alphabet wasn't a perfect fit for the Greek language, but the Greeks used some of the sound-signs that didn't appear in their language, turned them into vowels, and added a few letters of their own; for this we are quite grateful. The oldest Greek alphabet was also written from right to left like its source, but after some experimentation, left to right prevailed and ultimately that's why we read English in that direction.

Putting It Down

Although the Egyptians were masters at carving inscriptions in stone and the Mesopotamians produced an inscribed statue from time to time, most writing in the Near East was accomplished using ordinary materials. Apart from the clay which facilitated the cuneiform scripts, paper made from the papyrus plant was used in Egypt and exported from there. Parchment from processed animal skins was used for some of the most precious documents, including biblical scrolls. Unfortunately, some of these materials are highly perishable and have been lost forever to decay. Potsherds could serve as ready and resilient note paper and anything with a scratchable surface could be marked. Some of the earliest inscriptions are simple names scratched on objects to identify ownership or such things as the contents of a pot.

Preserving an Ancient Text

Unlike Ancient Egyptian, Akkadian, or Sumerian, the Hebrew language was never lost. With Aramaic and Greek as competition, its use in everyday life was probably minimal during the time of Jesus in the first century A.D. It was primarily used for reciting Scripture, prayers, and for study. The language was kept intact through the ages by rabbis, priests, and scholars.

As Jews spread out across the world and began speaking various languages, there was a fear that the original pronunciation of the biblical text might be lost in the process. As a result, a vowel-notation system was adopted that can be found used in most printed Hebrew Bibles. If you want to read a Torah scroll in a synagogue or a modern Hebrew book or newspaper, however, you'd better know the language well because they remain vowel-less!

Is That So!

The letters of the Hebrew script can also be used as numbers. Some folks with mystical leanings try to discern numerical patterns to bolster their belief that there are divine secrets to be found in the biblical text!

The Official Version

The authoritative complete text of the Hebrew Bible/Old Testament today, in Hebrew, is based on a manuscript known as the "Leningrad Codex" dating to about A.D. 1010 and housed today in St. Petersburg, Russia. The Codex was compiled and edited by a group of Jewish scholars known as the Masoretes, who not only carefully copied the text of the old books but made numerous insightful scholarly notations in the margins.

The Masoretes were also bound by strict rules in copying the texts, scribal rules that had been passed down through the centuries to ensure that the Word of God would not be changed as biblical texts were copied by hand over and over again, especially in the days before the printing press. These detailed rules are still in effect for those professional scribes who continue to produce handwritten Torah scrolls for synagogue use.

Cave Scriptures

While we're talking about Hebrew texts, it's worthwhile to mention one of the most famous discoveries in the history of archaeology, the Dead Sea Scrolls. Found in 11 caves near the Dead Sea beginning in 1947, the scrolls contain some of the earliest complete copies of biblical books. When all of the scrolls had been recovered, more than 25,000 scroll fragments were found, representing all or part of approximately 800 documents. More than 200 of these documents were copies of books in the Old Testament.

The Book of Psalms was well represented, with 39 copies, and Isaiah and the books of the Torah were also quite popular. Oddly, only a few examples of the so-called historical books of the Bible, such as Joshua, Judges, Kings, and Chronicles, were found. The rest were mostly nonbiblical books or hitherto unknown documents relating to a communal Jewish religious sect, perhaps the Essenes.

A facsimile of one of the Dead Sea Scroll fragments.

(After: John C. Trever, Scrolls from Qumran Cave 1 [1952], p. 154)

The Dead Sea Scrolls are important in many ways. They include the oldest copies of the Old Testament books and therefore offer an opportunity to see how the texts may have been altered through time. Although there are a few differences here and there, the scrolls confirm the general continuity of the biblical texts as passed down through the following generations.

The scrolls date from circa 250 B.C. to circa A.D. 70 and also enhance our understanding of a time that was crucial for the development of Jewish religion and Christianity that arose from it. One thing the scrolls reveal, for example, is that the Judaism of their time was considerably more diverse than previously thought.

This and That

The story of the discovery and subsequent study of the Dead Sea Scrolls is incredibly full of intrigue and drama. Much of their contents was kept from public view until the early 1990s! Excellent overviews of the scrolls can be read in *The Complete World of the Dead Sea Scrolls* by Philip Davies, George Brooke, and Phillip Callaway (Thames & Hudson, 2002) and in *The Mystery and Meaning of the Dead Sea Scrolls* by Hershel Shanks (Random House, 1998).

Because they date to around the time of Jesus, the scrolls provide insights into the cultural, political, and intellectual environment of his time. They also provide a glimpse of Jewish thought and practice before it changed forever with the destruction by the Romans of the Temple in Jerusalem in A.D. 70.

Saved from Destruction

Numerous fragments and copies of the individual books of the New Testament have survived from the second century A.D. onward but early collections of these books are rare. In 1844, Constantine Tischendorf (1815–1874), a scholar and collector of ancient manuscripts, discovered a real treasure trove while examining the material in the library of the famous St. Katherine's monastery at the foot of Mount Sinai (Gebel Mousa) in Egypt. One day he noticed a batch of papers in a basket next to a fireplace. They were pages from an ancient book, and they were being systematically burned.

Tischendorf immediately recognized from the script that these were pages from a very old Bible and asked whether he could have the rest. After several years of negotiation, he was able to retrieve the bulk of the manuscript; it proved to be the earliest known copy of the Bible to include the complete New Testament. This manuscript is called the *Codex Siniaticus* after the location of its discovery. The Codex dates to the fourth century A.D. and can be found today in the British Museum.

Hebrew Comes of Age

The story of the biblical language of Hebrew doesn't end with rabbis, preachers, and scholars. In the late nineteenth century, European Jews began to immigrate to Palestine to settle in the land of the Bible. One immigrant, Eliezer Ben Yehuda (1858–1922), argued that Jews living in a Jewish homeland should speak the language of their ancestors. Ben Yehuda had a remarkable career of adapting an ancient language for modern use. Such an epic project required the invention of thousands of new words to bring the language up to date with modern society. His efforts were incredibly successful. A modern and vibrant Hebrew, which was once only a biblical and liturgical language, is spoken by the approximately six million citizens of Israel and many others.

The Least You Need to Know

- ◆ Writing is one of the most profound of human inventions.
- ◆ The origins of writing are obscure, but they might have had to do with a need for accounting.

◆ Some of the ancient Near Eastern writing systems such as cuneiform and hiero-glyphs were cumbersome and involved hundreds of symbols.

◆ The development of the alphabet brought new simplicity to writing which spread far into the ancient world.

◆ Discoveries of early manuscripts add much to our understanding of the Bible, its text, and its influence.

Part 4

Daily Life in the Holy Land

Having discussed the lands and various people featured in the Hebrew Bible/Old Testament, it's time to look at some of the details of how the Israelites actually lived. At the center of their culture was a belief in God. The first chapter in this section will briefly examine the God of Israel and how he was worshipped, from simple altars to magnificent temples.

The ancient Israelites had basically the same life patterns as we do today, although the particulars differ somewhat. A chapter on daily life will describe how they went about their business from cradle to grave.

Ancient Israel was quite well organized. The year was guided by a calendar marked with Holy Days and the laws of God provided a framework for living within a society. We're going to examine some aspects of that organized society and then end this section with a chapter about one of the most famous cities in the world: the ancient Jewish capital of Jerusalem.

...Shalom, y'all!!!

Chapter 15

Worshipping the One God

In This Chapter

- ◆ The One God of Israel
- ◆ Worshipping the Supreme Being
- ◆ Temples and a Tabernacle
- ◆ The mysterious Ark of the Covenant
- ◆ Priests and rituals

Before beginning a description of the lifeways of the Jews in Bible times, it might be best to start with a few comments on the character upon which the whole book is centered: God. Who is this one God, this Creator, Law-Giver, Judge, and Loving Parent?

In this chapter, we're going to look at how the Jews worshipped the Supreme Being. It's a fascinating story of a temporary sanctuary, a Temple built and rebuilt, and a mysterious box known as the Ark.

The Sacred Name of the One and Only

There are many names for God in the Bible. The most important, though, is YHWH, a word that is probably related to the Hebrew verb "to be." So what's with the four letters? These four letters, as found in Hebrew, represent the personal name of God. The name is sometimes referred to as the Tetragrammaton and written with vowels as "Yahweh" or "Yahveh." The name is considered very sacred. In Jewish tradition, it is never pronounced nor spelled out with vowels, to avoid the possibility that this special name might be abused. When the name is encountered while reading the Bible, the word *Adonai*, which means "the Lord" or "my Lord," is substituted in its place. I will respect this tradition in this book.

YHWH: the personal name of God. Treat it with respect.

In the many names for God found in the Bible, YHWH is used descriptively in several cases. Here are just a few:

♦ **YHWH-Yireh:** "The Lord Will Provide"

♦ **YHWH-Rophe:** "The Lord Who Heals"

♦ **YHWH-Shalom:** "The Lord of Peace"

♦ **YHWH-Tsidekenu:** "The Lord of Our Righteousness"

All these names are interesting because they describe some of the traits of God.

God Communicates with Man

God is immediately encountered in the Bible in the first three words of Genesis in which the Creation story begins. We hear God speak the Universe into creation. God must have been in contact with Adam and Eve because they had their orders not to eat from the one special tree in the Garden of Eden. Our first recorded direct quote from God to humans came when Adam and Eve tried to hide after breaking the rules. God inquired, "Where are you?" The couple was banished from innocence and paradise forever—the first among millennia of humans to disobey God and suffer the consequences.

Throughout the Bible, God communicates in interesting ways. God spoke on one occasion to Moses via an attention-getting burning bush. God sometimes communicated directly to specific individuals. A series of prophets, for example, conveyed God's words of warning when people fell astray and occasionally offered words of hope. God often communicated indirectly through miracles, acts of nature, or other divine interventions. One could always pray to thank God, ask "Why me?" or ask for assistance. God would decide how to respond.

One of the most popular and poetic descriptions of God is given in Psalm 23 in which we, the people, are likened to sheep tended by God, a dutiful divine shepherd:

> The Lord is my shepherd; I shall not want. He maketh me to lie down in green pastures; He leadeth me beside the still waters. He restoreth my soul; He leadeth me in the paths of righteousness for His name's sake. Yea, though I walk through the valley of the shadow of death, I will fear no evil; for Thou [God] art with me; Thy rod and Thy staff [protective tools of the shepherd] they comfort me. (KJV)

Offerings and Thanks

In Genesis, Cain and Abel, the sons of Adam and Eve, each made an offering to God. God preferred Abel's animal sacrifice over Cain's "fruits of the earth," a subject that has been debated for centuries. In the story of the Great Flood, Noah built an altar immediately after finally getting off the boat and sacrificed animals to God. This practice of presenting offerings to God was common and widespread. God appeared to Abraham and he built an altar. Years later, two successive temples would be built to accept the offerings of his descendents.

Setting Down the Rules

When the Israelites left Egypt, the Bible tells us how Moses climbed a mountain to receive the laws of God. Just about everyone has probably heard of the Ten Commandments. These were written on tablets of stone and had to be replaced after an angry Moses smashed the first set on a pagan idol that the Israelites set up in his absence. The Commandments include demands to acknowledge and respect the One God. (We'll deal with some of the other commandments in the next couple chapters.)

Whereas most people have heard of the Ten Commandments, you might not be aware that Jewish tradition counts a total of 613 commandments to be found in the first five books of the Bible, the Torah. Three hundred sixty-five are considered negative commandments—"don't do this"—whereas the rest are positive—that is, "do this." Many of these laws have to do with the proper way to serve God, including ritual purity and the proper presentation of offerings, while others are ethical laws. The Bible also gives very specific instructions from God on how the Israelites were to build centers of worship.

> **Thus Saith**
>
> "What is it that God wants?" is an often-discussed question. Deuteronomy 10:12–13 offers some insights: "… what doth the Lord thy God require of thee, but to fear the Lord thy God, to walk in all of His ways, and to love Him, and to serve the Lord thy God with all thy heart and with all thy soul, to keep the commandments of the Lord, and his statutes, which I [God] command thee." (KJV)

A Portable Sanctuary

At Sinai, God instructed Moses to build a portable tentlike structure, or "tabernacle" that would serve as a worship center for the migrating Israelites. "And let them make me a sanctuary, that I may dwell in their midst." (Exodus 25:8, RSV)

The instructions for building the Tabernacle were quite specific, and the building materials, including acacia wood, goat skins, gold, silver, and bronze, were requested from the people. The end result was a rectangular structure about 145 feet long, 72 feet wide, and 7 feet tall, enclosed by curtains. Inside was another compartment divided into two sections by a veil. In the innermost chamber was the sacred Holy of Holies. Inside was placed the Ark of the Covenant, a special box containing the tablets of Law.

> **Logos**
>
> The glorious presence of God has been called the **She-kinah**. It was thought to be present in the Holy of Holies and on occasion was noted in the form of a cloud descending on such places as the Tabernacle and later in the Temple.

In front of the veil hiding the Holy of Holies was an incense altar, a bread table, and a seven-branched candelabra, all made of precious materials. In the courtyard outside was a washing bowl (laver) and an altar for burnt offerings.

The Tabernacle was sufficiently portable that it could be moved and set up as the Israelites wandered. Much of it could be carried on poles, and various groups were assigned responsibility for the different pieces. When it was re-erected, the Israelites camped around it in a specific order according to tribe.

That Special Box: The Ark of the Covenant

One of the most famous, and I should say popular, biblical artifacts of all times is a mysterious box that was constructed under God's specific orders. It was carried with the wandering Israelites as they made their way from Sinai, it helped them in battle and caused trouble for their enemies, and it was eventually kept in one of the most sacred and secret places in the world: the Holy of Holies of the Jerusalem Temple. And from there it disappeared! This box is commonly known as the Ark of the Covenant.

As was the case with the portable Tabernacle, God gave Moses specific instructions for the construction of the Ark. In short, what is described is a gold-gilded wooden box that can be moved about on two poles. Its close-fitting lid, called the "mercy seat," featured two golden angels with outstretched wings. Inside were placed the tablets of the Law. A verse in the New Testament (Hebrews 9:4) indicates that there was at one time also a gold urn containing a piece of manna and Aaron's staff. A scroll containing the Book of Deuteronomy was kept next to it.

The Ark of the Covenant.

(Courtesy of the artist, Chris Tyler)

A Point of Contact

The purpose of the Ark is as follows: "There I will meet you, and from above the mercy seat, from between the two cherubim that are upon the ark of the testimony, I will speak with you of all that I will give you in commandment for the people of Israel." (Exodus 25:22)

So it seems that the Ark was a symbolic throne for God. Being in the presence of the Ark, however, served as a sacred meeting point for an encounter with God. It also occasionally served as a visible reminder of God's power.

The Ark was not to be touched, and those who did suffered the price. A perplexing story in 2 Samuel tells how one day, the Ark was being transported on the back of a cart, instead of on its poles. When the cart began to tip, a man named Uzzah reached out to keep the Ark from tumbling to the ground. He was struck dead. Some might say that the very fact that the Ark was being carried on the cart was disobedience to God's word, and Uzzah's death brought this point dramatically home. On another occasion, curiosity seekers tried to take a peek into the Ark and 70 people died as a result.

Traveling with the Ark

The ark visited a number of places while the Israelites moved about Canaan. Apart from its place in the portable Tabernacle, the Ark was often carried into battle during the Conquest. The waters of the Jordan parted when priests carrying the Ark set foot into the river, and the Ark was paraded around the city of Jericho before the city's walls fell. For 14 years, it was stationed in the Tabernacle when it was erected at the site of Gilgal and afterward, it spent many years at Shiloh. Its power became legendary. The foes of the Israelites were well aware of its reputation and feared it. In Chapter 9, we saw what happened when the Philistines captured it! When David became king, it was time to make things permanent.

> **This and That**
>
> God obviously is not confined to, nor requires, a tent, a temple, or any other sort of structure. Such structures can, however, serve as a center of focus for humans.

The Bible tells us that David purchased a high spot on Mt. Moriah in Jerusalem, which was used as a threshing floor by a man named Araunah. This was also the traditional place where Abraham took his son Isaac to be sacrificed. It was at this spot that the Temple would be built. David, however, would not be the builder, because, as God explained to him, he was "a man of war, and [had] shed blood." He did, however, pass the plans on to his successor, Solomon.

The Holy Temple Is Built

When Solomon became king, he controlled the substantial empire built by David, his father. There was sufficient wealth and a relatively peaceful political environment to build a splendid monument, and the work began. Solomon's work was assisted by a Phoenician king, Hiram, who facilitated the harvesting of huge numbers of cypress and cedar logs from the forests of Lebanon. The logs were tied together like rafts and floated down the coast south where they could be transported inland to Jerusalem. According to 1 Kings, the amount of work involved in building Solomon's Temple was staggering, including many tens of thousands of laborers and craftsmen.

The dimensions of the Temple were about 90 feet long, 30 feet wide, and 45 feet tall. The walls were decorated with images of flowers, angels, and palm trees. Gilded olivewood doors, with the same decorative theme, led to the inner sanctum. The Holy of Holies was built of cedar and the walls and floor were gilded in gold. Inside were two identical figures of angels (cherubs) of olive wood overlaid with gold. Each stood 10 cubits (about 18 feet) tall high with a wingspan of 10 cubits.

A bronze specialist was brought from the Phoenician city of Tyre to lend a hand. He cast two elaborately decorated pillars, which he named Jachin and Boaz, set up in the vestibule of the Temple. He also produced an impressive array of ceremonial equipment. An enormous bronze tub holding the equivalent of "two thousand baths" was made which stood on the backs of four pairs of three bronze oxen, facing the cardinal directions. There were also 10 elaborate wheeled bronze stands to each hold a bronze laver with a capacity of "forty baths."

Other Temple furnishings were constructed from gold: an altar, a bread table, 10 candelabras of pure gold, incense dishes, lamp snuffers, fire pans, and sockets for the Temple's doors. The sheer wealth represented in the Temple is an important thing to remember. It would make it a prime target for foreign invaders seeking rich booty.

The whole Temple-building project was said to have taken seven years. Afterward, the Temple was dedicated with prayers and a whole lot of offerings, and the Ark was installed in the Holy of Holies.

People and Places
Certain secret societies trace their roots or teachings to the builders of Solomon's Temple. The Masons, for one, believe that some of their ideas and philosophies originated in the talented stonemasons of the Temple. Other groups believe that the building secrets of biblical times were maintained by medieval craft guilds that built the magnificent cathedrals of the Middle Ages.

Making Sacrifices

Offering rituals were held daily at the Temple as presided over by priests of the proper lineage. The Temple was primarily staffed by members of the tribe of Levi. Not having received land in the division of Canaan, they were given 48 towns and cities to live in. The Levites carried out all manner of religious functions but the actual priests had to be descendants of Aaron, the brother of Moses. During certain time periods, the High Priest served as a political figure as well.

On a typical morning, the fire was stoked and the altar was cleaned. The oil in the lamps was replenished and the incense lit. Twelve fresh loaves of bread were placed on their special table. The High Priest, bedecked in his special garments, could now proceed with the sacrifices.

There were a number of reasons for sacrifices and the offerings for each varied. The offerings typically involved unblemished animals including goats, sheep, cattle, and birds that were then sacrificed and burnt on the altar. There were other nonanimal offerings, too, including barley and wheat, wine, olive oil, and precious substances such as frankincense. In many cases, a portion of the offering went to the priests.

Here's a few of the occasions under which one might present an offering to God at the Temple:

- Sin offerings, to make one ritually clean after an intentional or unintentional offense

- Guilt, for various offences against people, breaking of minor laws, and so on.

- Free will, for no special prescribed reason

- Thanks to God for special things

- Peace

- Ordination of priests

- Festival offerings

On one day during the year, Yom Kippur (the Day of Atonement), the High Priest would enter the Holy of Holies alone. A smoke screen of incense prevented a clear view of the Ark, and two sin offerings were presented in the form of sprinkled blood; one representing the High Priest, and the other for the people. There the High Priest would utter the sacred name of God.

Is That So!

Two of the most curious objects noted in the Bible are called the Urim and Thummim. These were apparently two little plaques that were kept in a pouch under the upper garment of the priest. They were used to answer yes and no questions and were perhaps thrown like dice.

As was the case with the building of the Temple, instructions for the rituals performed therein are provided in amazing detail in the Torah, mostly in the book of Leviticus. Even the clothing to be worn by the priests is well described, giving us an amazing picture of the goings-on at this magnificent structure.

The Temple Takes a Beating

After the death of Solomon, the nation was split into the northern ten tribes of Israel, and the tribes of Judah and Benjamin in the south. The Temple was located in the southern kingdom, so for the most part, the northern division had to do without, and did so by building various worship centers, some of which were pagan. Even in the south, one of the kings, Menasseh, slipped into paganism and placed idols in the Holy Temple. This episode, however, was short-lived.

In another incident, the Egyptian king Sheshonq I (called Shishak in the Bible), attacked Judah and "came against Jerusalem." Solomon's successor Rehoboam seems to have thwarted destruction by paying off the Egyptian king. The tribute included Temple treasures.

As you may recall from Chapters 8 and 11 of this book, the Assyrians decimated the ten northern tribes and Jerusalem managed to survive. Later, in the year 586 B.C., Jerusalem was conquered by the Babylonians under the leadership of King Nebuchadrezzar, and its beautiful Temple was destroyed. Because the Temple was lined with gold-gilded wood, a thorough burning was probably useful in the destructive process. Many of the portable objects were carried off whole, and the Ark was never seen again.

> **This and That**
>
> It was popular among many of the ancient peoples of the Near East to establish "high places"—elevated platforms or altars—for the purpose of worship and offering sacrifices. The Israelites had them, too, but their use was discouraged after the building of the Temple in Jerusalem, which was to serve as the great center of worship.

Getting It Back Together

As we saw in Chapter 13, those Jews who had been held captive in Babylon were freed by the Persian king Cyrus and allowed to return home. Back in Jerusalem, priests of the proper lineage were sought, donations were obtained, and the Temple rebuilding began. A foundation was laid and wood again retrieved from Lebanon. There was some opposition to the Temple's rebuilding by some of Judah's neighbors who appealed to the Persian King Xerxes to have the work stopped. The building resumed, however, not long after Xerxes's successor Darius took the throne, and royal Persian money was used to assist in the project.

> **People and Places**
>
> A descendant of David named Zerubbabel deserves foremost credit for rebuilding the Temple after the Babylonian exile. He seems to have served as governor of the region of Judah, perhaps as appointed by the Persians.

The second Temple was by no means as splendorous as that of Solomon. For one thing, the Ark of the Covenant was gone. The Temple served its purpose, nonetheless, and the offerings and rituals continued, until the next crisis!

A Place to Gather

At some point, probably in the sixth century B.C. (scholars can't agree exactly when), community religious centers—synagogues—became established as an important part of Jewish life. People could visit there to hear the Torah read and receive instruction from learned men, rabbis. By the time of Jesus there were hundreds of synagogues, but the Temple remained the primary institution of the Jewish religion.

King Herod the Bad

You may recall how the Temple was abused by the Greek ruler Antiochus IV and the resulting rebellion by the Jews. After the victory over Antiochus, a dynasty of Jewish kings ruled in Jerusalem for several decades until the Romans appeared in their steady conquest of much of Alexander's old empire. You'll learn more about the Romans in Chapter 19, but to keep the history of the Temple going, let's jump ahead a bit. Unlike Antiochus, the Romans let the Jews continue their religious practices as long as they didn't rebel. They also appointed a client-king to rule over Palestine and the Jews, a man known as Herod the Great.

Herod the Great's personal reputation is pretty poor. He's generally considered to be a homicidal maniac, among other things; however, he was a great builder. With a penchant for architecture of a grand and elaborate scale, he built several palaces for himself along with public buildings. His crowning achievement, though, was his remodeling of the Temple Mount.

Herod expanded the Temple Mount into a huge plaza faced with mammoth blocks of carefully carved stone along its supporting walls. On top, the old rebuilt Temple of Solomon was essentially overwhelmed by Herod's new structure. Great staircases and gates were built leading up to the Temple and the end result must have been absolutely awesome. So immense and dramatic were his construction activities that his work is often referred to as "The Third Temple."

Herod, being the Roman toady that he was, installed a big Roman eagle crest over the entrance to the Temple as a sign of his submission.

A modern model of the Temple as enlarged by Herod can be seen at the Holy Land Hotel in Jerusalem.

(David Moyer collection)

History Repeats Itself

As was the case a couple centuries before, the Jews became disenchanted with their foreign oppressors, and a rebellion broke out against the Romans in A.D. 66. In A.D. 70, the Romans attacked Jerusalem and completely destroyed the Temple. The destruction was led by the Roman general Titus, who built a victory arch in Rome celebrating his conquest. The sculptured surface of the arch includes a scene of Temple booty, including a great menorah, being hauled away.

In A.D. 130, the emperor Hadrian rebuilt Jerusalem and renamed it Aelia Capitolina. A Temple to the god Jupiter was erected on the Temple Mount. When Christianity became the official religion of the Roman Empire in the fourth century, the Temple Mount was used as a garbage dump by Christians who could make a statement about Judaism and the pagan Romans at the same time.

In 638, a new era was initiated when the Arabs conquered Jerusalem. The Temple Mount thereafter became home to two impressive Islamic structures: the Dome of the Rock and the El-Aksa Mosque. The former, begun in 685, is topped by a huge dome, gilded in gold. This structure was built over top of a large exposed rock that legend says was the place where Abraham brought his son to be sacrificed. It is also the place, according to Islamic tradition, from which the prophet Mohammed rode his horse on a nocturnal visit to Heaven. Both the Dome of the Rock and the El-Aksa mosque remain in place today on Herod's immense Temple Mount.

Little if anything is left of Solomon's Temple. A portion of an old wall exists on the Temple Mount alongside blocks from King Herod's platform that might possibly be part of the original Temple.

Likewise, there is little or nothing to be seen of the rebuilt "Second Temple." A couple blocks here and there with a little writing have been found from King Herod's renovations. One inscription refers to a place of trumpeting which might have been from the spot where the priests would blow their horns on special occasions. The other is a warning sign, in Greek, that warns non-Jews to stay out of the sacred area.

Wailing No More

With the Temple destroyed, Judaism persisted nonetheless and developed on a different path. Instead of a centralized priesthood based in Jerusalem, Jewish rabbis and sages became the community leaders and teachers of Torah as Jews spread throughout the world. Such is the case today. The western wall of the Temple Mount, however, became a sacred site of prayer. It is called the *kotel* and has become a place of pilgrimage for Jews worldwide.

Is That So!

There is a tradition in which personal prayers are written on pieces of paper and shoved into the cracks of the Western Wall. There is even an organization in Israel that will do this for you if you send them a fax!

It has long been referred to as the Wailing Wall, a mournful declaration of the Temple's loss, and for many years it was inaccessible to most Jews. In 1967, however, the Israelis captured East Jerusalem from Jordan and the Wailing Wall was incorporated into the modern state of Israel. Although plenty of sorrow remains from the past and present, the wall is now often referred to as "the Western Wall" and remains available for prayer today.

And What of the Ark?

The last we heard of the Ark, it was in its rightful place in Jerusalem Temple where it was visited once a year by the High Priest. In 586 B.C., the Babylonians destroyed the Temple and the whereabouts of the Ark became unknown. It apparently was not available to be put in place when the Temple was rebuilt, and so that leaves us with a few possibilities: It was destroyed along with Solomon's Temple, it was taken to Babylon as booty and dismantled or destroyed there, or it remains hidden to this day.

The trip to Babylon story seems unlikely. Given the history of the Ark, one would expect tales of great doom to accompany its removal. It is not mentioned in the Book of Ezra with the inventory of the Temple implements given back when the exiled

Jews returned home. There are, however, a lot of people who think it still exists. Various theories suggest a hiding place under the Temple Mount in Jerusalem, a cave on Mt. Nebo in Jordan, and a church in Ethiopia … even that it is kept in a secret U.S. government warehouse!

The Least You Need to Know

♦ The one God of Israel goes by many names and is characterized, in part, as the Creator, Law-Giver, Judge, and Loving Parent.

♦ God communicated with humans from the very beginning.

♦ The Tabernacle and Temples were built with detailed instructions as worship centers for the presence of God.

♦ The Ark of the Covenant was a portable box built according to divine instructions and contained the tablets of law obtained by Moses on Mt. Sinai along with a couple of other special objects. Today its whereabouts are unknown.

♦ A variety of rites were performed in the Temple as described in detail in the Bible. Most involved offerings and sacrifices.

♦ Solomon's original Temple was destroyed, rebuilt, enhanced, and destroyed again.

Chapter 16

From Cradle to Grave

In This Chapter

- The way of life in ancient Israel
- Things to eat, things to drink
- Working for a living: men's and women's roles
- Clothes, wealth, and recreational pursuits
- Till death do us part

Because the Bible is such an awesome and powerful document, it can be easy to forget that it describes real people who lived real lives. Although of a different time and place, the ancient Israelites/Jews had the same basic life pattern needs as we do today.

The topic of daily life in biblical times is truly vast, with details galore. In this chapter, I can only hope to give you a taste here and a general picture of life in those days. So let's get started.

A Child Is Born

Let's start from the very beginning. The very first commandment in the Bible is "Be fruitful and multiply." A married couple was expected to reproduce and reproduce frequently. If children couldn't be produced, it was considered to be a sad situation indeed. To solve the childless issue, it was sometimes possible to adopt, marry a second wife, or use a surrogate mother. Children were born at home, assisted by midwives. Without the benefit of modern medicine, though, infant mortality, and that of the mother, was considerably higher than it is today.

The Mark of Circumcision

A Jewish baby is born. Hurray! If it's a girl, that's fine. If it's a boy, there are some extra considerations. On the eighth day of his life, he receives some minor surgery: circumcision. Why? Remember the story from Chapter 8 of this book about Abraham making a covenant with God? Actually, there were two parts to it. The first was the actual promise to be faithful to God. The second was a physical mark to be carried by all male holders of the covenant: circumcision. Abraham was 99 years old when he experienced the procedure himself and the tradition of circumcising Jewish baby boys continues to this day.

> **Is That So!**
>
> Just after Joshua entered the Promised Land by crossing the Jordan River, God ordered him to perform a mass circumcision on all the males who had been born during their years of wandering. A flint knife was used and the men were allowed to heal before the attack on Jericho.

If a couple's firstborn baby was a boy, he belonged to God. If the parents preferred to raise the boy as they pleased, as most did, they could redeem him from such service by paying a fee to the priests.

What's in a Name?

Picking a name for a baby was done as carefully as it often is today. Names could be inspired by such things as a beloved relative or hero, to honor God, after things in nature with favored characteristics such as strength or beauty, or even after abstract personal qualities. Here's a sample: Elijah (the Lord is my God), Ofrah (fawn), Gideon (mighty warrior), Shira (song), and Solomon (peaceful).

An amazing number of common English first names are biblical, including John, David, Mark, Daniel, Lisa, Anne, and Susan. Many of them have been "anglicized" from the original Hebrew or Greek and are a testament to the impact the Bible has had on Western society. You might be surprised to learn that in the original Hebrew, Solomon is "Shlomo," Isaac is "Yitzhak," and Joshua is "Yehoshua."

Growing Up

In biblical times, kids were basically raised to follow in the footsteps of their parents. When a boy was old enough, he might help his father in the fields or with whatever occupation his father was employed. Girls learned homemaking skills from their mothers. Parents and elders were to be respected. It was one of the commandments to "honor your father and mother" and disobedience was not tolerated. Education was mostly informal with instruction provided by the parents. By the time of Jesus, however, it was possible for boys to go to synagogue schools to study with religious teachers.

<table>
<tr><td>**This and That**</td></tr>
<tr><td>Some traditional Jewish practices have their origins after the time of the Bible. The bar mitzvah and bat mitzvah coming-of-age ceremonies for 13-year-olds which are common today were not conducted during Bible times.</td></tr>
</table>

Marriage

A marriage was either initiated by the groom-to-be or it was arranged. Marriages outside of the Jewish community were highly discouraged if not outright banned. (The rule didn't seem to apply to King Solomon with his many foreign princesses!) The parents had to agree and the groom paid a "bride price" to the father of the bride. The bride would then become a part of the husband's family. With hope, the babies would start arriving soon.

A marriage was considered a sacred thing and keeping it together was important. Adultery was taken very seriously and with grave consequences to the offenders. A man could divorce his wife if he could make a case that she was "indecent" but she could remarry. Jesus was very much against divorce, and you can read his opinion about that in Mark 10:2–11! If a wife became a widow, it was expected that she would marry her husband's brother or other close in-law.

In an interesting biblical marriage story, Jacob worked seven years to earn the right to marry his beloved Rachel but Rachel's father tricked him on the wedding night and gave him Leah instead. In exchange for an additional seven years of work, Jacob was allowed to marry Rachel as well.

Traditional Gender Roles

The Jewish family generally maintained traditional patriarchal gender roles. Men were considered to be the strong family leaders and the women were expected to be good wives and mothers. Women's work included cooking, weaving and sewing, supervising children, and helping occasionally in the fields as necessary. Men's work included serving in the military, plowing fields, or engaging in other strenuous occupations.

This idea of constrained gender roles seems to fly in the face of modern sensibilities but these roles seemed to work well in their time. There are actually a lot of strong and influential women in the Bible, both good and bad. There was the evil Jezebel, and the conniving Herodias who demanded the head of John the Baptist. On the other hand, Deborah was a great leader in the time of the judges and Mary the mother of Jesus is held in the highest regard.

Thus Saith

The thirty-first chapter of Proverbs includes a description of the good wife and mother. Here's an excerpt: "A good wife who can find? She is far more precious than jewels. The heart of her husband trusts in her, and he will have no lack of gain. She does him good, and not harm, all the days of her life … Strength and dignity are her clothing, and she laughs at the time to come. She opens her mouth with wisdom, and the teaching of kindness is on her tongue. She looks well to the ways of her household, and does not eat the bread of idleness. Her children rise up and call her blessed; her husband also, and he praises her: 'Many women have done excellently, but you surpass them all.'"

A Roof over One's Head

The majority of Jews in Palestine lived in hundreds of small villages or towns and most of the rest in cities. The average Israelite lived in a simple house made of mud brick composed of a small courtyard and two to four rooms. The interior could be secured by a wooden door and some even had locks. Sleeping, eating, and relaxing could take place on mats and skins placed on dirt floors.

Thus Saith

The Bible offers one of the world's earliest known safety laws: "When you build a new house, you shall make a parapet [a protective wall] for your roof, that you may not bring the guilt of blood upon your house, if any one fall from it." (Deuteronomy 22:8)

A typical house might contain a grain-grinder, cooking utensils, storage jars, and perhaps a loom. Food was cooked in an earthen oven in the courtyard. Animals could be kept outdoors or in.

The roofs were flat. Horizontal wooden beams were covered with branches, reeds, and mats and then plastered over. The largest homes might have a second floor supported by a few wooden or stone pillars on the inside. The roof provided additional living space. A roof could be a great place to sleep on hot summer evenings and a way to see what was going on next door or down in the street.

Some of the wandering biblical people lived in tents. They're great for people who want to pick up and go and they can be quite roomy and comfortable. Even today in the Near East, mobile groups like the Bedouin continue the tenting tradition.

As can be expected, people with more power and wealth tended to live in bigger houses. Such homes might feature walls of hewn stone, multiple rooms, and living quarters for servants.

Villages consisting of mud brick homes are still a common site in many areas of the Near East today.

(Courtesy of Lynn Cole)

City Life

Palestine was dotted with cities of various sizes, many of which had existed since the Bronze Age. Given the pattern of destruction and reuse characteristic of Palestinian history, a lot of these cities lacked what one might call an organized plan. Old buildings could be rebuilt, restored, and enhanced from the remains of previous structures. That's how we get those big tells! Later on, though, especially during Roman times, some new cities were planned with a degree of urban precision.

The old biblical cities were probably crowded and noisy places, but served important functions as administrative and trade centers as well as fortified refuges from enemies.

Let's Eat!

Let's talk about one of my favorite subjects: food! In Chapter 4, I mentioned some of the good stuff grown in Palestine during Bible times. Wheat and barley, dates, olives, beans, lentils, onions, garlic, nuts, and honey were regular meal ingredients. Goats, sheep, and cattle were common, but given their expense they were not on the table every day for the average Israelite.

There were two main meals a day plus some midday snacking. For breakfast, one might find bread, cheese, and fruit. A few dates, raisins, a piece of bread, or other small amounts of food could help tide over hunger until the big meal of the day, dinner! Dinner could consist of vegetables, vegetable soup, or stew, and meat or fish if some was available, guzzled down with water or wine. The meals were usually eaten sitting down on the floor.

The biblical Jews typically did not utilize eating utensils. Flat bread could serve as an edible plate and chunks of bread could be used to sop up soup.

Staying Kosher

Jews weren't allowed to eat just anything that was edible. The Torah contains a number of laws regarding appropriate and inappropriate foods. This is the basis of keeping *kosher*, which many Jewish people still do today. There are guidelines on what may or may not be eaten; many are listed in the eleventh chapter of Leviticus and the fourteenth chapter of Deuteronomy:

Logos

Kosher, or kashrut, means ritually clean or fit according to Jewish law. It applies especially to food but to other things as well.

- **Split hooves and cud.** "Whatever parts the hoof and is cloven-footed and chews the cud, among the animals, you may eat." This includes the ever-popular cows, goats, and sheep. Animals such as rock badgers, rabbits, and camels that chew the cud but do not have split hooves are forbidden. Pigs, which have split hooves but don't chew cud, are forbidden. Don't eat them and don't touch their carcasses.

- **Seafood.** "These you may eat, of all that are in the waters. Everything in the waters that has fins and scales, whether in the seas or in the rivers, you may eat …. But anything in the seas or the rivers that has not fins and scales, of the swarming creatures in the waters and of the living creatures that are in the waters, is an abomination to you." Some of the things to avoid included eels, catfish, lobsters, and shrimp.

- **Birds and bugs.** A number of predator, scavenger, and other birds were prohibited including eagles, vultures, sea gulls, and pelicans. And the ancient Jews weren't to eat winged insects that "go about on all fours" except for those "which have legs above their feet, with which to leap on the earth." Locusts, crickets, and grasshoppers were okay to eat. Weasels, mice, lizards, geckos, land crocodiles, chameleons, turtles, snails, and moles were also on the forbidden list.

If meat was consumed, it was not to contain blood, and there were rules for kosher and more humane slaughtering of edible beasts. Even today, kosher butcher shops exist for the purpose of preparing meat for human consumption according to biblical laws. Vegetables and mineral products (salt, and so on) were generally okay for all-around consumption.

A real mainstay of a kosher diet is the avoidance of eating dairy products at the same time as meat products. This is based on the law in Exodus that states "You shall not boil a kid in its mother's milk." Later Jewish law forbade all mixing of milk and meat in order that this commandment not be violated. This one requires a bit of thinking because it's not just a matter of knowing about what not to eat, but also knowing about ingredients and combinations of foods served at meals.

> **People and Places**
>
> Some people today might find these biblical food prohibitions rather strange. When you think about it, though, having cultural food preferences isn't all that strange. Americans, for the most part, don't eat dogs, cats, rats, horses, or insects. And raw meat or fish is not the norm. Some cultures are vegetarian by religious preference or otherwise.

Why Kosher?

Many readers of the Bible might ask questions such as "What's wrong with eating pigs and some of those other things on the list?" Let's look at some of the possibilities:

◆ To some, avoiding certain foods is an exercise in self-control, or maybe even personal sacrifice in accordance with divine law.

◆ To avoid certain foods can also be seen as a holiness issue. Certain things are set aside not because they are necessarily bad, but because obeying such prohibitions is an act of holiness that all similar believers share; some such prohibitions also separate the practices of believers from the practices of those who aren't.

◆ A classic explanation for pigs and shellfish involves health issues. Pigs can carry several diseases that can be passed on to humans. Consume some bad shellfish sometime and you will wish that you were eating kosher.

◆ It has been claimed that pigs are economically impractical; the cost-to-benefit ratio in terms of caring for them is in the negative. Also, unlike cattle, sheep, and goats, they are not particularly easy to herd, especially if you're in nomadic mode.

Thirsty?

When it came to drinking, water and wine were the most popular choices. In a country given to dry spells, water was a serious commodity. Wells were often communal and it would be a daily task for the women to draw water out of or descend into a well to retrieve water for their family. And it could take some real strength to carry a heavy ceramic jar back to the home! Going to the well was also the ancient equivalent of the office water cooler; it was a great place to share news and gossip.

Cisterns of different sizes were used to collect and store rain water. These could be carved out of the rock and plastered for waterproofing. Some truly huge ancient cisterns can be found in Israel that resemble large subterranean caves!

The average, everyday sort of wine consumed in biblical times had a low alcohol content. Getting drunk was considered to be in poor form if it caused one to behave poorly. High-quality wines from good grapes in Palestine were exported to many places in the ancient world. Milk was available from goats, sheep, cows, and camels and was useful for making butter, cheese, and yogurt.

" " Thus Saith

Fasting was sometimes practiced on special occasions such as Yom Kippur (the Day of Atonement), or to demonstrate sorrow. After his baptism, Jesus fasted for 40 days and was tempted with food by the devil. The classic metaphorical response by Jesus is often repeated today: "It is written, 'Man shall not live by bread alone, but by every word that proceeds from the mouth of God.'" (Matthew 4:4) On the other hand, a small family feast was welcome each Sabbath and a marriage was a good excuse for a party.

Going to Work

According to Genesis, man's first occupation was agriculture, and during biblical times, the majority of the Israelite men worked in this way. This was hard work and success was partly a matter of how well the weather cooperated. Palestine was not like Egypt or Mesopotamia with their giant rivers suitable for widespread irrigation. Irrigation was somewhat possible, but rain, dew, and mist were relied upon for much of the watering. Plows were used to till the land and sickles wielded to harvest its produce which was cached in jars and storage pits.

Famine was a concern, and we learn from such stories as those of Abraham and Jacob that families might pick up and move in times of drought. Insects such as locusts were dreaded as they could easily lay waste to one's hard-earned efforts.

There were also some interesting religious implications to agriculture. For example, a certain portion of a field's produce belonged to God and a certain percentage was tithed to the Levites. And one of the commandments mandated that agricultural fields were to be left alone every seven years thereby giving the soil a little rest! Several of the Jewish holy days have agricultural connections, including Passover, Sukkot, and Shavuot (see the next chapter).

Agriculture wasn't the only job outside the home. There were numerous other occupations one might expect in a complex society, of course, including potters, stonecutters, jewelers, carpenters, and so forth, along with political bureaucrats and religious functionaries.

Is That So!

The Israelite military could be characterized as a "citizen army." All able men 20 and over were eligible for military service when called up. There were several exemptions, including newlyweds. They provided their own weapons, which could include daggers, swords, spears, and javelins. Needless to say, the Old Testament records many opportunities when the weapons were put to use.

Sheep and goats continue to graze on old biblical lands.

(David Moyer collection)

What to Wear?

Apart from a kiltlike loincloth that laborers or soldiers might wear, dress in Bible times was quite modest. Men often wore a long, simple, close-fitting tunic made of wool or linen belted with a length of cloth wrapped around the body. Additional garb might include a cloak draped over the shoulder or robes for warmth or special occasions. As a reminder to keep the commandments, the Torah instructed the Jews to put tassels with a blue strand on the corners of their garments.

The women wore similar clothes that came to the ankle, and the head was often covered. Veils seem to have been optional. Leather sandals were the preferred footwear although going barefoot was an option in the home or among the poor. The average Israelite probably didn't change clothes very often, but females in the household could do the laundry or send it out to professional launderers.

Making clothes was considered women's work and many started from scratch, processing the flax for linen themselves or more often, spinning yarn from goat or sheep wool. The cloth could be dyed to add a bit of color. People of wealth might demonstrate that fact by wearing beautiful robes and other garments. And the priests of the Temple had their special clothes, especially the High Priest!

Though generally conservative, fashions changed a bit from time to time, especially under the influence of outsiders like the Persians, Greeks, and Romans. A popular Greek-inspired garment in the time of Jesus was a simple tunic made of a single piece of cloth.

An interesting biblical law prohibited the mixing of fabrics: "You shall not wear a mingled stuff, wool and linen together." (Deuteronomy 22:11) The holiness issues mentioned in our consideration of the pig prohibition might likewise be involved here.

When it came to hair, women wore theirs long and braided. In Old Testament times, men's hair tended to be longish but in the time of Jesus, shorter hair was popular. A certain Israelite religious group, the Nazarites, were forbidden to cut their hair at all! Sampson, you may recall, was one of them. Men wore beards. Jewelry was often worn, including bracelets and anklets, and was another way of exhibiting wealth.

A Measure of Wealth

In much of the ancient Near East, an individual's wealth might be measured in terms of his or her personal property including herds, servants, and even jewelry. Barter was the name of the game and established exchanges for commodities were known or negotiated. Weights and measures, therefore, was a serious matter and the Bible warned against cheating.

A common unit of exchange was in amounts of precious metal, especially small pieces of silver. Coinage didn't seem to be common in Palestine until the Persian period but coins would come into increasing use as standard currency during Greek and Roman times.

Taking a Break

The biblical Jews just didn't work, eat, and sleep. They knew how to have a good time once in a while. Family time, and festivals, of course, were often valued occasions.

Although we don't know a lot about specific activities, it would be safe to say that like children all over, the Israelite kids could contrive an imaginative collection of toys and games. Speaking of a future age to come, the prophet refers to a future Jerusalem where "the streets of the city shall be full of boys and girls playing in its streets." (Zechariah 8:5)

The Bible also mentions a number of musical instruments. David played the lyre, and harps were also known, as were flutes and trumpets. A special trumpet called a "shofar" was made out of a ram's horn. All of these could be accompanied by a variety of percussion instruments including cymbals, tambourines, rattles, and bells. Temple rituals were accompanied by singers and musicians although we don't have examples of the actual music played.

> **Thus Saith**
>
> Singing, dancing, and playing musical instruments could be used as a form of praise: "Praise the Lord! Sing to the Lord a new song, his praise in the assembly of the faithful! Let Israel be glad in his Maker, let the sons of Zion rejoice in their King! Let them praise his name with dancing, making melody to him with timbrel and lyre!" (Psalm 149)

Meet Your Maker

You can't live forever, and there were plenty of ways to die in biblical times. Surviving childhood without an accident or contracting a disease was by no means guaranteed. When death did occur, burial was required as soon as possible. Those in mourning could demonstrate their grief by putting on "sack cloth"—rough and uncomfortable clothing—and applying ashes to their body.

For the most part, the deceased were interred in family burial caves or tombs. The tombs could be hollowed out of rock and many featured shelves or niches on which the body could be laid out. Secondary burial was often practiced. After a body had reached a skeletal state, the bones could be collected from their laid-out position in the tomb and deposited in a pile with others, thus saving space for future occupants. By the time of Jesus, some folks' bones were being stored in stone boxes archaeologists call *ossuaries*.

Psalm 90:10 addresses our life span: "The years of our life are threescore and ten, or even by reason of strength fourscore; yet their span is but toil and trouble; they are soon gone, and we fly away." That's 70 years, or 80 if we're extra durable.

More Details?

As I mentioned at the beginning, the daily life of the biblical Jews is a big subject. Luckily, there are some good books to fill you in on a bit more. *Life in Biblical Israel* by Philip King and Lawrence Stager is outstanding, and *The Harper's Encyclopedia of Biblical Life* by Madeleine and J. Lane Miller might be considered a classic.

The Least You Need to Know

- Social and religious rules governed much of ancient Jewish life from birth to death.

- The average Israelite lived in a simple, mud brick dwelling and ate simply.

- In Israelite society, men and women had different roles that complemented each other.

- Lacking modern medicine, there was considerable variation in life span during biblical times.

- On a basic level, biblical people weren't all that much different from people today!

Chapter 17

An Organized Society

In This Chapter

◆ The Jewish calendar

◆ A year of holy days and festivals

◆ The Ten Commandments—and other important rules

◆ Government for the people

The first five books of the Bible, the Torah, were a source for organizing much of ancient Jewish life. In preparation for establishing the Israelites in the Promised Land, God set down the rules via Moses at Sinai. These rules were intended to create a civil and godly society.

Let's take a look at this well-ordered society, including its calendar, laws, and government.

The Cycle of Time

The 12-month Jewish calendar is lunar; that is, the months begin as the new moon appears. This differs from our Western calendar, which is designed on a solar basis so the seasons line up. This lunar method certainly is one good way of organizing time but has the drawback of not fitting quite in sync with the usual solar calendar year that governs the seasons. Consequently, the lunar calendar drifts and loses about 11 days every year. To compensate for this and to keep the calendar and seasons together, an extra month was regularly added.

The names of the months of the year were adopted from the Babylonian calendar system and applied to the Jewish year after the Jews returned from their captivity in Babylon. Prior to that, they just referred to them as the first month, second month, third month, and so on. The first month of the formal calendar is called *Nisan*, but the actual Jewish New Year, *Rosh Hashana*, doesn't occur until the first day of the seventh month, known as *Tishri*.

The months of the Jewish calendar. The additional month of Adar is occasionally added to adjust the imbalance between the lunar and solar calendar years.

Month 1 - Nisan
Month 2 - Iyar
Month 3 - Sivan
Month 4 - Tammuz
Month 5 - Av
Month 6 - Elul
Month 7 - Tishri
Month 8 - Cheshvan
Month 9 - Kislev
Month 10 - Tevet
Month 11 - Shevat
Month 12 - Adar I
(Adar II)

Holy Days and Festivals

The Jewish year included (and still does include) Holy Days. The month of Tishri has several of importance:

◆ **Rosh Hashanah** literally means the head of the year. It's the beginning of the holy calendar cycle and a birthday celebration for the universe. Unlike the raucous New Year's parties we know all too well in these modern days, Rosh Hashanah is actually a more solemn celebration in which to contemplate the year before and the year ahead.

♦ **Yom Kippur** is the Day of Atonement and begins ten days after Rosh Hashanah. Jews are to fast, refrain from work, and repent to God for sins.

♦ **Sukkot,** or the Feast of Booths, begins on the fifteenth day of Tishri. It is actually quite festive. It is both a harvest festival and a time to remember the years when the Israelites wandered in the desert, living in tents, before settling in Palestine. Jews are to celebrate the bounty of the land for seven days and live in tentlike "booths" or temporary houses for the duration. An additional eighth day known as Shemini Atzeret.

> **This and That**
>
> The Jewish calendar year begins with a traditional date for the creation derived from the counting of biblical genealogies. The Jewish year 5763 is included in most of our Western calendar year, 2003, until Rosh Hashanah occurs in late September and 5764 begins.

Reliving the Past

On the fourteenth day of the month of Nisan, Pesach is celebrated. Passover commemorates the Exodus story in which God delivered the Hebrew people from slavery in Egypt. The biblical Jews were to remember this profound story by eating unleavened bread for seven days and sharing the tale of God's deliverance. When the Temple was functioning, families traveled to Jerusalem to sacrifice a lamb. Over the years, a well-developed family ritual dinner or *seder* was developed for this very special holiday.

Seven Weeks Later ...

Seven weeks were to be counted from the second day of Passover to the beginning of the festival of Shavuot, or "weeks." (It is also known as "Pentecost.") Like Sukkot, the holiday was tied to agriculture—in this case, the "first fruits of harvest" and offerings to God were presented. It also celebrates the giving of the Torah.

> **People and Places**
>
> Sukkot, Passover, and Shavuot were all pilgrimage festivals that required a visit to Jerusalem to present offerings and give thanks.

And More Were Added

A number of holidays are found among Jews today that aren't found in the Bible, but were added later. Here are some of them:

- **Purim** celebrates the saving of the Jews from death during Persian times as presented in the Book of Esther. Today, it is celebrated by a reading of the story complete with audience participation (including hurrays and boos), and drinking is absolutely permitted.

- **Hanukkah** is the celebration of the rededication of the Temple (see Chapter 13) after it was desecrated by the Greeks. The story is in the apocryphal books of Maccabees but not in the Hebrew Bible.

- Although it's not mentioned in the Torah, the Torah does command that people not eat the fruit from new trees until the trees are at least four years old. **Tu B'Shevat** was the day from which the ages of the new trees were counted. Some Jews today celebrate this day by planting a tree.

- **Tisha B'Av,** the ninth day of the month of Av, is a sad day of memorial commemorating the two destructions of the Temple in Jerusalem that occurred on that same date centuries apart. Interestingly, it is also the date on which the Jews were expelled from Spain in 1492 and the day that World War I broke out, among other things.

A Day of Rest

One of the Ten Commandments ordered the Jews to rest one day a week:

> Remember the sabbath day, to keep it holy. Six days you shall labor, and do all your work; but the seventh day is a sabbath to the Lord your God; in it you shall not do any work, you, or your son, or your daughter, or your manservant, or your maidservant, or your cattle, or the sojourner who is within your gates; for in six days the Lord made heaven and earth, the sea, and all that is in them, and rested the seventh day; therefore the Lord blessed the sabbath day and hallowed it. (Exodus 20:8–11)

This commandment was to be taken very seriously. The Book of Numbers tells a story of how a man was caught gathering sticks on this day of rest. He was stoned to death.

The traditional Jewish Sabbath begins at sundown on Friday and lasts until sundown on Saturday. Later tradition has developed many specific rules about what is and what is not considered "work" and, therefore, what is permissible to do on the Sabbath. Today, driving, using money (shopping, paying bills), turning on electricity, and cooking are among the things not permitted in Orthodox Jewish households on the Sabbath.

This is not a big problem, though, and most Jewish families who observe the Sabbath look forward to it as a glorious time for family, a chance to rest, and an opportunity to worship God. In other words, it's an opportunity to spend some time devoted not to making a living, but to doing some living in very meaningful ways.

Obeying the Rules

Israelite/Jewish society was ultimately governed by divine law. Among the most famous and quoted of these laws are the Ten Commandments. The commandments can be looked at in two groups: those that govern the relationship between humans and God and those that govern the relationship between humans.

Moses descending Mt. Sinai with the Ten Commandments.

(Illustration by Gustave Doré)

The first four deal with divine relationship:

1. "You shall have no other gods before me." In the ancient Near East, a world rife with polytheism, God tells you there is only one real God.

2. "You shall not make for yourself a graven image … you shall not bow down to them or serve them …" Enough of that pagan idol worship already!

3. "You shall not take the name of the Lord your God in vain ..." Show some respect!

4. "Remember the sabbath day, to keep it holy." Take a day off once a week to honor God and to give yourself a break.

The rest of the Big Ten deal with how we should treat other people:

5. "Honor your father and your mother." This commandment recognizes respect for one's elders and encourages family harmony.

6. "You shall not kill." That word *kill* in this commandment means "murder," an unjust death.

7. "You shall not commit adultery." It will create pain and havoc in your family.

8. "You shall not steal." Plain and simple.

9. "You shall not bear false witness against your neighbor." Don't spread dubious rumors or lie to the judge.

10. "You shall not covet your neighbor's house; you shall not covet your neighbor's wife, ... or anything that is your neighbor's." You'll be a lot happier, and it might just help you from breaking some of the other commandments.

These latter commandments, especially, make a lot of sense even to nonbelievers, and I think most people would agree that murder, stealing, and adultery do not contribute to a healthy, peaceful society.

The Other 603 Plus

As you know, there are a total of 613 written commandments to be found in the first five books of the Bible, the Torah. Many of these laws have shaped attitudes prevalent in Western civilization and some have formed the basis of legal statutes.

Here are just a few of the less well-known ones found in the Book of Deuteronomy:

◆ Cross-dressing is typically considered to be bad form in much of Western society. Here's a verse that might have influenced this attitude: "A woman shall not wear anything that pertains to a man, nor shall a man put on a woman's garment; for whoever does these things is an abomination to the Lord your God." (22:5)

◆ "There shall not be found among you any one who burns his son or his daughter as an offering, any one who practices divination, a soothsayer, or an augur, or a sorcerer, or a charmer, or a medium, or a wizard, or a necromancer." (18:10–11) These were considered very pagan practices. So stay away from that Ouija board and quit calling the psychic hotline!

- "Cursed be he who misleads a blind man on the road." (27:18) It goes to show that mean-spirited people have been around for thousands of years!

- The eighteenth chapter of Leviticus records laws that forbid incest with a wide variety of relatives.

The following commandment found in Deuteronomy 6:3–9 is a strong statement of belief in and devotion to the One God. They also require that God and his rules be at the center of the believer's life and passed on to one's family:

> Hear, O Israel: The Lord our God is one Lord; and you shall love the Lord your God with all your heart, and with all your soul, and with all your might. And these words which I command you this day shall be upon your heart; and you shall teach them diligently to your children, and shall talk of them when you sit in your house, and when you walk by the way, and when you lie down, and when you rise. And you shall bind them as a sign upon your hand, and they shall be as frontlets between your eyes. And you shall write them on the doorposts of your house and on your gates.

Jewish tradition tells that along with the laws found in the Bible, Moses received an "oral Torah" that contains more rules and stories, some that offer specific instruction as to how to properly pray, observe the Sabbath, and so on. These laws are known as the Mishnah, the oldest part of the formal Jewish legal text known as the Talmud, which would be written down after the time of the Hebrew Bible.

You'd Need a Million More!

To cover all possible human offenses, it would be necessary to have thousands and thousands of rules. Many of the biblical rules, however, are examples of what can be called "case law." In Exodus 21:35, for example, there is a law concerning an unruly ox. Although this law would certainly be applied to a case where that very same incident occurred, the law would also serve as a model in judging other incidents of a similar nature.

Suffering the Consequences

Some of the biblical laws require that the offenders compensate the offendees in kind or money. Others require that the punishment fit the crime, including the famous penalty found in Leviticus 19: "When a man causes a disfigurement in his neighbor, as he has done it shall be done to him, fracture for fracture, eye for eye, tooth for tooth; as he has disfigured a man, he shall be disfigured." Some offenses, including murder, required the death penalty.

As you can imagine, given the many rules and often severe penalties, the Jews in general had good incentives to behave well, although the Bible points out many incidents where people fell short. You wouldn't have to witness too many stonings to realize that it's better to follow the laws than to break them. And part of the parents' job was to make sure their kids knew and understood the rules.

The Government of the People of God

The governing of the Israelites took several different forms, including rule by tribal elders, charismatic leaders, judges, and kings. When the twelve Hebrew tribes were in Egypt, they were governed amongst themselves by tribal elders. With the giving of the law at Sinai, the tribes really became one people under one law. Moses was God's appointed leader in the wilderness. It was a huge job and he eventually appointed "able men out of all Israel, and made them heads over the people, rulers of thousands, of hundreds, of fifties, and of tens. And they judged the people at all times; hard cases they brought to Moses, but any small matter they decided themselves." (Exodus 18:25–6)

Hearing the Cases

As they established themselves in Palestine, the Israelites established a court system in which political leaders such as town governors and military captains participated. Priests were involved in religious cases. This system of government by judges was in effect for a couple hundred years after entering Canaan to the establishment of the monarchy. During that time, a series of twelve heroic leaders, referred to as "judges," also emerged to save the Israelites from various oppressors. Their stories are told, not surprisingly, in the biblical Book of Judges.

A need for judges certainly continued thereafter, and a Jewish judicial system was in place throughout most of the years of biblical history that followed. Cases were typically heard, discussed, and decided at the city gates.

Give Us a King!

In 1 Samuel, we learn that the Israelites grew tired of this system of rule by judges and insisted on a king to rule over them. Samuel, repeating what God had told him, warned them that a monarchy might be even worse. The people insisted and a monarchy was established.

As the Bible informs us, the Israelites were united under the reigns of only three kings (Saul, David, and Solomon) and then split into two kingdoms under Solomon's successor, Rehoboam. The kings organized an army and put together royal households for themselves with numerous advisors and retainers. In short, they created big administrative bureaucracies to carry out their rule.

One can argue that the warning against establishing a kingship was justified. Solomon, for example, lived a very extravagant lifestyle and although there was the occasional good king to be found in both Judah and Israel, many were scoundrels. Some even facilitated or resorted to pagan worship.

The kings of the divided monarchy with their capital cities of Jerusalem (Judah) and Samaria (Israel) had an uneasy relationship. The dismantling of the ten tribes of Israel by the Assyrians in 721 B.C. obviously put an end to such disputes, and the Judean monarchy would likewise be terminated at the hands of the Babylonians.

Upon returning to Palestine after the Babylonian captivity, the Jews were given a certain amount of independence to conduct their affairs, albeit under Persian rule. As you learned in the Hanukkah story in Chapter 13, at least some Greeks tried to actively interfere with the Jewish culture. Several decades of relatively independent Jewish rule was allowed until the Romans came knocking. We'll see what that was about in the next chapter.

Logos

One might best characterize the Hebrew/Israelite/Jewish lifestyle as a **theocracy**, meaning rule by God. Although administered indirectly by people (except when God intervened), the laws came from God and were seen as divine commandments. To the Jews, God was the ultimate boss.

The Least You Need to Know

- The ancient Jewish calendar was based on a lunar, rather than a solar, cycle.
- The Jewish year featured a regular schedule of Holy Days.
- Israelite society was governed by strict divine law given at Sinai.
- An evolving system of government developed through the history of the Israelites, including rule by elders, priests, judges, and kings.

Chapter 18

Jerusalem: The City of David

In This Chapter

- ◆ Jerusalem: a special and holy city
- ◆ King David conquers the city
- ◆ Archaeological discoveries
- ◆ The arrival of the Greeks and Romans
- ◆ Battles, conflicts, and crusades
- ◆ An ancient city reaches into the present and future

When it comes to towns, cities, and other physical places in the Bible, Jerusalem takes center stage. Its importance in the world, though, extends far beyond its geographical borders in the region of Palestine. Jerusalem has been the site of some of history's greatest triumphs and tragedies.

People have been fighting over Jerusalem for thousands of years, and continue to do so. It is a city with a physical presence and a spiritual aura, a timeless city where the past, present, and future seem to converge. It is Jerusalem, the ancient City of David, the capital of the modern state of Israel, and, to some, a future world capital to be overseen by God himself in a new age.

Sacred to Billions

To Jews, Jerusalem was the original capital of the Hebrew tribes, united together in the Promised Land under the protection and authority of God. The Holy Temple was built there as a center of worship to the one God and was twice destroyed. A section of wall from the platform of Herod's Temple at the base of the old Temple Mount today serves as the holiest site in Judaism. Although Jews have been scattered over the centuries, Jerusalem has remained their spiritual center, and with the establishment of the modern state of Israel in the twentieth century, it has become the capital of the Jewish state.

> **Thus Saith**
>
> I was glad when they said to me, "Let us go to the house of the Lord!" Our feet have been standing within your gates, O Jerusalem! Jerusalem, built as a city which is bound firmly together, to which the tribes go up, the tribes of the Lord, as was decreed for Israel, to give thanks to the name of the Lord. There thrones for judgment were set, the thrones of the house of David.
>
> —David, Psalm 122:1–5

Jerusalem also played a vital part in the story of Jesus, and to Christians, it is the place where Jesus taught and died. Churches and monuments were built at every possible site that could be identified with him, and the city has been the destination of Christian pilgrimages for nearly 2,000 years. Great battles pitting Christians against Muslims and Jews were fought there in an effort to defend these holy places.

For Muslims, Jerusalem is the third most sacred city, after Mecca and Medina. The golden Dome of the Rock, built on the platform where the Holy Temple once stood, covers a rock that bears a traditional history relating it both to Abraham and Mohammed.

The name Jerusalem is interesting. In Hebrew, the name is Yerushalayim, which many say is a combination of the word for city and peace. The ending of the word for peace, *shalom*, is somewhat provocative, because it uses a dual grammatical ending, suggesting a double city. Some have interpreted the name to imply that Jerusalem is actually two cities: a physical city and a spiritual city. Some say that the latter is yet to come.

An Ancient Crossroads

Jerusalem lies on elevated land that stretches from north to south across the center of the Palestine region, about 35 miles from the Mediterranean coast. In ancient times, the city itself was situated at a convenient crossroads, with hilly flanks that made it easier to defend.

The areas surrounding the city provided suitable land for growing crops and trees and for grazing livestock. Very important to the city's ability to survive was an adequate and reliable water supply. This necessity was provided by the Gihon Spring, situated in a valley to the city's east.

> **This and That**
>
> On some old European maps, Jerusalem is pictured as the center of the world, and from a geographical standpoint, its location in Palestine does put it in a place where three continents come together: Europe, Africa, and Asia.

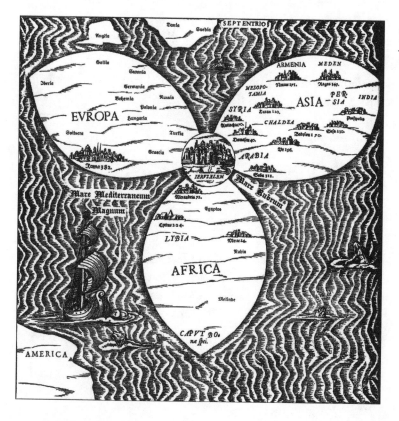

A map from 1580 showing Jerusalem as the center of the world.

One Old City

Archaeologists have found evidence of people living in Jerusalem as far back as 3000 B.C. A city was definitely there around 1800 B.C., and it is mentioned in the written correspondence of neighboring civilizations. In the time of King David, about 1000 B.C., the city was in the hands of a group of apparently Canaanite people called the Jebusites.

David Conquers a City

As we have seen, the land promised to the Hebrews was already occupied by other peoples, and the same was true of Jerusalem. It was something of a fortress, in fact, with its hilly location and fortified walls. How did David conquer such a place? The Bible talks about a water shaft that the Hebrews ascended in order to attack the city. What could that be all about?

One compelling idea is that the Israelite soldiers were able to infiltrate the Jebusite stronghold from the inside. A little way upslope from the outlet of the Gihon spring is a deep natural sinkhole in the limestone that drops down into the subterranean water. This sinkhole is called Warren's Shaft, after the English explorer who investigated it in the nineteenth century.

Earlier residents of Jerusalem had built an underground tunnel from behind the city wall leading into Warren's Shaft. That way, if the city were under attack, which wasn't an uncommon thing in those days, people could still visit the spring and obtain water by dropping a bucket down the shaft.

Could Warren's Shaft have been the ticket to conquering Jebusite Jerusalem? Might David's soldiers have accomplished the difficult rock-climbing feat of clandestinely ascending the shaft as a route to invasion? It's a fascinating question, and like many questions in the Bible, it is difficult to prove without additional archaeological data or information from ancient texts.

However they did it, the Israelites were victorious, and Jerusalem became the capital of the united Israelite tribes, gaining even more prestige when the sacred Ark of the Covenant was brought into town. Jerusalem was expanded, and a small portion of the remains of David's city have been excavated on the modern eastern slopes.

Thus Saith

2 Samuel 5:9 mentions that David "built the city [of Jerusalem] round about from the Millo inward." It's not clear exactly what the Millo was, but it could be a big stepped stone structure that has been discovered, which might have served as an ancient retaining wall.

After ruling from the city for 37 years, David died. A visitor to Jerusalem today will find a structure traditionally referred to as David's tomb. He's not inside, though. This tomb is relatively recent, dating to about the fourth century A.D.

Although it was customary to bury people outside the city walls, it's possible that an exception was made for David and a few other royals. Some rock-cut tombs within the confines of David's city walls have been found, and perhaps it was here that he was laid to rest. Tombs placed in special locations tend to belong to very special individuals.

Archaeologists have exca-vated some of the ancient ruins of Jerusalem dating to the time of David.

(David Moyer collection)

Holding the Fort

Jerusalem continued to prosper even after the Israelite Kingdom was divided and the ten northern tribes were led away by the Assyrians. It, too, was a target of the Assyrians, but the city survived the assault and the city population actually grew, due to an influx of refugees from the north.

The city was spared, thanks to the efforts of King Hezekiah (reigned 715–687 B.C.). He also prepared the city by building a 20-foot-thick wall to withstand a brutal assault. But his most famous accomplishment was an enduring marvel.

Hezekiah was well aware of the tactics of the Assyrians, who were more than willing to cut off food supplies and water to the cities they aimed to conquer. Dead or weakened people don't put up much of a fight. To insure that water would be available to the city of Jerusalem, Hezekiah initiated an amazing building project: a tunnel was carved from the Gihon Spring to provide water within the expanded city's walls.

The tunnel stretches for about one third of a mile, and two crews worked simultaneously from each end to meet in the middle. The route of Hezekiah's tunnel is by no means straight—in fact, it curves quite a bit. In addition, the tunnel maintains an appropriately gentle slope to keep the water moving. The real mystery is how the two teams were able to meet up at all.

Is That So!

The Bible tells how King Hezekiah prayed to God for help against a siege of Jerusalem. The next morning, he found 185,000 dead Assyrians outside the walls.

One solution to the puzzle might be that the tunnel diggers were following a natural geological fault or crack in the rock. In any case, an ancient inscription found at the exit of one end of the tunnel recorded the triumphant meeting of the two teams. They could apparently hear each other as they approached. The famous Siloam Inscription (named for the pool at one end of the tunnel) is not to be found in Jerusalem, however. It was chipped away from the rock, sold to an antiquities dealer, and eventually taken to Turkey, where it now resides in a museum in Istanbul.

The Babylonians Prevail

Although the people of Jerusalem were spared when the Assyrians attacked, they weren't so lucky with the Babylonians. As you know, the Babylonians were extremely successful in their final assault on the city, which took place in 586 B.C. Not only was Solomon's Temple destroyed, but archaeologists can confirm that much of the city was burned as well.

Barkay's Discoveries

An interesting archaeological discovery was made in 1979 when Israeli archaeologist Gabriel Barkay was investigating some old stone tombs outside the city walls. Underneath a collapsed ceiling, he found an amazing collection of human bones and artifacts. About 100 people were buried there, along with around 1,000 objects, including pottery and jewelry.

Is That So!

In the vicinity of Jerusalem have been found a lot of small clay fertility figures that are contemporary with the time the Temple was in use. This seems to indicate that not everybody was worshiping only one god.

Some of the pottery dates to the time period just after the Jews were said to have been taken away into Babylonian captivity. The grave appears to have belonged to members of the wealthy Jewish elite, and it shows that not all of them were deported. Some residents apparently continued a good life in the aftermath of the fall of Jerusalem.

A Blessing upon You

Perhaps the most remarkable objects recovered from Barkay's excavation were two amulets, each consisting of a rolled silver strip. When they were painstakingly unrolled, the strips revealed two versions of the priestly blessing from Numbers 6:24–26: "The Lord bless thee, and keep thee; The Lord make his face shine upon thee, and be gracious unto thee; The Lord lift up his countenance upon thee, and give thee peace."

The discovery of an ancient text of any kind from this part of the world is exciting, especially something relating to the Bible, but these are extra special. The two amulets date to around 650 B.C. and are the oldest known biblical texts!

The Greeks and Romans Arrive

When the Jews returned to Jerusalem after the Babylonian captivity, they not only rebuilt the Temple, but also engaged in other construction and restoration projects including building another city wall. And a couple centuries later, when the Greeks came to dominate Jerusalem, they brought along some of their culture, including a bit of architectural influence.

Some impressive tombs carved into the rock just outside the walls have elements that look as if they were borrowed from Greek temples. During Roman times, King Herod made dramatic changes to the city, including his spectacular remodeling of the second Temple.

Roman Wreckers

The time of the Romans was also the time of Jesus of Nazareth, and Jerusalem is famous for its role in his life. There are many sites and monuments to be found there, but I'll talk about some of those in future chapters. As noted earlier, the Romans destroyed the Temple in A.D. 70 during the Jewish revolt.

Another serious revolt took place against the Romans in the years A.D. 132 through 135. The rebels were led by a charismatic man named Simon Bar-Kokhba. Although successful in winning a number of skirmishes against the Romans, Bar-Kokhba's warriors were ultimately defeated. Thereafter, Jews were banned from Jerusalem.

Turnabouts

In A.D. 130, during the reign of the emperor Hadrian, Jerusalem was rebuilt and renamed *Aelia Capitolina*. A temple of the Roman god Jupiter was built on the Temple Mount. In just a couple hundred years, Christianity would become the official religion of the Roman empire, Jews would return, and Jerusalem would receive visitors from Europe seeking holy artifacts and hoping to locate sites mentioned in the Bible.

> **This and That**
>
> In the year (A.D.) 2000, the modern state of Israel honored the 3,000-year anniversary of the city of Jerusalem as the Jewish spiritual capital since the time of King David, circa 1000 B.C.

Fighting for God and Glory

During the first two millennia A.D., Jerusalem would be controlled by many different powers. The Arabs invaded Palestine in A.D. 635 and brought with them the new religion of Islam. In Jerusalem they built the Dome of the Rock and the El-Aksa Mosque on the Temple Mount, along with many other structures.

Jerusalem became an Islamic city and, as fellow "peoples of the Book," Jews and Christians were permitted to live in relative peace with their Muslim neighbors and rulers. Things were stirring in Europe, however, that would transform the holy city into a wild battleground.

The walled city of Jerusalem with the golden rotunda of the Dome of the Rock.

(Photo courtesy of John Petersen)

"Liberating" the Holy Land

Beginning in A.D. 1096, Christian armies formed in Europe to engage in eight major campaigns to "free" the Holy Land from non-Christian infidels. A request by a Christian emperor to send assistance to fight against the Turks in Palestine inspired Pope Urban II (1088–1099) to issue a call to arms.

In the speech that inspired the First Crusade, the pope reported that Christians were being killed and holy sites in Jerusalem and elsewhere in the Holy Land were being desecrated and destroyed. He promised those who died in their defense automatic forgiveness for their sins.

Huge armies left Europe, and in 1099, Jerusalem was taken by the Crusaders after a horrible slaughter of its inhabitants. Little Crusader kingdoms were set up in the region. The Muslims were not at all happy about this, and fought to win back the territory.

More Blood Is Shed

A Second Crusade was called in 1147 through 1149, and was a big failure. A Third Crusade (1189–1192) began after the great Islamic leader, Saladin, captured Jerusalem in 1187. The results of this Crusade were mixed, and the armies went home without recapturing Jerusalem. Christian pilgrims, however, were still permitted to visit the Holy City.

Five more Crusades took place between 1204 and 1291, and Jerusalem changed hands a couple of times in the process. The city would ultimately return to the Muslims. The Crusades were not just about religion, but also about greed, commerce, and power. Untold thousands died in the process, and not a whole lot was accomplished.

> **People and Places**
>
> Before the First Crusade began, a fanatical rag-tag peasant army, led by Peter the Hermit, rampaged through Europe on its way to Jerusalem, harassing Jews along the way. The army never made it. Along with another general, Walter the Penniless, these motley crusaders were eventually slaughtered by the Turks in Asia Minor.

A City Divided

Palestine was incorporated into the Turkish Ottoman Empire in 1516 and remained there until Jerusalem was captured by the British during World War I. Palestine became a British Mandate in 1922.

Tensions rose during the next couple decades due to an influx of Jewish immigrants, which the local Arab population found threatening. With more Jewish refugees hoping to move to their ancestral homeland, especially after the profound tragedy of the Nazi Holocaust, British policy failed to keep the peace.

War and Peace

In 1947, the United Nations partitioned Palestine into a Jewish state and an Arab state. Jerusalem was to be an international city. The Arabs never agreed to this plan, and when the state of Israel was declared on May 14, 1948, war broke out. The Jewish settlements in Jerusalem were cut off by Arab forces, but the Israelis eventually prevailed. Jerusalem, which was declared the capital of a new country known as Israel, was left divided.

> **Thus Saith**
>
> Pray for the peace of Jerusalem! "May they prosper those who love you! Peace be within your walls, and security within your towers!" For my brethren and companions' sake I will say, "Peace be within you!" For the sake of the house of the Lord our God, I will seek your good.
>
> —David, Psalm 122:6–9

The western sections were under Israeli control, and the ancient walled Old City, containing the Temple Mount, was in the hands of the Jordanians. In 1967, another war broke out, and the Israelis captured the Old City, along with other territories belonging to Jordan, Egypt, and Syria. Another war between Israel and several Arab states was fought in 1973, which Israel again survived.

The Palestinian Question

The Arab families who now live in, or who fled from, the areas captured by Israel in the wars have organized themselves under the name "Palestinians." A good many don't accept the original United Nations division of the land and have engaged in a long-term struggle with the State of Israel. Some have called for the utter dismantling of Israel, to be replaced by a secular, modern state of Palestine.

One of the biggest bones of contention in this biblical region is the ultimate status of the City of Jerusalem. The Palestinians would like to make Jerusalem the capital of what they hope will be a Palestinian state. They wish to regain control over the eastern part of the city, the part captured in 1967, which includes not only the sacred Western Wall and the Temple Mount, but many Jewish homes and establishments built in the last 30 years in the walled Old City's Jewish Quarter. The ultimate status of the city of Jerusalem will be one of the most difficult of the many issues to be settled.

The status of the city of Jerusalem remains internationally controversial. Many countries attempt to stay out of the dispute by placing their embassies in the modern Israeli city of Tel Aviv.

A Visit to the City

Jerusalem is a wonderful city today. The narrow streets and stone walls of the Old City exist side by side with a vibrant modern city. Jewish people flock to the Western Wall daily while Muslims pray at the mosques above. Thousands of Christians wander the city in awe of the sites where Jesus spent much time.

Jerusalem is also home to the Israel Museum, which exhibits a superb collection of artifacts from biblical times. The sites, sounds, and smells of Jerusalem are unforgettable. You'll find more information about visiting this amazing city in Chapter 22.

The Least You Need to Know

♦ The ancient and modern city of Jerusalem is held sacred by Jews, Christians, and Muslims.

♦ The city served as the capital of the Israelites in ancient times and serves as the capital of the modern state of Israel today. It has changed hands numerous times over the years.

♦ Archaeological discoveries have shed interesting light on the history of this amazing city, but much remains to be discovered.

♦ The city remains controversial to this day and plays a central role in the conflict between Israel and the Palestinians.

Part 5

The Holy Land in the Time of Jesus

The life and times of Jesus of Nazareth is the focus of the New Testament. Its story begins not too long after the Hebrew Bible/Old Testament ends. It is, however, a somewhat different world. The Greeks have had an effect and the Romans are now in charge. In this part, you'll learn a little about the Romans and the Jewish religious and political establishment during the time of Jesus. We also see how Jesus fit into that kind of environment. Last, I'll provide a few insights into how the word of Jesus spread outside of Palestine to produce eventually an amazingly diverse number of followers in the nearly two millennia since.

Chapter 19

The Romans Take Their Turn

In This Chapter

♦ A glance at Roman geography and history

♦ The rise and fall of the Roman Empire

♦ Rome comes to Palestine

♦ The accomplishments of Herod "the Great"

♦ Different Jewish groups

Traditionally, the Hebrew Bible is thought to have been written down after the Jews returned to Palestine after the Babylonian captivity. Ezra the Scribe is often cited as the editor about 450 B.C. The history recorded in the Hebrew Bible, therefore, ends at that point. Some of the apocryphal books record events that took place thereafter, notably during the period when the Greeks ruled the region. This period in between the Hebrew Bible/Old Testament and the Christian Scriptures/New Testament is sometimes referred to as the Intertestamental Period.

The Christian Scriptures of the New Testament begin a few hundred years after the Hebrew Bible ends. The New Testament, written in Greek, is quite a different library. These books concentrate on the life and teachings of a Jew named Jesus and his followers. Needless to say, Jesus has had an incredible impact perhaps best demonstrated by the fact that more than a billion people today claim to be his followers. And that he is respected by at least a billion more people of other faiths.

A lot of what Jesus said and did is best studied in the context of his time—that is, Jesus as a Jew living in Palestine under Roman rule during the first century A.D. Taken out of this cultural, political, religious, and temporal context, the story of Jesus can be confusing. That being the case, let's set the stage for the world of Jesus. For starters, let's take a look at the really big players in his world: the Romans!

A Little Geography

The Italian peninsula where the city of Rome would arise is quite a bit different from Greece, with its geographically isolated city-states. In Italy, especially in the north, there are large fertile areas. This can be good and bad. The Po River valley, for example, was not only good land for agriculture, but made a great entryway for the various marauding tribes who would dash in from time to time and sack Rome.

Italy wasn't all populated by the Romans, or even by the region's numerous local tribes. The Greeks, with their fondness for setting up colonies, were prominent in southern Italy. There were so many Greek settlements there, in fact, that the territory was known as *Grecia Magna*, or "Greater Greece." Greeks could also be found on much of the island of Sicily. Okay, that's the territory. Now it's speedy history time!

Is That So!

If there were an award for the most surviving antiquities from an ancient civilization, Rome might win. With its great empire and skilled builders, and a wealth of surviving artifacts, structures, and documents, Roman remains are found widely in Europe and the Mediterranean region. We know a good deal about these folks.

Roman Roots

There were a lot of tribes in north-central Italy in the first several millennia B.C., and one significant urban society, the Etruscans, provided the first kings of the growing city of Rome which is traditionally said to have been founded in the year 752 B.C. It was the sophisticated culture of the Etruscans, with their literacy and monuments, that formed the foundation of Roman civilization. Eventually, the Latin-speaking Romans dominated the Etruscans, as well as the rest of Italy, and conquered both the Western Mediterranean and the surviving empire of Alexander.

The First Republicans

According to traditional history, the monarchy in Rome was overthrown because of a gross abuse of power by a member of the royal family. It could have very well, however, been a coup on the part of wealthy nobles. What replaced the system of kingship was a kind of representative government. Much of the history of Rome can be seen in the evolution of this government, which featured two senior executives called consuls, a Senate, and several assemblies made up of free citizens.

The Senate and the Roman People

Roman society was divided up into at least three classes. The patricians were the wealthy upper class (probably no more than 10 percent of the population), the plebeians were the commoners, and then there were the slaves. The consuls and senators were typically patricians, and they held most of the power. A series of reforms gave the plebeians more of a say, including the appointment of two executive-level representatives called tribunes and a tradition that one of the two consuls would be a plebe.

> **People and Places**
>
> In the year A.D. 79, the volcano Vesuvius erupted near the modern city of Naples. The Roman town of Pompeii was buried under ash and Herculaneum was covered in a mud flow. As a result, both ancient towns were incredibly well-preserved through the ages and have provided scholars with a tremendous amount of information about Roman daily life and society.

A Good Idea Gone Bad

This nicely organized system of representative government and rule of law began to deteriorate as Rome began to expand its borders and the system was repeatedly abused. Then there were generals with loyal armies who after a successful campaign would turn around, march their armies into Rome, and make demands. The famous and charismatic Julius Caesar (100–44 B.C.) was one such leader with a large following.

Another commander, a fellow named Octavian (63 B.C.–A.D. 14), survived his rivals and was welcomed back at home, where immense powers were bestowed upon him by the Senate. He became the first emperor and was given the title Augustus, and the republican government thereafter would be mostly a charade as the emperor essentially became a dictator over the empire.

Building the Empire

Now let's take a step back and see how the vast Roman Empire came about. Well, it was built in stages. The first step was to conquer the neighbors, which the Romans did early on, beginning with the Etruscans and then the various tribes in Italy. The Greeks had to be dominated in the south in order to consolidate most of the peninsula. Way up in the north, the Gauls presented an annoying obstacle for most of Roman history.

Down with Carthage

With much of Italy proper taken care of, two major competitors still had to be squashed in the Mediterranean: the Carthaginians and the Greeks. The Carthaginians, you recall, began as a Phoenician colony on the North African coast and became a real power of their own. The Romans dealt with them in a series of three conflicts known as the Punic Wars that lasted from 264 to 146 B.C.

Is That So! _____

The Greeks had a profound effect upon the Etruscan and Roman civilizations, so much so that some scholars will say that Roman culture is really just an extension of that of the Greeks. Those who are less kind might characterize it as a bastardization of their beloved Greek civilization. The influence is not hard to see: Just look at the art, architecture, and much of the culture and literature.

Subduing the Greeks

With much of the Western Mediterranean cleared of those pesky Carthaginians, and the Greek colonists in that area no longer a real threat, the Romans turned east, where Alexander's mighty empire stood more or less intact. It was a Greek world out there, with the kingdoms established by Alexander's generals in control of vast territories, including Asia Minor, Persia, Egypt, and Palestine. The Romans sent armies out to thrash Greece itself while others gradually ate away at the Hellenistic world. The big finale finally came with the Roman acquisition of Egypt in 30 B.C.

Heading North

The Roman Empire was now immense, and the Mediterranean was essentially a "Roman lake." In the meantime, there was the rest of Europe to take care of, and much of Western Europe was touched by the Romans, including most of Great Britain. However, the Romans certainly weren't unopposed as they regularly fought the "barbarians" along their borders.

All Roads Led to Rome

But how to control such a vast area? The Romans were very clever. In the early days, a citizen of Rome was someone who lived in Rome or the immediate vicinity. As the empire began to grow, citizenship was extended to the conquered peoples, but on a sort of probational basis. If they behaved and fully submitted, they could be granted full Roman citizenship; otherwise they could be entitled to more or fewer privileges based on their behavior. The empire was divided up by into provinces ruled by Roman governors or their local lackeys.

Like the Persians, the Romans set up vast networks of roads that allowed troops to take care of any of the uppity conquered (such as the Jewish rebels in Palestine). Most important, they allowed taxes, tribute, booty, and a wide range of exotic goods to make it back to the homeland or to wealthy Romans everywhere. All this wealth helped those Romans who were so inclined to engage in the variety of vices for which Rome was noted. So dependent did Rome itself become on imports that a disruption in shipping could cause a serious crisis.

> **This and That**
>
> For a great introduction to Roman history and culture, take a look at *The Complete Idiot's Guide to the Roman Empire* by Eric Nelson (Alpha Books, 2002).

Large arenas such as the massive Coliseum in Rome demonstrate the architectural and engineering sophistication of the Romans.

(David Moyer collection)

The Romans were great builders. You can find a Roman road just about anywhere they traveled. The same goes for aqueducts and bridges. Roman engineers designed and built marvelous systems that could bring water from mountains or rivers to where it was needed, even if that meant spanning large ravines. They were masters of the arch, and the Roman aqueducts and bridges were so solid that many are still in use today.

The Romans have also been credited with the first wide-scale use, if not invention, of concrete. Concrete has the great advantage of being relatively portable (before it is mixed) and can be formed into all manner of shapes, including domes.

Emperors for Better or for Worse

Life seemed good in Rome in 27 B.C. when Octavian/Augustus began his rule of the empire. Augustus was quite popular and some consider these the best days for Rome, a creative and prosperous time. When he died in A.D. 14, though, his adopted son Tiberius became the emperor (ruled A.D. 14–37). Tiberius was not like dad, and was a bit mean-spirited and power-hungry.

His son and successor, Caligula, was genuinely insane, and Caligula's successor, Claudius, was a flake. Claudius' son Nero was also crazy. A power struggle after the death of Nero caused a crisis, and four people claimed the throne. A politician and military commander by the name of Vespasian (ruled A.D. 69–79) won out and thus started a new line of rulers. Some of them were pretty good but things went downhill fast, especially after the death of Commodus around A.D. 200.

During the third century A.D., plenty of Roman emperors came and went. Many were murdered and replaced. Attempts at reform were short-lived and Rome was getting so bad that even some of the emperors wouldn't live there. One such emperor, Diocletian, conceded that the empire was simply too large for one man to control and developed a system in which he would share his rule with three others. This idea was short-lived.

Another emperor, Constantine, attempted to improve the situation by dividing up the empire into numerous provinces and creating a huge bureaucracy to control it. He also formally moved the capital of the empire in A.D. 330 to the strategically located old Greek city of Byzantium at the westernmost juncture of Asia Minor and Europe proper. The city was renamed Constantinople in his honor.

> **People and Places**
>
> Augustus (ruled 27 B.C.–A.D. 14) and Tiberius (ruled A.D. 14–37) were the two Roman emperors in power during the lifetime of Jesus.

The empire was eventually divided into western and eastern halves, with the dividing line just east of Italy. The western empire collapsed in A.D. 476 when a German warlord by the name of Odoacer dethroned the last western emperor. The eastern half, known as the Byzantine Empire, would continue for another thousand years until 1453, when the Ottoman Turks captured Constantinople.

An Empire Falls

The so-called "fall" of the Roman Empire was more of a steady decline. Even though the fall of Rome is often fixed at the year A.D. 476, when a barbarian warlord conquered the city, the end of the empire really can't be pinned to one factor. Possible explanations include moral corruption and social laziness, environmental factors, and poor government; maybe all such factors played a role.

What did modern civilization inherit from the Romans? A bit of government and law, architectural and engineering skills, and some fine literature. The language of old Rome, Latin, was standard for both science and the Roman Catholic Church until relatively recently.

Meanwhile, Back in Palestine ...

Now that you know something about the Romans, let's go back to Palestine and see where they come in. After the Jews shook off the Greeks, they experienced a bit of independence that lasted about 80 years. The Jewish territory of Judah was greatly expanded during those years to incorporate a good bit of old Palestine. Political infighting amongst the rulers, though, did not help when the Roman general Pompey was engaged in collecting territories in the Eastern Mediterranean for Rome.

Pompey acquired Palestine in 63 B.C., and a Jewish king who promised loyalty to Rome was put in place. In 40 B.C., with the backing of Octavian and others, Herod ("the Great") was confirmed as king of the Roman provinces in Palestine and effectively took power three years later. By the way, there was more than one King Herod. Don't confuse Herod "the Great" who ruled from 37 to 4 B.C. with Herod Antipas, who ruled part of Palestine (4 B.C.–A.D. 39) during the time of Jesus' ministry.

Herod soon became greatly despised by a large number of his Jewish subjects. He was loyal to the unpopular Romans and was a megalomaniac. Plus he was mean and was quick to execute nearly anyone he found threatening or annoying.

Despite his many faults, Herod's greatest accomplishments were probably his construction projects, which were carried out with the advantage of Roman technology and engineering. Apart from greatly expanding the Temple (see Chapter 15), he built a palace and other buildings in Jerusalem resembling those that might be found in Rome. Some of his other projects include the following:

♦ Herod took an old Phoenician port and turned it into a magnificent harbor and city, which he named Caesarea in honor of Julius Caesar. Builders used concrete to construct a giant breakwater topped by warehouses; a planned city was also built nearby. A sophisticated Roman-style aqueduct brought water into the city.

The old Roman aqueduct built to bring water to Herod's port city of Caesarea still looks good after 2,000 years!

(David Moyer collection)

♦ Masada, a beautiful fortress and palace, was built on a desert mountaintop near the Dead Sea. (Ironically, this would be the site of a last stand by Jewish rebels against the Roman army in A.D. 73.)

♦ Herodium was an amazing fortified palace which featured an artificial cone-shaped mountain. The tomb of Herod was said to be part of the structure but it has yet to be found.

After the death of Herod in the year 4 B.C., the Jewish/Roman kingdom was divided among his sons. One of these sons, Herod Agrippa (ruled 4 B.C.–A.D. 39), ruled the area of Galilee that included Nazareth, the hometown of Jesus. Eventually, a Roman procurator, or governor, was assigned jurisdiction over the region that included Jerusalem. A man named Pontius Pilate served in this capacity during the latter years of Jesus' career.

Is That So!

As was common throughout the empire, taxes were collected from the various Roman subjects—a situation not well appreciated everywhere. The Romans were generally lenient toward people of other beliefs, including the Jews, allowing them to keep their temple and practice their religion as long as political stability remained intact. Threats to Roman control, however, were generally met with great brutality by troops stationed throughout the empire. Rebellions could be expected to end in massacres and executions.

Jewish Philosophies

By the first century A.D., there were several Jewish religious and political factions in Palestine. Although the Temple, spectacularly enlarged by Herod, continued the daily rituals, these factions were often at odds with each other. A volatile mixture of politics and religion was sure to complicate matters on occasions, and it did.

Pharisees

The Pharisees were a fairly popular group and promoted traditional religious practices. Although they insisted that the details of Jewish law be fulfilled, they were somewhat flexible in its interpretation. The Pharisees believed in the coming of a God-sent savior (the Messiah), life after death, heaven and resurrection, and a final judgment.

Sadducees

In opposition to the Pharisees were the Sadducees. This group believed in a very rigid interpretation of religious law. And all the business about heaven and resurrection? Forget about it! It's not surprising that they were often antagonists of the Pharisees. Many were priests, aristocrats, and wealthy individuals. They essentially disappeared after the Roman destruction of Jerusalem in A.D. 70.

Essenes

Yet another Jewish faction was called the Essenes. Not much is known about these people, who seem to be a marginal fringe-group. They reportedly lived in remote communes where they practiced agriculture and studied Jewish religious texts. Their beliefs were kept somewhat secret, but it seems clear that they wanted to separate themselves from the mainstream of religious practice that was centered in Jerusalem at the time. It is possible that the ruins found at Qumran near the site of the discovery of the Dead Sea Scrolls are the remains of an Essene community.

Zealots

There was also a political group referred to as the Zealots, whose goal was to rid Palestine of the Romans. They eventually attempted to overthrow their oppressors, and lost.

People and Places

The Samaritans were another Jewish group during New Testament times. They believed that only the Torah was Scripture and they built their own temple on Mt. Gerizim. Although sharing a common heritage, they were not very well liked by the other Jewish groups because they fell well outside the mainstream beliefs of the day. A small number can still be found in Israel today.

An Uneasy Climate

As you can see, Palestine in the first centuries B.C./A.D. was a complex and potentially volatile place. Most of the Jews wanted to be rid of the Romans, yet their survival depended on cooperation with them. It would be under this somewhat difficult set of circumstance that Jesus of Nazareth would live.

The Least You Need to Know

- ◆ Roman civilization borrowed heavily from the Greeks and the Etruscans.

- ◆ Although the Romans established a system of representative government, it was gradually transformed into an imperial dictatorship as laws were broken and power was abused.

- ◆ The Romans built a vast empire which especially benefited the Romans themselves, who were able to live a relatively luxurious existence.

- ◆ Palestine was added to the Roman Empire in 63 B.C., and Jewish kings such as Herod were allowed to rule as agents of Rome.

- ◆ There were several different Jewish sects in Palestine in the first centuries B.C./A.D., and they didn't necessarily all get along!

Where Jesus Walked

In This Chapter

- ◆ Jesus: the early years
- ◆ A controversial ministry
- ◆ Man, Messiah … or otherwise
- ◆ The Jesus of history
- ◆ Some interesting discoveries

As his followers, "Christians," will tell you, there has never been anything quite like the life and teachings of Jesus of Nazareth. There are deep theological meanings in most every story about Jesus and in every word he spoke. Theologians, philosophers, and historians have discussed his life and work for almost 2,000 years now with an immense variety of interpretations.

It's not the intention of this book to discuss the details and implications of such things as the virgin birth, miracles, and the resurrection, or what Jesus "really meant" when he said this or that. Although theological explanation might be occasionally necessary for explanatory purposes, in this chapter we're going to concentrate more on the situation of Jesus in his time and some of the evidence related to it.

The Gospel Truth

The "official" story of Jesus' life is found in the Christian portion of the Bible, the New Testament. Much of his life and teachings are described in the first few books of the New Testament, and the rest consists of commentaries about his teaching. The first four books are referred to as the *Gospels*.

The first three Gospel books, Matthew, Mark, and Luke, are very similar, suggesting that they may well have shared a common source or sources. Whereas these three books all have some of the characteristics of a historical narrative, the fourth Gospel, that of John, is quite different in its approach and spiritual tone.

Logos

The word *Gospel* is from the Greek word for "good news," and to Christians, the life and teachings of Jesus are considered to be good news for everybody.

Like all the other books in the Bible, we don't have the original manuscripts of the New Testament books. A few bits and pieces survive from the second century A.D., but the numbers greatly increase from that time on. These very early manuscripts are of great interest to scholars seeking to understand when and how these books were composed.

Born a Babe in Bethlehem

Before we examine some of the aspects of the life of Jesus, let's look at the origin of his name. The name Jesus in Hebrew is *Yeshua* and is similar to the name Joshua. The English name "Jesus" is derived from the Greek via Latin. "Christ" was not Jesus' last name. The word *Christ* is derived from the Greek word *christos*, which is a translation of the Hebrew term *mashiach*, or "Messiah." Thus, Christians will often refer to Jesus as Jesus [the] Christ, Christ Jesus, or just plain Christ.

People and Places

The town of Bethlehem is located just a few miles outside Jerusalem. Its name is composed of two Hebrew words, *Bet* and *Lechem*, which mean "House of Bread." It was David's hometown and the city in which, according to the Jewish prophet Micah, the Messiah was to be born.

The story surrounding Jesus' birth includes wondrous events involving angels, shepherds, and wise men from afar. At its core, we find a Jewish couple, Joseph and his pregnant fiancée Mary, traveling to Bethlehem to register for a Roman tax census. When they couldn't get a room at the local inn, Mary gave birth in a stable, and the baby's first cradle was a lowly manger.

When was Jesus born? We're not exactly sure, but it seems clear that he was born out of sync with our modern calendar. The Gospel of Luke tells us that Jesus was born while the Jewish king Herod the Great was still alive, which gives us an important clue. Because Herod is known to have died in 4 B.C., the birth of Jesus must have taken place in that year, or prior to it. A Roman census is mentioned in Luke, and some have argued that this event took place in 6 or 7 B.C. All this, of course, leads to the situation of Jesus having been born perhaps four years before his official calendar "birthday."

The newborn baby Jesus in the manger.

(Illustration by Gustave Doré)

In any event, we know King Herod was apparently still around when Jesus was born. According to the Gospel of Matthew, Herod was informed that a future "king of the Jews" had been born and perpetrated a massacre of all male children two years or younger in the vicinity of Bethlehem. The parents of Jesus were tipped off and fled with the baby to Egypt.

The Unclear Early Years

Upon the death of Herod, Jesus and his parents returned and settled in the town of Nazareth in the Galilee region. There's not a whole lot about his childhood in the Bible. His father was a carpenter, and he had brothers and sisters. His brothers were James, Joseph, Judas, and Simon; the names of his sisters are not recorded in the Bible. Jesus had a traditional Jewish upbringing, including being circumcised on the eighth day after his birth.

There are stories about the early years of Jesus that don't appear in the Bible. These other "Gospels" include miraculous childhood incidents and sayings, but have been rejected as not authentic and lacking in theological value by the compilers of the New Testament.

As far as the Bible is concerned, we next find Jesus at age 12 accompanying his parents to Jerusalem to celebrate Passover. On the way home, they notice that he's missing and return to Jerusalem to search for him. When he's eventually found, he's at the Temple, dazzling the scholars. When his worried parents reprimand him, he answers, "Did you not know that I must be in my Father's house?" (Luke 2:49) He went home with his parents and was no doubt a good boy, although they must have had quite a time raising such a child.

This and That
Jesus probably spoke two languages, possibly three. The standard language of the region during his lifetime was Aramaic. The Scriptures, in which he was well versed, were written in Hebrew. He may also have spoken Greek, a language widely spoken in the region as a result of the Hellenization brought by earlier Greek rulers.

After the story about the Temple, the Bible provides no details regarding the life and whereabouts of Jesus from age 12 to 30, when he began his ministry. Given the profound impact of what we know of his life, it's not surprising that all manner of theories have appeared to explain what was going on during the undocumented years. Some say that he dutifully worked with dad in the carpenter's shop. Others claim he was on a spiritual quest. Was he, for example, living an ascetic life in the desert with a group of monklike Jews known as the Essenes? We don't really know, and there is no evidence to firmly indicate what he might have been doing.

The Ministry Begins

Jesus' ministry is thought to have begun when he was around 30 years old, and may have lasted up to three years before his execution. It begins with an encounter with an interesting fellow known as John the Baptist, who seems to have been a bit of a wild man. The Bible describes him as living in the desert, wearing clothes of camel hair, and eating locusts and wild honey. John had his own ministry going. He preached that people should repent of their sins and presided over a ceremony of symbolic purification in water, or baptism.

As recorded in the Gospels, Jesus was baptized by John and thereafter received a divine commissioning: "And when he came up out of the water, immediately he saw the heavens opened and the Spirit descending upon him like a dove; and a voice came from heaven, 'Thou art my beloved Son; with thee I am well pleased.'" (Mark 1:10–11)

It isn't the place of this book to go into depth about all of Jesus' teachings; there are scores and scores of other volumes that address these. (Two good resources are *The Complete Idiot's Guide to the Bible*, now in its second edition, by Jim Bell and Stan Campbell; and *The Complete Idiot's Guide to the Life of Christ* by William Grimbol.) In summary, however, he taught love and compassion and was a great advocate of forgiveness. Like John the Baptist, he preached about the need for repentance and lived his life as an example for others to follow.

Jesus was based in his home territory of Galilee and in particular, the town of Capernaum, where he preached in the synagogue. As he toured about, he collected a dozen close enthusiastic followers, or disciples. As the teachings of Jesus touched hearts, his followers steadily grew in number.

> **Thus Saith**
>
> Jesus was once asked what was the greatest commandment. This is how he answered: "You shall love the Lord your God with all your heart, and with all your soul, and with all your mind. This is the great and first commandment. And a second is like it. You shall love your neighbor as yourself. On these two commandments depend all the law and the prophets." (Matthew 37–40)

Today, the ruins of a third- or fourth-century synagogue can be seen in Capernaum. Archaeologists have found the remains of an even earlier one underneath, perhaps dating from the time of Jesus and maybe the very one in which he taught. The disciples came from a variety of backgrounds. Several were fishermen who worked the waters of the Sea of Galilee, which is featured in several great stories of the New Testament. In 1986, when the water in the Sea of Galilee was low, the remains of an ancient boat were discovered dating to around the first century A.D. Although it can't be proven that this interesting artifact has anything directly to do with a Bible story, the "Jesus Boat" is an exciting relic reminiscent of the life of Jesus.

Jesus teaching in a synagogue.

(Illustration by Gustave Doré)

Miracles and Signs

The ministry of Jesus is heavily punctuated with accounts of wonderful activities including many healings, exorcisms, and even a couple raisings from the dead. To many theologians, these miracle stories are not simply devices to convince people that Jesus is divine, but contain within them metaphorical meanings of great spiritual significance.

Running into Trouble

A lot of what Jesus did and said flew in the face of the dominant Jewish groups of his day, the Sadducees and especially the Pharisees (see Chapter 19). Jesus highly criticized the Pharisees as pious fools and hypocrites. He taught that it wasn't enough just to go through the motions of following God's law, but it was necessary to live the spirit of the law as well.

The Pharisees considered Jesus a radical, a heretic, and a blasphemer. Among other things, Jesus broke social rules and seemed to ignore the rigidly interpreted religious laws of his day. For example, he readily socialized with prostitutes, tax collectors, and lepers. The Pharisees condemned Jesus for "working" on the Sabbath even when he assisted individuals who needed his help. Rumors that he might be more than just a man were considered blasphemy.

Is This the Messiah?

Judaism has long had a tradition that at some time in history, when things are really bad, God will send a deliverer, a savior who will right wrong and establish a godly kingdom. Some of the prophets of the Old Testament spoke of such an individual, or *Messiah*, and longed for the day of his coming.

In the Old Testament, some of the prophets described the coming Messiah, and Christians believe that Jesus is a perfect match to the picture from his birth to his resurrection. The Messiah, for one thing, was expected to be a descendent of David, and there are genealogies in the New Testament that make an effort to trace the lineage of Jesus back to this royal ancestor. But is he really the Messiah?

His followers seemed to believe so, and Jesus is reported to have implied it on several occasions. Skeptics, however, will say that some of the verses describing the Messiah were taken out of context, or even mistranslated when applied to Jesus. More important, the Jews of his time, as is still the case today, do not believe that Jesus fulfilled their requirements of the anticipated Deliverer.

Logos

The **Messiah** is an awaited savior sent from God to deliver his people from oppression and to restore the world. Prophecies predicting his coming are found in the Old Testament. Christians believe that this Messiah is Jesus.

The heavily taxed and Roman-dominated Jews of first-century Palestine were looking for a strongman-leader, a charismatic and powerful king who would relieve them of their oppression. This was their expectation of the Messiah. Instead, peaceful Jesus came along, speaking in parables, and this was certainly not what many were seeking at the time. Jesus himself promised that after his death he would come again, and the scenarios for this return call for physical restoration and judgment of the kind that the Jews expect.

Man or God?

Being the Messiah is one thing, but was, and is, Jesus also God? Jesus occasionally referred to himself as Son of Man or Son of God; others will say that we are all children of God, and such titles were not uncommon in the culture of Jesus' day. Some see it spelled out in the opening verses of the Gospel of John that are in some ways as profound as those of Genesis:

> In the beginning was the Word, and the Word was with God, and the Word was God. He was in the beginning with God; all things were made through him, and without him was not anything made that was made. In him was life, and the life was the light of men. The light shines in the darkness, and the darkness has not overcome it … The true light that enlightens every man was coming into the world. He was in the world, and the world was made through him, yet the world knew him not. He came to his own home, and his own people received him not. But to all who received him, who believed in his name, he gave power to become children of God; who were born, not of blood nor of the will of the flesh nor of the will of man, but of God. And the Word became flesh and dwelt among us, full of grace and truth; we have beheld his glory, glory as of the only Son from the Father … And from his fullness have we all received, grace upon grace. For the law was given through Moses; grace and truth came through Jesus Christ. No one has ever seen God; the only Son, who is in the bosom of the Father, he has made him known.

Many Christian interpreters believe that "the Word" was Jesus, who was one and the same with God.

This and That

Although millions of Christians follow Jesus as their Messiah, there are many who do not believe that Jesus is God or even the Messiah. To Muslims, Jesus is one in a line of great prophets leading up to the last and highest, Mohammed. Jews do not feel that he met the criteria for the Messiah that many are still waiting for.

The Final Days

The Gospels tell us much about the last days of Jesus and provide insights into some of the political and religious dynamics of the day. The Jewish authorities were growing tired of Jesus and wanted him eliminated. His growing number of followers were likewise disliked and making many nervous, especially when the Messianic term *king* was implied.

The story begins when Jesus and his disciples traveled to Jerusalem for Passover. At what was likely a Passover meal, Jesus informed his disciples that his time was short, although he had been dropping clues about his departure for some time. That same night he was arrested by an angry mob who took him to the High Priest, Caiaphas. He was questioned and considered to be blasphemous and the Jewish high religious court, the Sanhedrin, likewise found him guilty.

Under Roman rule, the Jews weren't allowed to execute someone for such an offense so they sent him to the Roman governor, Pontius Pilate, in hopes of a harsh judgment. Pilate found no reason to have Jesus executed.

Because Jesus was from Galilee, Pilate turned him over for judgment to the Jewish king of that region, Herod Antipas, who then sent Jesus back to the Roman officials. Pilate seemed to be somewhat sympathetic to Jesus, but he finally gave in to cries for his execution, and, as he said, washed his hands of the whole thing. Although Jesus was basically found innocent, it was expedient to have him executed. And he was.

Jesus was executed in a most cruel and painful Roman form of torture: crucifixion. Crucifixion involved the suspension of the condemned person from a crossbar affixed to a vertical post. The individual's arms were spread out and the hands were tied to the bar, and the feet to the post. In its most brutal form, as practiced on Jesus, nails were driven though the hands or wrists and feet to assist in pinning the condemned to the structure.

The crucifixion of Jesus.

(Illustration by Gustave Doré)

Is That So!

How did Jesus die? There have been medical studies to suggest that crucifixion causes eventual asphyxiation, an inability to breathe. Others have disputed this and suggest shock caused by the Romans' penchant for breaking the legs of the condemned on the cross causes death (although the Gospels don't report that Jesus' legs were broken). It's plausible that some crucified people might have survived for days before succumbing to dehydration and exposure.

Short Stay in the Tomb

Jesus was removed from the cross and taken to a respectable tomb donated by a man named Joseph of Arimathea. The typical Jewish rock-cut tomb was closed with a heavy stone and placed under guard. The disciples and relatives of Jesus were thoroughly distraught. A few days later, the Gospels tell us, visitors to the tomb were surprised to find the guards gone and the stone rolled away from the entrance. An angel at the tomb reported that Jesus had risen from the dead.

Even those who had witnessed the various miracles Jesus performed during his lifetime found it difficult to believe that he was no longer dead, but it is said that he appeared on a number of occasions to his surprised and overjoyed disciples. After 40 days of sporadic visits, Jesus was seen to ascend into heaven, and he promised that someday he would return.

The Ultimate Sacrifice

The death and resurrection of Jesus are of the utmost importance to Christian theology. Jesus is seen to represent an unblemished (in this case, sinless) sacrificial lamb. Like the lambs sacrificed once a year during Yom Kippur to atone for the people's sins, Jesus, as the Son of God (if not God himself), took on the burden of the sins of humanity.

This ultimate sacrifice is seen as eternal by those who are willing to believe and ask God for forgiveness. The resurrection demonstrates the unique status of Jesus and gives hope to believers that they too will experience a resurrected life in heaven after death.

The Historical Jesus

There are some skeptics who have a hard time believing that Jesus actually existed. Lest there be any concerns that we're dealing with a King Arthur, Achilles, or some other legendary character, most scholars agree that an individual named Jesus did actually exist in Palestine during the first century A.D.

For those who question the historical reliability of the New Testament, there are a few outside sources that also attest to his existence. The best-known mention of Jesus is found in the writings of the Jewish historian Flavius Josephus. In his record of Jewish history, *The Antiquities of the Jews* (18:63–64), he writes:

> At this time there was a wise man who was called Jesus. And his conduct was good, and [he] was known to be virtuous. And many people from among the Jews and the other nations became his disciples. Pilate condemned him to be crucified and to die. And those who had become his disciples did not abandon his discipleship. They reported that he had appeared to them three days after his crucifixion and that he was alive; accordingly, he was perhaps the Messiah concerning whom the prophets have recounted wonders. And the Christian community named after him has survived to this day.

This famous statement by Josephus is somewhat controversial. Other translations have been made that have him demonstrating "surprising feats" and boldly asserting that "He was the Messiah" who had been "restored to life." There has been some obvious Christian editing in such versions, as there is no evidence that Josephus was a believer and, thus, he would not be expected to make such bold statements.

In the centuries that followed the time of Jesus, some enthusiastic Christians visited the Holy Land in an attempt to visit the very places where biblical events took place. One such tourist, Helena, the mother of the Roman emperor Constantine, visited Palestine in A.D. 326 and identified a number of such places. The exact spot of Jesus' birth, for example, was noted in Bethlehem.

Churches were built and rebuilt and a few visitors today might be skeptical that they really match locations from the life of Jesus. The Church of the Holy Sepulcher in Jerusalem, for one, is a huge, ornate, domed edifice inside a crowded walled city built over the alleged site of the tomb of Jesus. Investigations, however, have shown that the supposed tomb seems to date to the appropriate time and could very well be authentic.

People and Places

Flavius Josephus (c. A.D. 37–100) was a Jew living in Palestine during the first century A.D. Although he participated in a revolt against the Romans, he was captured and later became a Roman translator and historian. Two of his principle works, *The Jewish Wars* and *The Antiquities of the Jews*, provide valuable insights into the history of his times.

Pieces of the Past

Helena and many others who followed also sought souvenirs from the life of Jesus to bring back to Europe. The Crusaders were particularly known for this and alleged pieces of the "True Cross," nails from the crucifixion, and even supposed bones from the disciples of Jesus were removed and cherished back home.

Perhaps the most famous Holy Land "souvenir" is the Shroud of Turin, a piece of cloth bearing an image of a crucified man, which some purport to be the burial cloth of Jesus. While some have proclaimed it to be a medieval forgery, others remain convinced that it is indeed the burial cloth of Jesus. Whatever it might be, the process that produced the image on the cloth remains somewhat of a mystery. The Shroud of Turin is housed in a church in Turin, Italy.

Any discovery related to the time of Jesus usually generates considerable excitement. Do you remember those stone burial boxes called *ossuaries* that I mentioned in Chapter 16? Some of them have provided some very interesting connections with the story of Jesus!

Bones of the High Priest

In 1990, contractors came across a tomb in a Jerusalem neighborhood dating to around the time of Jesus. The tomb contained several stone boxes containing bones. One held the remains of a man about 60 years old whose name is identified on the box as Joseph son of Caiaphas. It's probable that this could be the family burial place of the very High Priest who presided during the last days of Jesus.

Another Roman Victim

In the 1970s, a Jewish tomb was found in Jerusalem with an ossuary containing the bones of a young man crucified during the first century A.D. Interestingly, two bones of the foot were found pierced through with a large nail. A fragment of wood was attached to the back as if ripped off when the body was torn free from the cross. One of the victim's lower leg bones appeared to have been shattered by a hard blow. This discovery provides one of the few pieces of physical evidence for the brutal Roman practice of crucifixion.

The Brother of Jesus?

In October 2002, some exciting news was announced. Another ossuary from the vicinity of Jerusalem was presented to the public for the first time. Scratched on its surface in the Aramaic script is the name, "James, son of Joseph, brother of Jesus."

The authenticity is being argued but it looks pretty good! If it is real, it's possible that this could be the earliest known evidence for Jesus (and his brother) outside of the Bible.

What do these artifacts mean? To many, they might confirm what the biblical traditions already say; Christianity, however, is based on faith and such discoveries are really only icing on the cake. For skeptics, they are points to ponder. For archaeologists, they are yet more interesting pieces of a giant ancient puzzle.

 Thus Saith

The truth is, it is not Jesus as historically known, but Jesus spiritually arisen within men, that is significant for our time, and can help it.

—Albert Schweitzer, *The Quest of the Historical Jesus* (1906)

Some Final Comments

The life and teachings of Jesus changed history. But did this all really happen, and if so, what does it mean? Who was this man named Jesus and what was he really trying to say? These questions were asked during his own time, and continue to be asked nearly 2,000 years later.

The Least You Need to Know

- ◆ Jesus was born in a town called Bethlehem sometime around 4 B.C. Not much is known of his early years, and there are few stories of his childhood in the Bible.

- ◆ The ministry of Jesus is characterized by a variety of miracles and righteous teachings emphasizing love, compassion, and a sincere adherence to the spirit of God's law.

- ◆ Christians believe that Jesus was the Messiah as prophesied in the Old Testament.

- ◆ According to the Gospels, Jesus was crucified, died, and was resurrected.

- ◆ Whatever you might believe about who Jesus is or was, he was a real person who lived during the first century A.D.

- ◆ Archaeological discoveries relating to the life and times of Jesus continue to be made.

Chapter 21

Building the Church

In This Chapter

♦ Life after Jesus

♦ A man named Paul

♦ Missionary activities

♦ Persecution and rebellion

♦ A little church history

The death and resurrection of Jesus was not the end, but just the beginning. The New Testament books that follow the Gospels record the spread of the message of Jesus and provide the foundation for the development of the Christian faith.

Although Jesus and his followers were Jews living in Palestine, the faith would quickly spread elsewhere. What would become known as Christianity developed as a universal religion available to anyone who would accept it.

Sharing the Word

The book that immediately follows the Gospels is called the Book of Acts, or the Acts of the Apostles. It is one of the most amazing books of the New Testament. Stories of incredible events abound. Jesus departed, and his followers were left to make sense of it all and to spread the word.

Not long after Jesus ascended into heaven, his most devoted followers got active. There were now about 120 of them, led by the disciple Peter. On the Jewish festival of Shavuot (also known as Pentecost), the disciples were gathered and Acts tells us that amazing things began to happen: "And suddenly a sound came from heaven like the rush of a mighty wind, and it filled all the house where they were sitting. And there appeared to them tongues as of fire, distributed and resting on each one of them. And they were all filled with the Holy Spirit and began to speak in other tongues, as the Spirit gave them utterance." (Acts 2:2)

This would be quite startling to the cosmopolitan crowds of Jerusalem, who heard preaching in their own diverse languages coming from this group of apparently ordinary people.

The speaking in tongues, along with Peter's dramatic teaching on the subject of repentance, resulted in a large number of converts on that very day. And the wonders didn't stop with verbal communication abilities. The disciples were able to heal people by invoking the name of Jesus. Peter was even able to raise a fellow Christian from the dead.

These sorts of activities didn't please the established religious authorities, who hoped the Jesus phenomenon would be over after his death. Not surprisingly, the disciples found themselves in jail from time to time. On one occasion in Jerusalem, Acts tells us that an angel let them out of a locked prison, after which they were found back at the Temple preaching.

Bad Boy Turned Good

One of the most unlikely candidates to be a follower of Jesus was a man named Saul, from Tarsus in Asia Minor. Saul was a highly educated and observant Jew, a Pharisee and a Roman citizen no less, who looked at these renegade Christians as blasphemers against his own religion. Intolerant of these radicals, Saul actively persecuted Christians when the opportunity arose, and even sought permission from the high priest in Jerusalem to punish any he might find while on a trip to Damascus in Syria.

Saul Sees the Light

Saul got a big surprise on his way to Damascus when he was hit with a big heavenly light and heard the voice of Jesus. "Saul, Saul, why do you persecute me?" He was thereafter blind for three days, after which he regained his sight and converted to Christianity. One can only imagine the fear and skepticism that must have arisen among the Christians on hearing that Saul was now one of them. Saul, who would later be better known by his Roman name Paul, began preaching in the synagogues of Damascus, and even had to be smuggled out of the city so he himself wouldn't receive the treatment he had formerly dished out!

The conversion of Saul of Tarsus.

(Illustration by Gustave Doré)

Sharing the Gospel

Paul went on to become the premier spreader of the Gospel to the non-Jewish world. He traveled far and wide and preached in such far-flung places as Arabia, Syria, Cyprus, Asia Minor, Macedonia, Athens, and Rome itself. He typically went to the synagogues first, where the message of Jesus would be understood in its Jewish context. In his wake were left many new congregations of believers in Jesus.

Much of the New Testament outside of the Gospels and Acts consists of letters written by Paul to various newly established Christian communities who required spiritual guidance and support. These include letters to congregations in such places as Ephesus and Galatia in Asia Minor; Thessalonica, Philippi, and Corinth in Greece; and Rome.

Jesus for Everyone?

With its roots in Judaism, there were some big questions that needed to be answered if the word of Jesus was going to spread. For example, was Jesus only for the Jews? This was answered quickly. The teachings of Jesus were not just for Jews, but for everyone. Another big question: How Jewish should non-Jewish Christians be? After all, the teachings of Jesus were rooted in the Hebrew Bible, whose prophecies served to legitimize Jesus as the Messiah among his followers.

Among Jewish converts, that last question wasn't too much of an issue, but to the outside world, like the Romans, Greeks, and assorted other non-Jews, such issues as kosher food and circumcision and full adherence to other Jewish laws might be big obstacles to conversion.

Kosher No More

The kosher food issue is dealt with in Acts 10:9–16, which describes how Peter fell into a trance and had a vision, in which a giant sheet descended from heaven containing all kinds of food, including reptiles and other biblically unclean beasts of all sorts. A voice accompanying the vision revealed that all foods were now clean.

Beyond the Physical

Circumcision, too, had to be addressed. It might be a fair statement that however appealing the Christian message was, the idea of such a physical initiation among the grown men of the non-Jewish world was not. Like many of the teachings of Jesus, circumcision became understood as a purely spiritual demand and not a necessary physical one.

Thus Saith

Paul addressed the circumcision issue with the following: "For in Christ Jesus neither circumcision nor uncircumcision is of any avail, but faith working through love."
—1 Galatians 5:6

It was decided that it was more important to be circumcised in one's heart than in one's body. That is, the covenant between God and an individual was more importantly personal. One could be physically circumcised as a cultural reflection of Abraham's original covenant, but the actual spiritual relationship with God was the matter of overwhelming substance.

Convicted for Their Convictions

The followers of Jesus tended to be an outspoken lot, unafraid to address their detractors. The religious authorities in Jerusalem, in particular, were not amused by these bold upstarts who had few qualms about chastising even the most senior of officials. Imprisonments and beatings took place, and it wasn't very long before the Christians began accumulating martyrs.

For example, a man named Stephen, who boldly proclaimed his faith before the authorities, was thrown out of town and stoned to death as an accused blasphemer. This would start a trend of sorts, and many of the early followers of Jesus met unpleasant deaths. All but one of the original disciples of Jesus are said to have met horrible deaths: Six were crucified, one hanged himself, and the others were stoned, stabbed, or beheaded.

The persecution of Christians became quite a sport in the Roman world in certain times and places. Some of the Roman emperors, such as Caligula and Nero, found ready victims among those who refused to bow down to the official gods of the state. Many Christians were publicly executed in arenas full of cheering crowds. Burning at the stake and being fed to wild animals were not unusual forms of execution.

People and Places
The Roman emperor Nero (reigned A.D. 54–68), whom most historians agree was genuinely insane, is said to have blamed the Christians for a massive fire that broke out in Rome during his reign. Needless to say, the Christians were merely a ready excuse, and many were unjustly executed as a result.

The Jews Rebel

As you know, there was a tremendous amount of resentment against the Roman occupation of Palestine during the time of Jesus. Militant Jews plotted against the empire and sporadic outbreaks of violence occurred, but two major rebellions against the Romans would change the Jews and their religion forever.

The first major Jewish rebellion took place between A.D. 66 and 73. In A.D. 70, the Romans under the emperor Vespasian attacked Jerusalem and completely destroyed the Temple. Fighting continued, and in A.D. 73, one of the most dramatic recorded events of the rebellion occurred. Groups of Jewish rebels holed up on Herod's mountaintop fortress of Masada were finally subdued when the Romans patiently built a ramp up its steep flanks. The traditional story tells that the rebels committed suicide rather than become slaves to the Romans, and the huge ramp up the side of Masada can still be seen today.

In A.D. 130, the emperor Hadrian rebuilt Jerusalem and renamed it Aelia Capitolina. A temple to the god Jupiter was erected on the Temple Mount, and two years later, a second major rebellion took place that was led by the clever and charismatic Simon Bar-Kokhba. Although there were some initial successes, the rebellion failed in 135 and thousands were slaughtered by the Romans.

There were some who saw Simon Bar-Kokhba as the promised savior of the Jewish people, the Messiah who would defeat the Romans, serve as king, and initiate a new Messianic age. The horrible defeat of his rebellion and his own death proved that any such hopes were sadly misplaced.

When the Romans destroyed the Temple, they destroyed the very center of Jewish worship and the religion of the Jews was thereafter forever changed. What arose in its place, however, was what is called "Rabbinic Judaism." Instead of a central place of worship with a staff of priests and sacrifices, the synagogues and their teachers, rabbis, took on a new and important role in shaping the Jewish faith. A new kind of Judaism would emerge and spread to many parts of the world as Jews fled oppression or otherwise settled in different lands.

The Believers Multiply

Despite the persecution, the message of Jesus spread far and wide, and many churches were established. Mark, the supposed author of the Gospel of Mark, is credited with establishing the Christian church in Egypt. The disciple Peter is considered to be the original patriarch of the church founded in Rome. As such, he was the first pope of the Roman Catholic Church, the largest Christian group in the world today.

The ruins of a Greek temple in Corinth, Greece. Because of the missionary efforts by Paul and others, the teachings of Jesus spread from Palestine into the non-Jewish world where many gods were worshipped.

(David Moyer collection)

In an ironic change of events, the Roman Empire that once tortured and executed the followers of Jesus became formally Christian under the emperor Constantine in the fourth century A.D. In the battle of Zeus and Jupiter against Jesus, Jesus won.

Coming to an Agreement

As the original followers of Jesus died off, there were still some important questions left to be answered. Some of these involved the very nature of Jesus and his associa-tion with God. Several contrary ideas flourished and to settle the matter, the emperor Constantine held a conference in A.D. 325 at Nicaea, located in modern-day Turkey. One of the results was a creed that outlined the Christian beliefs that would be considered official or "orthodox." Among other things, the Nicene Creed, as it is known, defines Jesus as one person of a Trinity which sees God, Jesus, and the Spirit of God which works through humans (the "Holy Spirit") as three persons of the same one God. Other conferences were held and the center of the Church was established at Rome with the pope as its spiritual leader.

Thus Saith

With all its fidelity to the spirit and style of the Jewish scholars of his time, the teaching of Jesus did nevertheless pass beyond the boundary, to stand in a place of its own. Had it not done so, it most probably would not have created a world religion.

—Sholem Asch, *What I Believe* (1941)

A Church Evolves

Christian philosophy and history developed in a number of different ways that this book couldn't even begin to tackle. In summary, there were still significant differences in belief, however, and power and politics proved to be huge factors. In 1054, several of the churches in the eastern portion of the old Roman Empire split off from Rome and today are referred to as Eastern Orthodox churches. Each has its own patriarch, or spiritual leader, analogous to the Roman Catholic pope.

Meanwhile, most of Western Europe fell under the domain of the Roman Catholic Church. In the 1500s, critics of the beliefs and practices of the Church began a move-ment known as the Reformation. The result was the formation of a number of "Protestant" churches which became separated from the overwhelming power of Rome. Reformation leaders such as Martin Luther (1483–1546) and John Calvin (1509–1564) inspired churches that include the Lutherans, Presbyterians, and Methodists, which continue to thrive today.

Another major split with the Roman Catholic Church occurred in 1533, when English King Henry VIII refused to take orders from the pope and set up the Church of England, also known as the Anglican Church. Although the Anglican Church was following in the Protestant spirit, its members do not consider themselves Protestants, and even today it continues to be closer to the Catholic churches than Protestant churches in many important issues of doctrine and worship style.

The Christian church continued to change as European colonization of the Americas opened up new prospects for the Christian religion. The New World became a haven for religious groups escaping persecution in Europe, or just looking for a place to do their thing.

With the establishment of the United States, a country guaranteeing religious freedom, new groups were formed, old ones split, and the end result is the dizzying variety we find today. Meanwhile, the Roman Catholic Church is still alive and well, and there is scarcely a place on this planet to which one religious group or another hasn't sent a missionary to spread the Word.

Something for Everyone

Check the telephone directory of any big city and you will see dozens of different churches listed. All are followers of Jesus with their own special history or their own special spin on the meaning of Christianity. Who's right? Is this what Jesus had in mind? Maybe not, who knows? But it certainly is a testament to the wide appeal of Jesus' teachings.

Is That So!

Whereas the tendency for religious groups is to split, an interesting exception occurred in 1988. Three separate branches of the Lutheran church—the American Lutheran Church, the Lutheran Church in America, and the Associated Evangelical Lutheran Churches—combined to form a single body, the Evangelical Lutheran Church in America. Still other groups of Lutherans remain outside this body.

In this modern age, it's interesting and hopeful to see a number of groups trying to find common ground rather than perpetuate divisiveness. Many Jews, Christians, and other groups, within and among themselves, are attempting to engage in meaningful dialogue.

Some Christian groups, long at odds with each other, participate in what is known as the *ecumenical* movement. Their aim is to find understanding and unity with each other so they can all get along and maybe even learn to appreciate one another, despite their seemingly irreconcilable differences.

Today, the Word is still being spread. New churches are still founded and the Bible continues to be translated and published in new ways and in different languages. And all of this, from a wandering teacher in Palestine with a profound message 2,000 years ago!

Logos

The **ecumenical** movement, or ecumenism, involves dialogue between different religious groups in order to find common ground and understanding.

The Least You Need to Know

♦ The disciples of Jesus carried on his ministry after his death by spreading the word and performing miracles.

♦ Paul, a former oppressor of Christians, became an early missionary and one of the most important interpreters of the spiritual philosophy of Jesus.

♦ The Roman defeat of the Jews in Palestine set the Jewish religion on another course.

♦ The Christian church has evolved through a series of religious and political refinements and disputes to its present diverse forms.

Part **6**

The World of the Bible Today

We're going to wrap things up with just a couple more chapters to help you pursue what I hope is a heightened interest in the Bible and its world. The Holy Land is an exciting and fascinating place to visit today and Chapter 22 will give you a few travel tips. And if your interest has indeed been stimulated, the last chapter will give you a number of suggestions on how you can go about learning more about the wonderful and intriguing subject of the world of the Bible.

Chapter 22

Visiting the Holy Land

In This Chapter

◆ Some modern Israeli history

◆ A visit to the Jewish state

◆ A glimpse of Jordan

◆ Checking out Egypt

◆ Learning a few simple phrases

It's interesting reading about the world of the Bible, but seeing the sights and sites themselves is truly a special experience. Few return from such a visit to the Holy Land without agreeing that it was very informative, if not inspirational.

In this chapter, you'll find a bit of information about the Holy Land today and what you might expect if you choose to travel there. There is an incredible amount to see and it's really not that hard to make it happen.

Welcome to Israel

As you know, much of the action in the Bible took place in Palestine, a region that has been under many jurisdictions over the last thousands of years. Today, it is the country of Israel along with some adjacent territories.

Israel is a fascinating place. It's about the size of New Jersey and home to around 6.4 million people. Like America, it is an amazing cosmopolitan democracy and melting pot with citizens from all over the world. To understand the place, and to set the stage for comments about traveling there, a little historical review is very helpful.

Coming Home

As described in earlier chapters, the Israelites/Jews in the Promised Land suffered deportations by the Assyrians and Babylonians, culturally destructive practices under the Greeks, and the destruction of their center of worship under the Romans. Although a good many Jews persisted and stayed in Jerusalem and elsewhere in Palestine, many left for all parts of the world.

Holding on to Jewish heritage was often a difficult thing to do in Christian Europe, in the Islamic Near East, and elsewhere, but many persisted in maintaining their traditions nonetheless. In the late nineteenth century, the Zionist movement was born in Europe with the goal of establishing a Jewish homeland somewhere in the world where Jews could be free from persecution. Many areas were considered, including sites in North and South America, Africa, and Asia, but Palestine, where Jerusalem and many other important historic and religious sites lay, was the strong and sentimental favorite. Large waves of Jewish immigrants, especially from Europe, began coming to Palestine to settle and work the land. The region was then under the jurisdiction of the Turks, and many Arab residents complained about the newcomers while others sold them their land.

Logos

The term **Diaspora** is often applied in reference to the widespread dispersal of Jews throughout the world. Jewish populations can even be found in China, where a community was established centuries ago!

Palestine became a protectorate of the British as a result of World War I. Although the British gave a nod to continued Jewish immigration, they also told the Arab inhabitants that they would try to limit it. There were many outbreaks of violence, including against the British who were increasingly anxious to leave the situation. After World War II, the newly created United Nations addressed the problem by dividing the land of Palestine essentially into two pieces with the intent of creating side-by-side Jewish and Arab states. Jerusalem was divided in half with the Jews in the western portion. The Arab countries did not favor this arrangement and there was more violence, especially after the state of Israel was declared on May 14, 1948, with Jerusalem as its capital. Many Arabs in the new country left Israel feeling either unwelcome or with claims that they were forced out.

Wars and More Wars

After Israel was declared, several Arab countries joined together to try to wipe out the newborn state but failed. In 1967, another large-scale war took place and the result was to have a long-term effect in the region. Israel not only defeated several Arab armies, but it captured land from its neighbors including the Sinai Peninsula and the Gaza Strip from Egypt, the West Bank of the Jordan River from Jordan, and the Golan Heights from Syria. To the great joy of the Israelis, they also captured East Jerusalem, including the Temple Mount. Israel occupied these areas which included millions of Arabs who had fled in 1948 and were unhappy with the situation.

An even more intense war broke out in 1973 and Israel once again survived. Eventually a peace treaty was made with Egypt in 1979 and the Sinai was returned, but the Israelis continued to occupy the other territories which many saw as security buffer zones. Others, however, saw these lands as part of God's gift to the Jews as spelled out in the Bible and they began building settlements there. At present, there are numerous settlements in the occupied territories, especially in the West Bank. By the way, Jordan followed Egypt's example and made peace with Israel in 1994.

Map of modern Israel, including the occupied territories.

People and Places

Israel's population is approximately 80 percent Jewish and 15 percent Muslim; the rest are Christian or of other religious faiths. During the last two decades, the Jewish population increased by nearly one million due to large immigrations of people from such places as Russia and Ethiopia.

The Violence Continues

The former occupants of pre-Israel Palestine and those who live in the occupied territories have organized themselves under the name "Palestinians" and would like to be free of the Israeli occupation. Although many are quite peaceful, others resort to violence. While some Palestinians will settle for the creation of a peaceful Palestinian state in the territories, others will settle for nothing less than the destruction of Israel itself.

In 1987, a Palestinian uprising, or "intifada," took place. A serious peace deal came close just a few years ago but the terms were rejected by the Palestinian leadership. A second uprising took place beginning in 2000 and of this writing, it is still going on. This second set of events has been exceptionally violent, especially with a regular stream of suicide/homicide bombers sponsored by Palestinian extremist groups. The Israelis often retaliate and the cycle of violence continues.

This and That

For a more detailed explanation of the Middle East situation, see *The Complete Idiot's Guide to Middle East Conflict, Second Edition,* by Mitchell G. Bard (Alpha Books, 2003).

Is there hope for peace? I'd like to think so. There has to be an end to violence but there are some difficult things to settle, including the issue of Jewish settlements in the occupied territories and the status of Jerusalem, which the Palestinians would like to have as their capital as well. Peace for Israel and all its neighbors? It might just happen.

Let's Go on a Trip

With this historical summary in mind, it's a lot easier to understand some of the special situations involved in visiting Israel. Especially the fact that the country is very security oriented. If you fly to Israel, you will be extensively interviewed and your belongings will be thoroughly searched. You might receive another interview when you arrive and likely one when you leave. There will probably be soldiers at most places you go and even off-duty soldiers with weapons. Once you can get used to such security measures, though, Israel can really be a pleasant place!

To check on current safety concerns in the vicinity of Israel, contact the U.S. State Department, which issues regular bulletins. For general country information, see www.state.gov/r/pa/ei/bgn. For travel warnings, see travel.state.gov/travel_warnings.html.

Getting There

Israel can be reached on several major air carriers from Europe. El Al, Israel's national airline, also has direct flights from the United States, including New York and Los Angeles. If you're traveling around the Middle East, it's usually possible to cross into Israel by land from Egypt or Jordan. Some cruise ships also visit the country, usually calling at the Mediterranean port of Haifa.

There are also numerous tours available to the Holy Land. There are Jewish tours, Christian tours, and loads of other theme tours as well. The advantage of going on such a tour is that the planning is done for you. You'll probably be picked up at the airport, taken to hotels, and put on buses to visit a variety of sites. You won't get lost and guides will explain what you're seeing. If you don't like traveling with a lot of people or having your life planned, this might not appeal to you. Having said that, a well-organized tour will efficiently take you to the main attractions and if you fall in love with Israel, as many people do, you can always come back with a little experience under your belt. The same advice applies to Egypt or nearly any foreign country. See your travel agent or do a search on the Internet to find a tour that sounds just right.

> ### People and Places
>
> In modern Israel, it helps to know who is who because on Friday, the Muslim shops are closed; on Saturday, the Jewish shops are closed; and on Sunday, the Christian shops are closed.

Exploring on Your Own

Many people enjoy the challenge of planning and carrying out their own trip. Fortunately, there are several good guidebooks available to help you along. If you choose to go on your own, keep a few things in mind: The official languages of Israel are Hebrew and Arabic. Fortunately, English is a preferred second or even third language and it's usually possible to find someone with whom to communicate. Still, knowing a few native words in any foreign country is a great ice-breaker and a way of showing that you are truly interested in a foreign land. (See the end of this chapter for a few.) Keep in mind, though, that you can't necessarily go anywhere you want anytime you want. In a volatile place like Israel and elsewhere in the Middle East, things you can visit one day might be inaccessible the next.

My Two Cents' Worth

I am often asked which of the two options I prefer: traveling with a tour or alone. Being the independent type, I generally favor traveling alone, but I have also participated in tours that have been really great. If I had to offer one recommendation to a first-timer without a lot of travel experience outside of North America or Europe, I'd have to suggest the tour, especially for women traveling alone or in a small group. Again, you will get a good look at the most famous stuff and will have an opportunity to see whether this is a place you might wish to revisit.

> **This and That**
>
> Some of the Jewish immigrants to Palestine set up socialist working communities called *kibbutzim*. The first, called Degania Alef, was established in 1910. All property is owned by the kibbutz and is allocated to its members as needed. A stay on a kibbutz is a great way to spend time in Israel without spending much money. You will, however, be required to work!

Some tours allow free time so that you can explore a bit on your own. And there are dozens of ways that tourists on their own in any foreign land can "get into trouble," so to speak, and a tour will help you avoid such things. However, having spent a great deal of time traveling, I prefer to go on my own. On the other hand, you can do both. Start with a tour and schedule a few days afterward to explore a bit after you've gotten a feel for things.

Visiting the Holy City

There are dozens and dozens of places of interest to see in Israel and the territories. Take Jerusalem, for example:

- The Western Wall of the Temple Mount, the most holy site in Judaism

- The golden Dome of the Rock, one of the most holy sites in Islam

- Numerous sites related to the life of Jesus, including the Garden of Gethsemane, the Via Dolorosa, and the Church of the Holy Sepulcher

- Archaeological sites dating from the time of David and before and after

- The Israel Museum, home to many of the most important and interesting archaeological treasures from the Holy Land

- The Shrine of the Book, an exhibition of the Dead Sea Scrolls

- Yad Vashem, a somber memorial to the victims of the Holocaust

The Western Wall of the old Jewish Temple in Jerusalem is a sacred place of prayer for Jews from around the world.

(Courtesy of John Petersen)

Ancient sites and modern cities exist side by side in Israel and this is certainly true in Jerusalem. To the north in the Galilee region are more sites of Christian interest. In the West Bank, one can visit both modern and ancient Jericho and the site of Qumran, where the Dead Sea Scrolls were found. If you want to be baptized in the Jordan River in the manner of Jesus, that can be arranged. How about a mud bath in a resort near the Dead Sea or a visit to the dramatic mountaintop fortress of Masada? Yes, there is plenty to see and experience in Israel!

A trip to Israel can often be combined with visits to a couple other Biblical lands, Egypt and Jordan, both of which have made peace treaties with the Jewish state. Both are relatively easy to get to from North America or Europe. Egypt and Jordan are overwhelmingly Islamic, and Arabic is the language spoken. Keep in mind that there is no one universal form of spoken Arabic. There are a number of dialects, some of which are barely understood by other native speakers. The Arabic spoken in Egypt, for example, is different from that spoken in Morocco, which is different than the Arabic spoken by Palestinians or Saudis.

Thus Saith

The Israeli government is a parliamentary democracy composed of representatives of numerous political parties of all slants and then some. Politics is a subject of great discussion in Israel and thus the old comment, "Ask three Israelis a question and you'll get four opinions."

Welcome to Jordan!

On the east side of the Jordan River and the Dead Sea is, of course, Jordan. Jordan (formerly Transjordan) was home to the likes of the Moabites and Edomites. Jordan's modern capital, Amman, was the ancient capital of the Ammonites. A particular attraction of great international fame is the ancient Nabatean city of Petra. The country is vast and beautiful, with archaeological sites of all ages and numerous cultural activities and recreational opportunities. For a taste of the possibilities, see the website of the Jordan Tourism Board at www.see-jordan.com.

Although Israel has peace treaties with Egypt and Jordan, there are some serious misgivings regarding the Palestinian situation, so don't be surprised if you hear some angry comments from the locals. America's deep friendship with Israel is also regularly criticized.

The ancient Nabatean city of Petra is one of Jordan's most famous sites.

Egypt's Pyramids, Temples, and Tombs

There is no place in the world like Egypt! It's a crowded, noisy, fascinating place full of friendly people and natural beauty. It's also probably the world's biggest archaeological site. Most tourists gravitate to Cairo, Luxor, and Aswan but there are beautiful resorts on the Red Sea and the city of Alexandria has its own special charm. Like Israel and Jordan, lots of people fall in love with Egypt. Go on a tour or go on your own; either way, you'll have an interesting time.

One Big City

Cairo, Egypt's capital, is home to at least 16 million people. It's a lively place and the city never seems to sleep. There is much to see in this sprawling metropolis and for the tourist, there is no better place to start than at the Egyptian Museum, truly one of the most amazing collections of antiquities to be seen anywhere in the world. Located off Cairo's central square, it is a very large building and packed with exquisite items from Egypt's pharaonic past. Gallery after gallery will take you through the ages, and many of the original objects to be seen will be immediately recognizable to anyone who has taken a course in art history. There are sculptures in wood and stone, coffins, furniture, jewelry, and objects of daily life, and there is the mummy room (perhaps not for the squeamish). The museum's many highlights include the treasures from the tomb of Tutankhamen; the gold still gleams 3,000 years later!

For those who are fascinated with Islamic history and monuments, Cairo alone has enough to keep you busy for a long time. There are also Christian monuments here and there, especially in a section of the city known as "Old Cairo," and a Coptic Museum. The old Ben Ezra synagogue can also be found, a rare remnant of Jewish life in Egypt. Consult a guide book for the details.

Built to Last an Eternity

Outside of Cairo are two famous sites, Giza and Sakkara, where you'll find ancient cemeteries and artistic and engineering marvels. Giza, of course, is home to three famous pyramids, including the biggest and most controversial of them all, the Great Pyramid of Khufu (Cheops). The famous sphinx is there, as are many beautifully decorated tombs dating to Egypt's Old Kingdom. At Sakkara, the famous Step-Pyramid of Djoser is found among other impressive monuments and tombs.

The awesome Great Sphinx and the Pyramids at Giza are located just outside Cairo.

Is That So! _____

One of the most fascinating artifacts to be found in all of Egypt is a 4,600-year-old boat made from cedar wood which was found in a sealed pit at the base of the Great Pyramid. The boat is 142 feet long and is believed to have played a role in the funerary rites of the deceased King Khufu. It can be found in a special museum at the side of the pyramid.

King Tut's Hometown

There's a good reason Luxor is on just about everybody's itinerary to Egypt. It's the site of ancient Thebes, and astounding things can be seen on each side of the lovely Nile. The huge Luxor Temple and the massive temple complex of Karnak can be found on the east bank of the river. Remarkable mortuary temples to the likes of Hatshepsut, Rameses II, and Rameses III can be found on the west.

The Egyptians believed that the land of the dead was off in the west where the sun sets, and that's why a good many of the cemeteries are situated on that side of the river. The west bank of the Nile at Luxor contains thousands of tombs. A number of decorated tombs belonging to important ancient officials can be found there along with two major royal cemeteries, the Valley of the Kings and the Valley of the Queens. The Valley of the Kings contains the dramatic tombs of a veritable Who's Who of the Egyptian New Kingdom.

Way Down South

Quieter and smaller, to the south is Aswan—a real favorite for many people, where the pace of life seems much slower. There is much to see, including an excellent new Nubia Museum. South of Aswan can be seen the beautiful temple of Philae, saved from the flooding waters of the massive Aswan Dam which was completed in the 1970s. Even farther south are the huge temples of Abu Simbel, likewise saved from the dam and reconstructed on higher ground.

Egypt's people are friendly and generous and have a lively sense of humor. Don't ever expect things there to be just like you enjoy them at home, though. Egypt has its own speed and style. As can be said about virtually any new place you might visit, do your homework before you go so you'll know what you're getting into. Learn some of the cultural expectations on how to dress and behave, become familiar with the history, and get excited about trying new foods. You'll be glad you did.

This and That
A great way to see parts of southern Egypt is on a Nile cruise. These luxury boats ply the Nile usually between Luxor and Aswan, with stops at archaeological sites along the way.

Other Bible Lands

Outside of Israel, Jordan, and Egypt, other parts of the Near East can often be problematic to visit. Lebanon has improved dramatically in the last decade but can still be troublesome on occasion. Syria will deport you if it finds evidence in your passport that you have been in Israel. Iraq (Mesopotamia) and Iran (Persia) have much to offer but current hostilities suggest that it might be worth waiting until the political situations there improve. Keep in mind, though, that the average citizen in all of these countries just wants to live a happy life, and this we have in common.

Want to walk in the footsteps of Paul and trace the development of the early Christian church? Turkey, Greece, and Italy are waiting for you! There are even specialized Christian tours that will take you to such places as Ephesus, Corinth, and Rome! Check with your travel agent or surf the web. Or buy a good guidebook and plan your own trip.

The Polite Visitor

Last but by no means least, I would like to leave you with a few polite phrases that should be in the vocabulary of foreign visitors, wherever they may roam. Here are a few words in English followed by their equivalents in (Egyptian) Arabic and Hebrew:

- Hello!, "sa'ida!" "shalom!"

- Please, "minfadlak" (to a male), "minfadlik" (to a female), "bavakasha"

- Thank you! "shukran!" "todah!"

- My name is …, "ismi …," "shmi …"

- Yes, "aywa," "ken"

- No, "la'a," "lo"

- Good-bye! "masalama!" "shalom!"

The Least You Need to Know

- The modern state of Israel has been controversial since its very inception.

- Despite sporadic political turmoil, a visit to Israel is a fascinating way to explore the world of the Bible.

- Jordan offers beautiful scenery and stunning ancient monuments.

- Egypt is one of the most interesting tourist destinations on the planet.

- Do your homework, plan your trip carefully, and have a great time!

Chapter 23

Expanding Your Knowledge

In This Chapter

- ◆ Where to find more information
- ◆ Learning ancient languages
- ◆ Going on a dig
- ◆ The Bible on the Internet

We've covered a lot of ground in this book, but actually we've only skimmed the surface. For nearly every subject mentioned herein, there are dozens of books and articles and a wide variety of opinions. Hopefully, your interest in the subject of the Bible has greatly increased.

In this final chapter, I'd like to provide some suggestions on ways you can further your interest in the fascinating world of the Bible.

More to Read: Books and Magazines

As I mentioned, there is a wealth of books on various subjects. I've listed a number of very good volumes in Appendix B, and Appendix C also contains more information about some of the materials I mention in this chapter. I'll take advantage of the opportunity here, however, to shamelessly plug a few relevant books in the *Complete Idiot's Guide* series:

- *The Complete Idiot's Guide to the Bible, Second Edition* (Jim Bell and Stan Campbell)

- *The Complete Idiot's Guide to Biblical Mysteries* (Donald P. Ryan)

- *The Complete Idiot's Guide to Jewish History and Culture* (Benjamin Blech)

- *The Complete Idiot's Guide to the Life of Christ* (William R. Grimbol)

- *The Complete Idiot's Guide to Ancient Egypt* (Donald P. Ryan)

- *The Complete Idiot's Guide to the Roman Empire* (Eric Nelson)

- *The Complete Idiot's Guide to Lost Civilizations* (Donald P. Ryan)

There are a few really good magazines that deal with the world of the Bible (see Appendix C for subscription information). For all the news about the latest archaeological discoveries and scholarly debates, *Biblical Archaeology Review* is hard to beat! It comes out six times a year and there is usually something of interest for everybody in nearly every issue. And they're certainly not afraid to be controversial!

Biblical Archaeology Review is published by the *Biblical Archaeology Society*, an organization whose stated goal is to "educate the public about archaeology and the Bible through magazines, books, visual materials and seminars." They also produce two other magazines that are useful to those interested in the Bible: *Bible Review* and *Archaeology Odyssey*. *Bible Review* typically contains articles with insights and interpretations of various biblical stories and other texts. *Archaeology Odyssey* presents material on the ancient Near East and Mediterranean worlds (Greece, Rome, and so on).

Another magazine, *Near Eastern Archaeology* (formerly called *Biblical Archaeologist*), is a bit more scholarly than those noted earlier but very readable nonetheless. It comes out four times a year as published by the *American Schools of Oriental Research*.

> **People and Places**
>
> Hershel Shanks, the editor of *Biblical Archaeology Review*, used his magazine as a powerful forum that greatly helped in finally making the Dead Sea Scrolls accessible to the public.

Archaeology Magazine is very popular and is published by the *Archaeological Institute of America*. It contains articles about archaeology from around the world, including the biblical lands.

If Egypt is of special interest, *KMT Magazine*, "a modern journal of Egyptology," is outstanding and appears four times a year.

Back to School

Lots of churches, synagogues, colleges, and universities offer opportunities to further explore the Bible. Many universities host departments of religion or theology with a variety of course offerings. Classes might range from biblical geography to the most in-depth of abstract discussions about the finer points of textual meaning. Courses on the history and archaeology of the Near East can often be found in history, humanities, and sometimes even art departments. Some larger universities have departments of Near Eastern studies in which the civilizations of the Bible are addressed. And if you want to be a religious professional, there are seminaries serving nearly every denomination and the Bible will be the majority of your curriculum.

Also, many churches and synagogues offer adult education classes and Sunday schools. Check your local religious institutions for details.

It's All Greek to You!

A great way to study the Bible is to read it in the languages in which it was written. That would be Hebrew for the Hebrew Bible/Old Testament and Greek for the New Testament. Apart from colleges, universities, and seminaries, Hebrew and Greek are occasionally taught at religious institutions. Hebrew is in regular use in the liturgy and Bible readings of synagogues today, and Greek can be heard in the liturgy of modern Greek Orthodox churches.

It's also possible to go out and learn on your own. EKS Publishing, for example, specializes in producing materials for the teaching and learning of biblical Hebrew. One of its books, *The First Hebrew Primer* (Third Edition), is excellent for classroom use or self-teaching.

Another book that is often recommended is *Biblical Hebrew: Step by Step* by Menaham Mansoor. It is published by Baker Book House. For those wanting a bit more detail in their studies, *Biblical Hebrew: An Introductory Grammar* by Page Kelley (Wm. Eerdmans Publishing Co.) will provide you with a very firm foundation. An accompanying *Handbook* to that volume provides an answer key so you can check your work.

If it's Greek you want to try, James Found's *Basic Greek in Thirty Minutes a Day: New Testament Greek Workbook for Laymen* (Bethany House) has often been recommended as a way to get a taste. *Mastering New Testament Greek* by W. Harold Mare (Wipf & Stock Publishers) and *Learn New Testament Greek* by John H. Dobson (Baker Book House) have both received good reviews. For a bit more in-depth coverage, *Basics of Biblical Greek Grammar* by William D. Mounce (Zondervan Publishing House) might serve you well.

Once you get through any of these introductory books, there are plenty of more advanced grammars to keep you busy for a long time to come! And if you want to learn some of the other languages of the greater Bible world, there are books out there to teach you Sumerian, Akkadian, Ancient Egyptian, Aramaic, and others from the region, including Ugaritic!

If it's Bible languages you want to study on your own, make sure that you're buying books that deal with the ancient stages of the language. Both modern Hebrew and Greek, especially the latter, are a good bit different in grammar and vocabulary than their ancient counterparts!

What Are You Doing This Weekend?

A great way to learn more about the Bible, its world, and its teaching is to attend services at religious institutions. And there are many to choose from! Most services will feature a sermon, often based on a Bible story, and some good speakers will discuss the ancient cultural and historical surroundings of their given topic.

A visit to a service at your local religious establishment is an excellent way to learn more about the Bible.

The Jewish Sabbath begins at sundown on Friday and ends at sundown on Saturday. Many synagogues will have an "Erev Shabbat" service on Friday evenings and other services on Saturday. It's a great way to hear the Bible, prayers, and liturgy read in

Hebrew. A few Christian churches also meet on Saturday, including the Seventh-Day Adventists. The majority of Christian congregations, however, meet on Sunday and several meet on other days in addition! Take a look around. Compare and contrast. Listen to some Hebrew or Greek being read if you like. Most churches and synagogues are more than happy to have you visit!

> **This and That**
>
> It's a good idea to call before visiting a new religious congregation. You might feel lost if you attended a service that, for example, was conducted completely in Hebrew. You also might feel like a party-crasher if you stumbled into a church's annual financial meeting or an unanticipated bar mitzvah.

On the Tube

There are a surprising number of programs on television dealing with religion, the Bible, and archaeology. The quality varies from the sensationalist to the scholarly, and the better ones tend to be found on educational channels. Being full of provocative stories, miracles, and outright mysteries, the Bible provides a wealth of possible content for the TV producer. Scan the schedules and maybe you'll find a good one.

Occasionally, you can find some good biblical preaching on television, especially Sunday morning. Again, quality varies and so does style. Some might even ask you to send a little money, but that's entirely up to you.

> **This and That**
>
> For the ultimate learning experience, visit the Holy Land ... when it's safe. If you've read the previous chapter, then you've got a few ideas on how to go about doing it.

Dig This!

Would you like some genuine excitement and adventure? Both are possible when you combine two of the world's most interesting subjects, the Bible and archaeology. Every summer, and occasionally in other months as well, a couple of dozen digs in Israel and Jordan actually recruit volunteers to help them excavate the world of the Bible. No kidding! In fact, many rely on this sort of participation to carry out their projects. Typically, the volunteers pay a fee which funds their room and board and helps support the general expenses of the dig. No experience is generally necessary, as the volunteers are supervised by professional archaeologists, graduate students, or other competent personnel. The volunteers tend to be adults, 18 years old on up, and come from all walks of life.

Is That So!

Lots of people would like to volunteer to work on digs in Egypt. Unfortunately, Egypt prefers only professionals working with their precious monuments. Keep in mind, too, that archaeological digs can be affected by changing political situations. Most of the Israeli excavations inviting volunteers were cancelled in the summer of 2002 due to security concerns.

There are usually a variety of sites from different time periods and environments from which to choose to fit your schedule and interests. Many digs offer lectures and travel programs to visit other places of interest. Some can actually offer college credit for your efforts. Where do you sign up? A good list of summer digs can be found annually in the January/February issue of *Biblical Archaeology Review*. It can also be found online at www.bib-arch.org/bswbDigBAR.html.

Eager volunteers working hard at the site of Ashkelon, Israel.

The Bible Online and on Disc

The Internet has allowed anyone with the proper equipment to access an incredible amount of material on almost every subject including the Bible and its world. There are not, however, universal standards for quality. A search for information on any given subject might turn up authoritative, useful, and even uplifting data on one hand, or baseless musings or vulgarity on the other. It's a mixed bag, and learning how to surf the web to separate the wheat from the chaff, so to speak, is increasingly becoming an art. A few good websites can be found in Appendix C.

Perhaps more useful than the Internet, and certainly less surprising, is the existence of an increasing number of Bible software programs that allow one to explore the Bible in numerous ways. Typically these programs are on CD-ROM, which can hold a vast amount of information. Here's a sample:

- PC Study Bible
- QuickVerse
- Bibleworks
- Power Bible

The *Power Bible CD* is an excellent example of Bible study software. It is inexpensive and includes 16 Bible translations (including versions in Spanish, French, and German), 3 Bible dictionaries, 5 topical reference works, 18 commentaries, and more than 700,000 cross-references. Different translations of Bible verses can be viewed side by side, and search engines will help you find just about anything. Information on this useful product can be obtained at www.powerbible.com.

Go Right to the Source

You want to learn more about the Bible? Read it. Many different translations are out there to fit nearly anyone's taste. There are also a variety of commentaries that you can read along with the text to help you get some ideas about what it might all mean. Other resources provide schedules that will get you through the Bible, cover to cover, in a year.

Shalom!

I hope you have enjoyed this book and its fascinating topic. I know that whenever I study the Bible, my appreciation for its numerous interesting facets and insights increases. No matter whether you are an earnest believer, a seeker of knowledge, or just curious, there is much to be gained in its study. And you can bet that there will be more discoveries and insights in the future that will shed ever more light on the fascinating world of the Bible!

The Least You Need to Know

♦ There are many ways to pursue a study of the Bible, including taking classes at schools or religious institutions.

♦ Learning a biblical language is a wonderful way to gain insights into the Bible.

♦ It's possible to volunteer on archaeological projects in Israel and Jordan and actually take part in the exploration of the Bible world.

♦ Modern technology has brought the study of the Bible to televisions and computers.

Appendix A

Glossary

A.D. (*anno Domini,* "the year of our Lord")   The number of years since the birth of Jesus.

agnostics   Those who acknowledge the possibility that God might exist, but aren't sure.

antediluvian   The world before the Deluge (the Great Flood).

anthropology   The study of human cultures.

Apocrypha   Additional books found in some Bibles that aren't universally accepted.

apologetics   The defense of one's beliefs as practiced by apologists.

archaeology   The interdisciplinary study of the human past.

Arkologists   Those who are interested in locating the remains of Noah's Ark.

Assyriology   The study of ancient Mesopotamia.

atheists   Those who don't believe that God exists.

B.C. ("Before Christ")   Refers to the number of years before the birth of Jesus.

B.C.E. ("Before the Common Era")   The religiously neutral term referring to the same time period as B.C.

B.P. ("Before Present")   The number of years prior to the present. Essentially it means "years ago."

Bible A collection of books held sacred, particularly by Jews and Christians. The word *Bible* is derived from the Greek word *bibla*, which means "books."

biblical archaeology The use of archaeological techniques to illuminate the world of the Bible.

Bronze Age An archaeological period in Palestine characterized by the building of cities and the use of bronze, extending between 3300 and 1200 B.C. It is subdivided into Early, Middle, and Late Bronze periods.

bulla (plural **bullae**) A clay seal bearing a stamp with an individual's name, typically used to seal documents.

canonization The process by which potential parts of a book, or a group of books, are accepted or rejected on the basis of their appropriate merits.

C.E. ("Common Era") The religiously neutral equivalent of A.D., the number of years since the birth of Jesus.

Chalcolithic A cultural period in which copper becomes a component of the Neolithic lifestyle. As a time period in the chronology of Palestine, it extends between 4500 and 3300 B.C.

Christ As derived from the Greek word *christos*, Christ means "Messiah."

Christians Followers of Jesus and his teachings.

complex society A human society characterized by such features as class, wealth, and status differences; political, economic and religious elites; craft specialists; relatively large populations and cities; and writing.

concordance A volume that lists words in the Bible and where they occur.

Creationists Those who believe that God created the earth as described in the Book of Genesis.

cuneiform Wedge-shape scripts, typically impressed in clay, which were used to write such languages as Sumerian, Akkadian, and Old Persian.

deists Those who believe in the general concept of the existence of God.

Diaspora A term often applied in reference to the widespread dispersal of Jews throughout the world.

ecumenism Engaging in dialogue between different religious groups in order to find common ground and understanding.

Egyptology The study of ancient Egypt.

Gospel   Greek for "good news," a Gospel is one of the four books of the New Testament—Matthew, Mark, Luke, and John—that describe the life and teachings of Jesus.

Hebrew Bible   The books of the Bible originally written mostly in Hebrew and known to Christians as the Old Testament.

Hebrews   The Hebrew-speaking descendants of Jacob's twelve sons who would themselves become the patriarchs of twelve tribes. These people are often referred to as the children of Israel or the *Israelites*. Today these people are called "Jews," after the tribe of Judah.

Hellenistic   An adjective referring to those things that are Greek. Hellenization is the process of spreading Greek culture.

hieroglyphs   A kind of writing that uses pictures for its symbols, such as that used by the Egyptians.

Hittitology   The study of the ancient Hittites as practiced by Hittitologists.

Intertestamental Period   The time period between the Hebrew Bible/Old Testament and the Christian Scriptures/New Testament.

Iron Age   An archaeological period in Palestine extending between 1200 and 586 B.C. It is divided into Iron I and Iron II periods.

kashrut   Rules relating to Jewish dietary laws.

kosher   Ritually clean or fit according to Jewish law. It applies especially to food, but refers to other things as well.

Levant   The countries bordering the Eastern Mediterranean including Egypt, Israel, Lebanon, and Turkey.

maximalists   Those who believe in the general historical accuracy of the Bible.

Messiah   An awaited savior sent by God to deliver his people from oppression and to restore the world. Christians believe that this Messiah is Jesus.

Middle East   The predominantly Islamic and Arabic-speaking countries found bordering the Eastern Mediterranean and parts farther east including Egypt, Israel, Jordan, Syria, Lebanon, Saudi Arabia and the Gulf States, Turkey, Iraq, and Iran. Essentially synonymous with the term Near East.

minimalists   Those who argue that there is little compelling evidence that many of the events described in the Bible actually happened.

monotheism   The belief in one God.

mtDNA   A type of DNA inherited unmixed from one's maternal line that can provide evidence of long-term inheritance.

Near East   *See* Middle East.

Neolithic   A cultural period characterized by permanent settlements and the tending of plants and animals. Stone tools are widely used, and pottery and other new kinds of tools reflect this way of life. As an archaeological time period, the Neolithic in Palestine extends between 8000 and 4500 B.C.

New Testament   The Christian addition to the Hebrew Bible/Old Testament relating to the life and teachings of Jesus of Nazareth.

Old Testament   A Christian term for the Hebrew Bible.

ossuary   A receptacle for holding the bones of the dead.

Paleolithic, or "Stone Age"   As a lifestyle, it is characterized by the use of stone tools and hunting and gathering. As an archaeological time period in the Palestine region, it extends from about 1,000,000 years ago to about 10,000 years ago.

Palestine   A geographical term for the region in the vicinity of the modern state of Israel and some adjacent territories.

Passover   A Jewish festival commemorating the Exodus story.

Pentateuch   A Greek term referring to the first five books of the Hebrew Bible/Old Testament.

Pesach   Same as Passover.

Pharaoh   The ruler of ancient Egypt.

polytheism   The belief in many gods.

Rosh Hashanah   The Jewish New Year.

scientific creationists   Believers in God who look at the findings of science to demonstrate and confirm their belief in biblical creation.

scroll   A rolled-up manuscript which is unrolled for reading.

Semite   Someone who speaks a Semitic language as their native tongue, including Akkadian, Arabic, and Hebrew.

Shavuot   A Jewish harvest festival that also celebrates the giving of the Torah.

stratigraphy   The study of layers, or "strata," in the earth.

Sukkot   The Jewish Festival of Booths, which commemorates the Israelites wandering in the wilderness after leaving Egypt.

Sumerologist   Someone who specializes in the study of ancient Sumer.

synagogue   A Jewish religious community center.

Tanach   The Hebrew name for the Hebrew Bible, or Old Testament.

tell (or **tel**)   A mound made up of the accumulated debris of human occupation.

Tetragrammaton   The four Hebrew letters, YHWH, that represent the personal name of God.

theocracy   A system of government under rule by God's laws.

Torah   The first five books of the Old Testament, sometimes referred to by its Greek name, the Pentateuch.

Yeshua   The name "Jesus" in Hebrew.

Yom Kippur   The annual Jewish Day of Atonement.

Zionism   The political movement advocating the establishment and perpetuation of a homeland for the Jewish.

Appendix B

Select Bibliography

Looking to read some more? There are tens of thousands of books dealing with the Bible. For starters, check out some of these great tomes that can fill you in on some more of the details!

Achtemeier, Paul J., ed. *Harper's Bible Dictionary*. San Francisco: Harper & Row, 1985.

Aharoni, Yohanan. *Land of the Bible: A Historical Geography*. Philadelphia: Westminster Press, 1979.

Aharoni, Yohanan, and Michael Avi-Yonah. *The Macmillan Bible Atlas*. New York: Macmillan, 1977.

Bahn, Paul, ed. *The Cambridge Illustrated History of Archaeology*. Cambridge: Cambridge University Press, 1996.

Bard, Mitchell G. *The Complete Idiot's Guide to Middle East Conflict, Second Edition*. Indianapolis: Alpha Books, 2003.

Bell, Jim, and Stan Campbell. *The Complete Idiot's Guide to the Bible, Second Edition*. Indianapolis: Alpha Books, 2003.

Ben-Tor, Ammon. *The Archaeology of Ancient Israel*. New Haven: Yale University, 1992.

Blech, Benjamin. *The Complete Idiot's Guide to Jewish History and Culture*. Indianapolis: Alpha Books, 1999.

———. *The Complete Idiot's Guide to Understanding Judaism*. Indianapolis: Alpha Books, 1999.

Boardman, John, et al. *The Oxford History of the Classical World*. Oxford: Oxford University, 1986.

Buttrick, George A., ed. *The Interpreter's Dictionary of the Bible*. Nashville: Abingdon, 1962.

Crawford, Harriet. *Sumer and the Sumerians*. Cambridge: Cambridge University, 1991.

Currid, John D. *Doing Archaeology in the Land of the Bible*. Grand Rapids: Baker Books, 1999.

Curtis, John. *Ancient Persia*. London: British Museum, 1989.

Danker, Frederick W. *Multipurpose Tools for Bible Study*. Minneapolis: Augsburg Fortress, 1993.

Davies, Philip R., George J. Brooke, and Phillip R. Callaway. *The Complete World of the Dead Sea Scrolls*. London: Thames and Hudson, 2002.

Davies, W. V. *Reading the Past: Egyptian Hieroglyphs*. Berkeley, University of California, 1987.

Devries, LaMoine F. *Cities of the Biblical World*. Peabody: Hendrikson, 1997.

Doré, Gustave. *The Doré Bible Gallery*. Chicago: Clarke & Co., 1888.

Dothan, T., and M. Dothan. *Peoples of the Sea: The Search for the Philistines*. New York: Macmillan, 1992.

Finegan, Jack. *The Archeology of the New Testament: The Life of Jesus and the Beginning of the Early Church*. Princeton: Princeton University, 1992.

Friedman, David N., et al. *Anchor Bible Dictionary*. New York: Doubleday, 1992.

Fritz, Volkmar. *An Introduction to Biblical Archaeology*. Sheffield: Sheffield Academic Press, 1994.

Grimbol, William R. *The Complete Idiot's Guide to the Life of Christ*. Indianapolis, Alpha Books, 2001.

Hanson, K. C., and Douglas E. Oakman. *Palestine in the Time of Jesus: Social Structures and Social Conflicts*. Philadelphia: Fortress, 1998.

Harris, Roberta L. *The World of the Bible*. London: Thames and Hudson, 1995.

Healey, John F. *Reading the Past: The Early Alphabet*. Berkeley: University of California, 1990.

Hoerth, Alfred J. *Archaeology and the Old Testament*. Grand Rapids: Baker Books, 1998.

Hoerth, Alfred J., et al. *Peoples of the Old Testament*. Grand Rapids: Baker Books, 1994.

Kee, Howard Clark, et al. *The Cambridge Companion to the Bible.* Cambridge: Cambridge University, 1997.

King, Philip J., and Lawrence E. Stager. *Life in Biblical Israel.* Louisville: Westminster John Knox.

Laughlin, John C. *Archaeology and the Bible.* London: Routledge, 2000.

Lieber, David L., ed. *Etz Hayim: Torah and Commentary.* Philadelphia: Jewish Publication Society, 2001.

Lloyd, Seton. *The Archaeology of Mesopotamia: From the Old Stone Age to the Persian Conquest.* London: Thames and Hudson, 1984.

Macqueen, J. G. *The Hittites and Their Contemporaries in Asia Minor.* London: Thames and Hudson, 1986.

Mazar, Amihai. *Archaeology of the Land of the Bible, 10,000–586 B.C.E.* New York: Doubleday, 1990.

Metzger, Bruce M., and Michael D. Coogan, eds. *The Oxford Guide to People and Places of the Bible.* Oxford: Oxford University, 2001.

———. *The Oxford Companion to the Bible.* Oxford: Oxford University, 1993.

Miller, Madeleine S., and J. Lane Miller. *Harper's Encyclopedia of Bible Life.* Edison: Castle, 1996.

Moyers, Bill. *Genesis: A Living Conversation.* New York: Doubleday, 1996.

Murphey-O'Connor, Jerome. *Oxford Archaeological Guides: The Holy Land.* Oxford: Oxford University, 1998.

Negev, Abraham, and Shimon Gibson, eds. *Archaeological Encyclopedia of the Holy Land.* New York: Continuum, 2001.

Nelson, Eric. *The Complete Idiot's Guide to the Roman Empire.* Indianapolis: Alpha Books, 2002.

Oates, Joan. *Babylon.* London: Thames and Hudson, 1986.

Packer, J. I., et al. *Nelson's Illustrated Encyclopedia of Bible Facts.* Nashville: Thomas Nelson, 1980.

Plaut, W. Gunther, ed. *The Torah: A Modern Commentary.* New York: UAHC, 1981.

Price, J. Randall. *The Stones Cry Out.* Eugene: Harvest House, 1997.

Pritchard, James B. *Ancient Near Eastern Texts Relating to the Old Testament.* Princeton: Princeton University, 1969.

Rast, Walter E. *Through the Ages in Palestinian Archaeology: An Introductory Handbook.* Philadelphia: Trinity Press International, 1992.

Reade, Julian. *Mesopotamia.* London: British Museum, 1991.

Reader's Digest. *The Bible Through the Ages.* Pleasantville: Reader's Digest, 1992.

Roaf, Michael. *Cultural Atlas of Mesopotamia and the Ancient Near East.* New York: Facts On File, 1990.

Rogerson, John, ed. *The Oxford Illustrated History of the Bible.* Oxford: Oxford University Press, 2001.

Ryan, Donald P. *The Complete Idiot's Guide to Lost Civilizations.* Indianapolis: Alpha Books, 1999.

———. *The Complete Idiot's Guide to Biblical Mysteries.* Indianapolis: Alpha Books, 2000.

———. *The Complete Idiot's Guide to Ancient Egypt.* Indianapolis: Alpha Books, 2002.

Shanks, Hershel. *The Mystery and Meaning of the Dead Sea Scrolls.* New York: Random House, 1998.

———. *Jerusalem: An Archaeological Biography.* New York: Random House, 1995.

———, ed. *Ancient Israel.* Upper Saddle River: Prentice Hall, 1999.

Shaw, Iain, ed. *The Oxford History of Ancient Egypt.* Oxford: Oxford University, 2000.

Stern, Ephraim. *The New Encyclopedia of Archaeological Excavations in the Holy Land.* Westwood: Prentice Hall, 1993.

———. *Archaeology of the Land of the Bible: The Assyrian, Babylonian and Persian Periods.* New York: Doubleday, 2001.

Tubb, Jonathan N. *Bible Lands.* London: Dorling Kindersley, 1991.

———. *Canaanites.* Norman: University of Oklahoma, 1998.

Walker, C. B. F. *Reading the Past: Cuneiform.* Berkeley: University of California, 1987.

Zohary, M. *Plants of the Bible.* Cambridge: Cambridge University, 1982.

Appendix C

Resources for Further Exploration

Following are some other resources, besides books, that can help you pursue an interest in the world of the Bible. These include some information about magazines, Bible software, some Internet websites, and even a few movies you might enjoy.

A word of caution about the Internet sites: Websites come and go in the anarchistic world of the information highway. Sometimes they change addresses or disappear altogether. The website addresses in this appendix were current as of early October 2002. Needless to say, I am not responsible for their content, except, of course, for my own material on my own site.

Magazines

Here's the information for contacting those magazines I mentioned in Chapter 23.

Biblical Archaeology Review, *Bible Review*, and *Archaeology Odyssey* can be ordered by contacting the *Biblical Archaeology Society* at:
4710 41st Street NW
Washington, DC 20016
202-364-3300
www.bib-arch.org/

To order *Near Eastern Archaeology* (formerly called *Biblical Archaeologist*), contact:
ASOR Subscriber Services
PO Box 531
Canton, MA 02021-0531
1-800-821-7823
www.asor.org/pubs/nea/index.html

To order *Archaeology*, contact:
877-275-9782
www.archaeology.org/

To order *KMT Magazine: A Modern Journal of Egyptology*, contact:
PO Box 1475
Sebastopol, CA 95473-1475
707-823-6079
www.egyptology.com/kmt/

For some good instructional materials for learning biblical Hebrew (including *The First Hebrew Primer*), contact EKS Publishing Company at:
1029A Solano Avenue
Albany, CA 94706-1617
877-743-2739
www.ekspublishing.com/

Bible Study and Exploration Software

There is now lots and lots of software of interest to students of the Bible. The following companies can help you explore that option.

Bible and other software of Jewish interest
www.jewishsoftware.com

Discount Bible Software
www.discountbible.com/

Discount Christian Software
www.christian-software.org/

Power Bible
www.powerbible.com/

Online Resources

Here's a nice sample of Internet sites. Half the fun of the web is the surfing, so use these as a starting point for further exploration of the Bible and the ancient Near East.

General Sites

Bible 101 Biblical Studies Unit
www.bible101.org

Bible History On-Line
www.bible-history.com/

Biblical Studies Info Page
www.biblicalstudies.info/

Catholic Encyclopedia
www.newadvent.org/cathen/

Christian Answers to Biblical Archaeology Questions
www.christiananswers.net/archaeology/home.html

Christianity Today
www.christianity.net/

Jewish/Roman World of Jesus
www.uncc.edu/jdtabor/

Judaism and Jewish Resources
shamash.org/trb/judaism.html

Lambert Dolphin's Web Links
www.ldolphin.org/

Resource Pages for Biblical Studies
www.torreys.org/bible/

Organizations and Institutions

American Bible Society
www.americanbible.org/

American Schools of Oriental Research
www.asor.org

Biblical Archaeology Society
www.bib-arch.org/

British School of Archaeology in Jerusalem
britac3.britac.ac.uk/institutes/jerus/index.html

Gideons International
www.gideons.org/

Israel Exploration Society
www.hum.huji.ac.il/ies

Israel Museum
www.imj.org.il/

Palestine Exploration Fund
www.pef.org.uk

Wycliffe Bible Translators
www.wycliffe.org/

Ancient Languages and Texts

Ancient Biblical Manuscripts Center
www.abmc.org

Ancient Greek Language Resources
www.umass.edu/fclrc/greekancient.htm

Ancient Texts Relating to the Bible
www.usc.edu/dept/LAS/wsrp/
educational_site/ancient_texts/

Biblical Hebrew Resource Page
www.reslight.addr.com/biblehebrew.html

Evolution of Alphabets
www.wam.umd.edu/~rfradkin/
alphapage.html

Greek Language
www.greek-language.com/

History of Writing
www.historian.net/hxwrite.htm

Orion Center for the Study of the Dead Sea Scrolls
orion.mscc.huji.ac.il

Shrine of the Book
www.imj.org.il/eng/shrine/

West Semitic Research Project
www.usc.edu/dept/LAS/wsrp/index.html

Bible Lands and Places

Bible Lands
www.silk.net/RelEd/biblegeo.htm

Bible Places
www.bibleplaces.com/

Egyptian Ministry of Tourism
www.egypttourism.org/

Geography and the Bible
www.bible-history.com/geography/
helpful_maps.html

Israel Ministry of Tourism
www.infotour.co.il/

Jerusalem Archaeological Park
www.archpark.org.il/

Jordan Tourism Board
www.see-jordan.com/

Lebanese Ministry of Tourism
www.lebanon-tourism.gov.lb/

Virtual Jerusalem Tour
www.md.huji.ac.il/vjt/

The Ancient World

ABZU—Ancient Near East Resources on the Internet
www.etana.org/abzu/

AncientNearEast.net
www.ancientneareast.net/

Ancient World Web
www.julen.net/aw/

Egyptology.com
www.egyptology.com/

Egyptology Resources
www.newton.cam.ac.uk/egypt

My website (Don Ryan)
www.plu.edu/~ryandp/

Okeanos: Ancient Near Eastern Studies
faculty.washington.edu/snoegel/okeanos.html

Oriental Institute: University of Chicago
www-oi.uchicago.edu/OI/

Recommended Reading on the Ancient Near East from the Oriental Institute
www-oi.uchicago.edu/OI/DEPT/RA/RECREAD/REC_READ.html

Let's Go to the Movies!

With the advent of modern technology, interpretations of the Bible have found their way onto the big screen many times. Movies with biblical themes were a big hit even before they figured out how to add sound to silent films. Both *The Ten Commandments* (1923) and *Ben Hur* (1926) were originally produced as silent movies before coming again to the screen in full color, sound, and spectacle in 1956 and 1959 respectively.

Films have been made on such subjects as *The Last Days of Sodom and Gomorrah*, *David and Bathsheba*, and several involving Moses. And there are now numerous made-for-television films on a whole variety of biblical characters. The historical accuracy in Bible films varies considerably but so does the quality of the acting. So here are just a few of the classics, all of which are at least available on video.

- *The Bible … in the Beginning* **(1966).** A dramatic attempt to tell stories from Genesis including the Creation, Noah's Ark, and Abraham.

- *The Ten Commandments* **(1956).** This all-star screen spectacular starring Charlton Heston is arguably one of the greatest films ever made.

- *Prince of Egypt* **(1998).** A well-researched Disney cartoon retelling the story of the Exodus.

- *Samson and Delilah* **(1949).** The story of the biblical strongman starring the sturdy Mr. Victor Mature. The scene where he wrestles the lion is my favorite part.

- *Ben Hur* **(1959).** Set in the time of Jesus and also starring Charlton Heston. The chariot racing is incredible!

- *The Greatest Story Ever Told* **(1965).** And that story here is Jesus.

- *The Robe* **(1953).** Richard Burton stars as a Roman centurion touched by the life of Jesus.

And if you like a little singing and dancing in your life, you might enjoy three Bible-inspired musicals that made their way from the stage to the screen:

◆ *Godspell* **(1973).** A musical adaptation of the Book of Matthew including tunes such as *Day by Day*, which became a popular hit single.

◆ *Joseph and the Amazing Technicolor Dreamcoat* **(1999).** What started out as a short choral piece by Andrew Lloyd Webber and Tim Rice became a popular international musical. The new video starring Donny Osmond is actually quite excellent!

◆ *Jesus Christ Superstar* **(1973).** Another Lloyd Webber and Tim Rice creation, the last days of Jesus are portrayed in this compelling "rock opera" which has been both highly praised and damned. Dancing hippies and Roman soldiers in chrome-plated construction helmets complement this musical, which was filmed on location at dramatic sites in Israel.

Index